CW01499433

PREFACE

MY interest in Hockley arose as a result of a file missing in the Library of the United Grand Lodge of England. Ellic Howe whilst researching his paper on *Fringe Masonry* (*Ars Quatuor Coronatorum*, Vol. 85, 1972) asked for the Hockley file, but it was not to be found. As a result I had to start from scratch to find the information he required. A strange picture began to develop. On the one hand, there emerged a typical middle-class Victorian professional man who, late in life, developed an interest in Freemasonry; on the other, an avid collector of occult knowledge, a practical Spiritualist, and an acknowledged expert on all matters arcane. This phenomenon of a double *persona* continued to fascinate me long after Mr Howe's research was complete. The search proved difficult, for although Hockley's name appears in studies of nineteenth-century occultism and Spiritualism it is always as a passing reference and never in detail. Many details indeed have still proved elusive.

To Ellic Howe I owe much, not least an endless fascination with the stranger areas of the history of ideas to which he introduced me. To R. A. Gilbert I owe not only his contribution on the Hockley MSS, but also his many useful suggestions when various lines of research dried up. Michael Cox has shown infinite patience during the long gestation period of this work, for which I am very grateful. For their assistance with many enquiries on details of Hockley's life I would like to thank: Dr Charles Rondle; Mr A. G. Davies; Miss Sheila Kertesz, Archivist of the Sir John Cass Foundation; Mr Martin Hayes, Local History Librarian, Croydon Public Libraries; Mr J. W. Pavey, Registrar of the Institute of Chartered Accountants; Miss Valerie Vaughan, Librarian, National Portrait Gallery; Mr Timothy D'Arch-Smith; and the Secretaries of the various Masonic groups to which Hockley belonged.

March 1985   J. M. HAMILL

£2-00

The Rosicrucian Seer

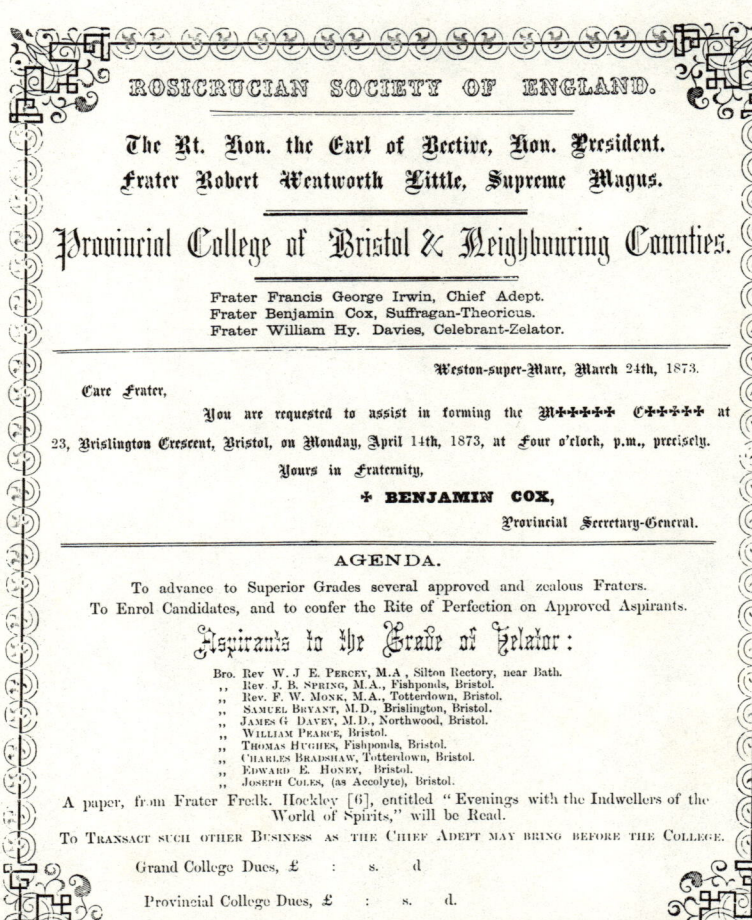

ROSICRUCIAN SOCIETY OF ENGLAND.

The Rt. Hon. the Earl of Bective, Hon. President.
Frater Robert Wentworth Little, Supreme Magus.

Provincial College of Bristol & Neighbouring Counties.

Frater Francis George Irwin, Chief Adept.
Frater Benjamin Cox, Suffragan-Theoricus.
Frater William Hy. Davies, Celebrant-Zelator.

Weston-super-Mare, March 24th, 1873.

Care Frater,

You are requested to assist in forming the M✠✠✠✠ C✠✠✠✠ at 23, Brislington Crescent, Bristol, on Monday, April 14th, 1873, at Four o'clock, p.m., precisely.

Yours in Fraternity,

✠ BENJAMIN COX,

Provincial Secretary-General.

AGENDA.

To advance to Superior Grades several approved and zealous Fraters.
To Enrol Candidates, and to confer the Rite of Perfection on Approved Aspirants.

Aspirants to the Grade of Zelator:

Bro. Rev W. J E. Percey, M.A , Silton Rectory, near Bath.
,, Rev. J. B. Spring, M.A., Fishponds, Bristol.
,, Rev. F. W. Monk, M.A., Totterdown, Bristol.
,, Samuel Bryant, M.D., Brislington, Bristol.
,, James G Davey, M.D., Northwood, Bristol.
,, William Pearce, Bristol.
,, Thomas Hughes, Fishponds, Bristol.
,, Charles Bradshaw, Totterdown, Bristol.
,, Edward E. Honey, Bristol.
,, Joseph Coles, (as Accolyte), Bristol.

A paper, from Frater Fredk. Hockley [6], entitled "Evenings with the Indwellers of the World of Spirits," will be Read.

To Transact such other Business as the Chief Adept may bring before the College.

Grand College Dues, £ : s. d

Provincial College Dues, £ : s. d.

Bristol Rosicrucian College summons for 14 April 1873 mentioning the reading of Hockley's 'Evenings With the Indwellers of the World of Spirits' (see p. 132).

The
Rosicrucian Seer
Magical Writings of Frederick Hockley

Edited with an Introduction by
JOHN HAMILL

With a Note on Hockley's Manuscripts by
R. A. Gilbert

THE AQUARIAN PRESS
Wellingborough, Northamptonshire

First published 1986

© THE AQUARIAN PRESS 1986

All rights reserved. No part of this book may be reproduced or utilized in any form or by any means, electronic or mechanical, including photocopying, recording or by information and retrieval system, without permission in writing from the Publisher.

British Library Cataloguing in Publication Data

Hockley, Frederick
 The Rosicrucian seer: the magical writings of
 Frederick Hockley
 1. Occult sciences—Early works to 1900
 I. Title   II. Hamill, John   III. Gilbert, R. A.
 133   BF1410

ISBN 0-85030-289-7

*The Aquarian Press is part of the
Thorsons Publishing Group*

Printed and bound in Great Britain

FOR ELLIC HOWE

CONTENTS

1
INTRODUCTION

FREDERICK HOCKLEY is claimed as a major influence in the Occult Revival of the nineteenth century but little is known of the man, his life, or what happened to his near-fabled library and manuscript collection. Even after five years' research only a patchwork of details of his life has emerged. Indeed, it often seemed as though Hockley did not wish to be traced. Despite his moving from one set of rooms to another his addresses can be carefully plotted for certain periods of his life but never for those periods necessary for tracing him in the census returns! Nor does his name appear in any London or Croydon *Directory*, rate list or electoral register. Indeed, until the registration of his death and proving of his will Hockley does not appear to have officially existed.

For details of his birth the only source traced is his own copy of Sibley's *Uranoscopia*[1] in which he entered his own birth details on a nativity chart as 'Nat. Oct. 13th. 2h.20 am 1808 Lat. 51 32N'. Where he was born or what his parentage was has not been established. By his own admission[2] he was educated up to the age of eight at Captain Webb's School at Hoxton. After that, his early life becomes something of a mystery. From two sources[3] it appears that he worked for John Denley the occult bookseller in Catherine Street, Covent Garden, but in what capacity is not certain. From a comment in a letter to the Irwins his work may have involved copying occult manuscripts for customers, and he may even have manufactured manuscripts for Denley to sell. The copying and production of manuscripts was to occupy him for much of his life. Certainly in the Irwin letters Hockley remembers Denley with affection and considered his period with him as his education in occultism and the beginning of his 'bibliomania', as he called his avid collecting of books and manuscripts.

From his evidence to the Dialectical Society (*see* Part 5) we learn that he began his experiments with the crystal and magic mirror in 1824 at the age of sixteen. He was also a practised astrologer and follower of Mesmer's ideas on animal magnetism and its use for medical treatment. Attracted to the general developing interest in Spiritualism, he experimented with all its various manifestations but soon became convinced that scrying with the crystal or mirror was the only true form of spirit communication and the method least capable of being tampered with by charlatans and publicity seekers.

He married, but details of his wife have proved elusive. From a comment to Irwin it appears that she died in the 1850s, but the records at St Catherine's House, surprisingly, list many female Hockleys dying in that decade. She shared her husband's interest in Spiritualism and may herself have possessed mediumistic powers. The Revd C. M. Davies records an amusing use of the powers she had.[4] It would seem that in his youth Hockley was addicted to the pleasures of the turf, often over-staying his time at race meetings. He possessed an ancient spell by means of which it was possible to summon anyone to his presence, no matter how far away they were. Hockley's wife discovered the spell and began to use it to summon the erring Fred from the racetrack! In the words of the Revd C. M. Davies: 'All of a sudden he would feel an uncontrollable desire to go home. Whatever the hour of night or day might be, he must set off at once. He felt sure his wife was working the spell, and afterwards found out that such was the case.' Hockley obviously had a great affection for his wife and spent the thirty-odd years between her death and his own in trying to contact her through the spirit world. As his *transition notice* in Light[5] shows, he was eventually successful. 'He maintained his interest in Spiritualism to the end, one of his last visits being to Mr. Eglinton,[6] through whose mediumship he received, in writing between slates, a cherished communication from his long departed wife intimating that he would speedily rejoin her.'

Whatever Hockley's position had been with Denley, by the early 1840s he was practising as an accountant in partnership with two others. Where or how he received his training is not known. He was not involved with any of the professional bodies in existence at this time. Again the Directories give no clue. His business address, certainly by the 1870s, was 3 Raymond Buildings, Grays Inn. It appears in all the Directories, but as chambers housing law firms. From this, and his mention to

Irwin of a difficult Chancery suit, it would seem that Hockley and his partners worked for a legal practice. From the letters we also know that his work took him out of London on occasion, including an annual trip to Northumberland.

From the 1850s he was much involved in Spiritualism, coming into contact with Mr and Mrs Everitt (who were to remain lifelong friends), Lord Stanhope, Robert Owen (the Social Reformer), D. D. Home, the Revd Stainton Moses *et al.* Whilst convinced of the veracity of some Spiritualists he was not unaware of the many charlatans, misguided enthusiasts (the 'harpies' as K. R. H. MacKenzie called them) and the simple publicity seekers involved in the Spiritualist movement. He was very free with his own knowledge and the contents of his library, with the exception of the records of his own work with the crystal. Whether or not he had actual pupils is difficult to determine. Certainly MacKenzie and Davies both regarded him as their first Master in matters Spiritualist and occult. It was to Hockley that MacKenzie immediately rushed on his return from seeing Eliphas Lévi in Paris, Hockley recording MacKenzie's account of the visit.[7] In the 1840s he began to publish occasional reports of his experiences with the crystal and magic mirror in the form of letters to the editor of *The Zoist* and to Robert Owen's *The New Existence of Man upon Earth.* As the editors of the main Spiritualist journals were all known to him it is surprising that he did not contribute more to them. Surprisingly he published no books. The Irwin letters infer that he was preparing a history of the Grand Stewards' Lodge and definitely state that he was preparing for publication an edited version of the philosophical revelations of his principal spirit guide, the Crowned Angel of the Seventh Sphere. Neither work appeared in print.

In 1864, at the relatively late age of fifty-six, he was initiated into Freemasonry. This gave him an additional point of contact with Irwin, to whom he had first been recommended by the Everitts on Spiritualist matters. The letters resulting from the introduction are the main source of information on Hockley. They reveal him as a kindly man ever willing to share his knowledge and library and possessing the knowledge and kindness to take time to advise others on the forming of their own collections. They also show that, despite his deep involvement in Spiritualism and his knowledge of and belief in the occult, he maintained a healthy sense of proportion and perspective, as well as a sense of humour with regard to

Spiritualism, occultism, and their practitioners. They reveal his depth of knowledge of occult literature (although Davies states that Hockley knew no other language than English) and the resultant ability to detect when an author was summarizing or merely plagiarizing a little known writer's work, as in his dismissive comments to Irwin on Madame Blavatsky's *Isis Unveiled*. Except with regard to Freemasonry, he does not appear to have been a joiner of groups or societies, his Corresponding Membership of the Theosophical Society being an 'honour' from Col. Olcott in 1877.

The letters also show a marked concern with his own and other's health, and the problems of regularly removing from one set of rooms to another accompanied by his large library. Why he should have had to move so often has not been discovered. An insomniac, he constantly suffered from headaches and eyestrain, probably a result of many years studying and meticulously copying and deciphering old manuscripts. The implication from the letters is that he was rarely at home, constantly attending meetings and seances. His last few years were dogged by increasing ill-health and he died at the age of seventy-seven on 10 November 1885. The cause of death, registered by a cousin who was present, was stated to be 'natural decay and exhaustion'.

As befits an accountant, his will was short and precise. He left a little over three and a half thousand pounds, household goods, his books, manuscripts, mirrors and crystals. He ordered his library to be sold and the proceeds, together with the remainder of his estate after a few personal bequests, were to be divided between distant relatives. His crystal and mirrors were bought by James Burns and Co., but their ultimate fate is not known. The fate of his books and manuscripts is also a mystery. A. E. Waite[8] was in error when he stated that Irwin bought Hockley's library. Much of it, in fact, was bought by George Redway, who issued a special catalogue compiled for him by Arthur Machen (see p. 26).[9] Some items turn up in Redway's catalogue of the library of Walter Moseley,[10] including the manuscript of the Crowned Angel's *magnum opus*. Neither catalogue, however, contains anything like the 1,000 volumes Hockley claimed to have had in 1869, or even a small part of his own manuscripts. Of the thirty or more notebooks in which he recorded his scrying experiments few can be traced in addition to the extracts copied by Irwin in the 1870s.

Hockley was given his first crystal in 1824 and by the time he

gave his evidence to the London Dialectical Society in 1869 he
had amassed thirty manuscript volumes containing the answers
to more than twelve thousand questions he had asked of his
spirit guides in the mirror or crystal. To his sorrow, like the
great Dr Dee, he was unable himself to see anything in the
crystal and had to make use of what he termed a 'speculatrix'.
He appears to have met with most success when using young
girls, particularly one Emma Louisa Leigh. He came into
contact with her in the early 1850s in Croydon where she lived
with her father, Edwin Wavell Leigh, a retired Excise Officer, at
195 Cherry Orchard Lane.[11] She was about thirteen years old
when Hockley met her and died in 1858 at the age of twenty.[12]
It was through her that Hockley received the Crowned Angel's
*magnum opus, Metaphysical and Spiritual Philosophy; or the
connection with and influence over material bodies by Spirits.*

Hockley approached crystal or mirror scrying with an almost
religious awe. Indeed his experiments were to have a profound
effect on his own religious beliefs, turning him from a Unitarian
to a Trinitarian Christian with a firm belief in the mystery of the
Virgin Birth. Before use, the crystal or mirror had to be
consecrated with prayers and dedicated to the service of God.
Consecrated calls, again invoking the name of Christ, were to be
given three times to summon whichever spirit guide was
required. Once the Spirit's message had been received, a special
discharge was to be given three times, again invoking Christ and
his Angels, followed by prayers of thanks. Despite all the care
taken to avoid calling up evil spirits, they occasionally came
through and had to be speedily discharged (*vide* his report
'Raising the Devil', p. 129). Again, despite all the care taken,
even the Crowned Angel was not above giving Hockley the
required ceremonial for calling up very dubious spirits. As
Hockley took down verbatim what his speculatrix reported
seeing, what is remarkable is the quality and depth of
information received. It seems unlikely that a teenage girl with,
presumably, an average Victorian female's education, could have
invented the religious and philosophical information Hockley
transcribed.

Many seekers after arcane knowledge sought initiation into
Freemasonry, in the erroneous belief that knowledge of the
rituals of Freemasonry would set them on the path to
discovering the key to all knowledge. Surprisingly, Hockley did
not take this step until his fifty-fifth year, although some of his
contacts, professional, Spiritualist and occult, must have been

Freemasons. The answer is possibly to be found in an extract
copied by Irwin from Hockley's 'Crystal MS No. 7'. Irwin
simply copied the answers received from the Crowned Angel
but it is easy to construct the probable questions. Hockley
appears to have asked the Crowned Angel's opinon as to his
becoming a Freemason. The answers are, to say the least,
surprising.

'I have a great objection to your being a fellow of a FM Lodge
unless you could at once become a member of that sacred society
of which the Fathers are at Jerusalem.'
[Why?]
'It is not only folly but wickedness in joining a society who do
no possible good but a great deal of harm.'
[What is the sacred society?]
'They are followers of the Rosy Cross.'
[Where are they?]
'The Society is in France and unless you went there and were
Installed a Brother you could not possibly become one. Napoleon
the 1st Emperor of France was a member of that Society.'
[What is their purpose/what do they study?]
'They study the occult sciences after an interview with an
invisible power, which they have at stated times. The Elders
travel to Jerusalem.'
[Where do they meet?]
'You have seen their place of meeting in the Crystal—it is in
the [blank] they then return to the rest of the Society with the
instructions they receive from the invisible agent—upon this they
act. They are not limited to the wealthy for Jean-Jaques Rousseau
was one of its firmest supporters. I will show you visions that will
tend to enlighten you, but in the meantime I hope you will not
join an English Lodge.'

Hockley either met an *invisible power* in France (the letters show
he had been to Paris), or chose to disregard his Guardian
Spirit's warning, for on 21 March 1864 he was initiated into
Freemasonry in the British Lodge No. 8, then meeting at the
Freemason's Tavern, Great Queen Street, London. He appears
to have taken a liking to the ritual of the Craft for as soon as he
had taken the Third Degree, of Master Mason, he became a
member of the Emulation Lodge of Improvement. This is a
Lodge of Instruction at which the ceremonies and the catechi-
tical lectures of the Craft (in which the ceremonies, symbols and
emblems of the Craft are explained and moralized upon) are
rehearsed, the ultimate goal being the ability to render them by
heart and without error. His progress in British Lodge No. 8

was rapid. Within fifteen months of his initiation he became its Junior Warden and its Master in 1867, serving for the customary twelve months. His proficiency in the ritual must have been equally rapidly attained for he was a regular attender at the Emulation Lodge of Improvement and served on its Committee from 1866 to 1868, ceasing to attend after he had installed his successor as Master of British Lodge.

His Lodge was, and still is, one of the nineteen London Lodges having the special privilege of nominating each year a Grand Steward for appointment by the Grand Master. The Grand Stewards serve for one year and have the responsibility of arranging the Grand Festival banquet held annually immediately after the investiture of the new Grand Officers and the re-installation of the Grand Master. Additionally they had to cover the cost of the event, although a nominal ticket price was charged, which made appointment as a Grand Steward an expensive honour. In contrast to the usual garter blue silk-edged and -lined apron and collar of other Grand Officers, the Grand Stewards, present and past, since 1731 had been permitted to wear red collars and red silk edging and lining to their aprons. Hockley was given the British Lodge nomination as a Grand Steward in 1867 and was invested with his collar and jewel at the Annual Investiture held on 24 April 1867. The Minutes of the Board of Grand Stewards show him to have been a regular attender, taking his full part in the arrangement of the Grand Festival held on 29 April 1868. As a Grand Steward he was entitled to join the Grand Stewards Lodge. Formed in 1735, and standing without number at the head of the Register of lodges since 1792, the membership was limited to those who had served the office of Grand Steward. Joining in 1867 Hockley became its Junior Warden in 1875 and from 1877 until his death was its Secretary. He was so assiduous in the performance of his duties as Secretary that the members in 1885 voted unanimously to present him with a special jewel, as Masonic medals are called, as a token of their esteem. He died, unfortunately, before the jewel was finished, but as a mark of their sincerity and as a lasting memorial to him the jewel was completed, accepted by the lodge and ordered to be worn by successive Secretaries, which it still is today.

Hockley, as the letters show, had a long professional connection with Alnwick in Northumberland, spending three or more weeks there each year. He came into contact with local Freemasons and on 27 September 1870 was elected a joining member of the Alnwick Lodge No. 1167. His proposer and seconder into this lodge reflect his life's passion and his profession for the proposer, Henry Hunter Blair, was a printer and bookseller and the seconder, Edward Thomas Turnbull, was a local banker. Visiting the town only once a year he was unable to take a full part in the lodge's affairs, but he attended when possible and remained a member for the rest of his life.

As an extension of his work in British Lodge No. 8 he was Exalted into Royal Arch Masonry in the British Chapter No. 8 on 1 December 1865. The Craft and Royal Arch in England are thematically and administratively linked, the latter being said to be the completion of the former. As with the Lodge he was a regular attender at the Chapter, taking minor offices but never putting himself forward for the Principal's Chairs, the three Principals being the rulers of a Chapter. It is surprising that he did not, because the Royal Arch is a much more mystical Order than the Craft and, as such, would have had much more appeal to Hockley. Many are put off taking office in the Royal Arch by its rather daunting and complicated ritual, but Hockley, having been a member of the Committee of the Emulation Lodge of Improvement, certainly had a facility for learning ritual.

Surprisingly, in an age when new and 'revived' Masonic degrees and Orders were proliferating, Hockley remained aloof from them all; perhaps he was all too aware of the spuriousness of the claims of antiquity of origin put forward by many of them. More surprisingly, for a 'Rosicrucian', he had no contact with the Societas Rosicruciana in Anglia (SRIA) until six years after its formation, and then in a curious way. The SRIA had been 'revived' in 1865 by Robert Wentworth Little, and despite claims by W. Wynn Westcott, in his official history of the Society, that Hockley and K. R. H. MacKenzie had assisted at its formation, the letters to Irwin clearly show that Hockley's first contact with the SRIA was through Irwin's Bristol College of which he was elected a member in 1872. It seems clear that Irwin accepted Hockley as a true Rosicrucian Adept, for there appears to have been no necessity for him to go to Bristol to be inducted into the Zelator Grade of the SRIA. Upon his being elected a member of the College, *in absentia*, Irwin by post advanced him to the VII Degree of *Adeptus Exemptus*, the highest grade Irwin could confer in his College. Hockley never attended the Bristol College but was pressed by Irwin to prepare a paper for them. He sent a copy of one of his crystal experiments, 'Evenings with Indwellers of the Spirit World'. A verbatim account taken down exactly as Hockley's seer reported it to him, it does not appear to have gone down at all well with those present at the Bristol College, when it was eventually read. It was to be another three years before Hockley sought membership of the Metropolitan (London) College, of the SRIA, in 1875. Once elected, Hockley was not to be a regular attender and never gave a paper. He did, however, exhibit at one meeting the Rosicrucian certificate and diary of Sigismund Bacstrom.[13] He had possibly stayed aloof from the Metropolitan College because of his quarrel with and temporary dislike of K. R. H. MacKenzie, who was Assistant Secretary-General and was probably scheming to gain control of the SRIA to make it a more practical, magical Order. Additionally, from the evidence of talks to the College printed in the *Rosicrucian*, Hockley would have found little to stimulate him at their meetings. His knowledge and experience were far greater than any of his co-members. It is clear from his letter of 10 March 1872 to F. G. Irwin that he saw practical Spiritualism via the crystal as the most important work to be undertaken by a true Rosicrucian.

It is difficult to establish what it was in Freemasonry that appealed to Hockley. To a man of his sensibility the basic principles of Craft Masonry, Brotherly Love, Relief and Truth, and the practice of ceremonies which attempt to instil in a candidate a 'system of morality, veiled in allegory and illustrated by symbols', would have had an attraction. To a certain extent the Craft ritual is a means towards the same end that the Rosicrucians were seeking: the perfection of man in the physical world and the preparation for and contemplation of the eternal world which will open to all mankind at the close of their physical existence. It may also have been a part of his public *persona*, the successful and respectable professional man enjoying membership of an eminently respectable society. This would not, however, explain the assiduity with which he attended to his Masonic duties. The Secretaryship of a Lodge, as with that of any voluntary society, is a time-consuming and often thankless task, and being honorary entails no financial reward. Possibly Hockley needed to be actively involved rather than simply a spectator on the sidelines. Perhaps the clarity and orderliness of Masonic ceremonial and organization appealed to his accountant's mind.

That there was a belief in a Rosicrucian tradition stemming from the publication of the *Manifestos* in the early seventeenth century is beyond doubt. Whether the movement actually existed, or whether the many personalities labelled Rosicrucians believed themselves to be so, are questions too large to be considered here. The *Manifestos* and the traditions built upon them are capable of an almost limitless interpretation of their symbolism, whilst the introduction of 'Secret Chiefs' was a masterstroke permitting the most outrageous claims to be made which could be neither proved nor disproved. English Rosicrucianism was said to encompass Dr Dee, Robert Fludd, John Heydon, Thomas Vaughan, William Backhouse and Elias Ashmole—indeed anyone who had any interest or skill in mathematics, natural science, astronomy, astrology, or alchemy. By the nineteenth century the Rosicrucian idea was to a great extent a spent force in England but its nineteenth-century apologists claimed for it a major revivalist in the person of Ebenezer Sibley, whose works were to be called in as evidence of the continuing tradition. Sibley was to be quickly followed by Francis Barrett, whose seminal work *The Magus* (1801), a plagiarism of plagiarisms, greatly revived interest in astrology, alchemy, and magical operations and was probably largely responsible for the later nineteenth-century revival of practical occultism. The tenuous Rosicrucian thread and the, later, belief in a continuing Rosicrucian presence in England was given a seeming veracity by the presence in England of Sigismund Bacstrom with his certificate attesting to his initiation into a Rosicrucian group by the Comte de Chazal on 12 September 1794 in Mauritius. Godfrey Higgins' *Anacalypsis* (1836) was claimed as a further proof of the continuing tradition. Higgins stated that he had been invited to join a Templar and Rosicrucian Order in London. Higgins was a Freemason and I have no doubt that what he was referring to were the *Masonic* Knights Templar and Rose Croix degrees. The latter is now the 18th degree of the Antient and Accepted [Scottish] Rite of Freemasonry, which in Higgins' time did not exist as a coherent Rite in England. The Rose Croix degree was generally worked within Knights Templar Encampments and was variously referred to as the Rose Croix, Rose Cross, Rouge Croix, Rosae Crucis or Rosie Cross degree. Intensely Christian in content the Rose Croix had nothing about it, even in Higgins' time or earlier, to link it with the ideas or traditions of Rosicrucianism, other than a very confusing set of alternative names!

In *Ritual Magic in England* (1970) Francis King, without any supporting evidence, claimed a definite line of continuity from Sibley to Barrett, then through a pupil of Barrett's Magical

Academy at Marylebone to Hockley. That Hockley knew the works of Sibley is undoubted, copies bearing his signature are in various libraries and he is known to have copied Sibley's MSS for himself, and to have received copies done by other hands. His knowledge of Sibley was enhanced by his working with Denley, who purchased many of Sibley's books from Lackington, who in turn had bought Sibley's library from his nephew, to whom Sibley had left it in the hope that he would preserve it as a working library. The ungrateful heir sold it within two months of receiving it.

Hockley's connection with Barrett is explained in notes copied by the late Gerald Yorke from Hockley papers in the possession of the late John Watkins. Discussing *The Magus*, Hockley wrote: 'The above which is an abridgment of the title sufficiently gives the scope of the work which consists of an unacknowledged compilation from other Authors. In fact, all that is of real value is taken from C[ornelius] Agrippa & the Clavis or Key to unlock the Mysteries of Rabbi Solomon, and an ancient Work on Telesmata of great rarity which only exists in MS of which, however, there are a large number of copies extant. For compiling this book my late friend John Denley, the Occult Bookseller of Catherine Street, lent Barrett the whole of the materials, and my friend complained that B[arrett] never recompensed him even with a copy. At the sale of Lackington's stock in 18[18] Mr Denley bought the MS blocks, plates and copyright, which were for several years in my possession. Barrett, notwithstanding his professorship of Magic, lived and died in poverty.'

Hockley knew Bacstrom both from his Rosicrucian certificates and diary, which he owned, and from his contact through the crystal. He may have known Higgins personally and certainly knew his works. Whether this is proof of an actual and continuous Rosicrucian presence in England I leave to others to decide. That Hockley intimately knew their writings is true, but reading other's books does not prove a Rosicrucian apostolic succession.

That Hockley believed himself to be at least working within a Rosicrucian tradition is shown in the letters to the Irwins. His search for the Rosicrucian path to Utopia was not, however, by the performing of complex magical rituals but by Spiritualism, invoking the spirits of both Angels and his Rosicrucian predecessors who had crossed the Great Divide. He believed, in particular, that contacting spirits by means of the crystal and

mirror was the means by which man's earthly knowledge could
be expanded to prepare him for the final journey in which
perfection would be completed and man's earthly and spiritual
goodness would be dissolved into oneness with the Godhead in
a perfect entity. His Spiritualist definition of Rosicrucianism is
perhaps the true explanation of his standing apart from the
SRIA, which has always been a forum for the discussion of ideas
and has *never* involved itself in practical experiments, whatever
its members may have indulged in outside its meetings. Those
members of the SRIA who were drawn more towards practice
rather than theory later joined the Golden Dawn. Hockley's firm
belief that the Rosicrucian path lay through the crystal would
probably have met with little support amongst the generality of
the SRIA's membership.

Hockley is claimed as a member of another very shadowy
Rosicrucian group, which may have formed the model for the
Golden Dawn: the Fratres Lucis, also known either as the
Brotherhood of the Cross of Light or the Order of the Swastika.
The Fratres Lucis had its origins in 1873 when between 31
October and 9 November Count Cagliostro, by means of
Herbert Irwin and the crystal, gave to F. G. Irwin the history
and rituals of the Order. Cagliostro informed Irwin that the
Order had originated in fourteenth-century Florence, from
whence it spread to Rome, Paris, and Vienna. Among former
members were, he claimed, Vaughan, Fludd, the Comte de St
Germain, Mesmer, Martinez de Pasquales, Swedenborg, and
Cagliostro himself. The objects of the Order were the study *and*
practice of 'natural magic, Mesmerism, the science of life and
death, immortality, Cabala, alchemy, necromancy, astrology and
magic in all its branches'. Not content with claiming Cagliostro
as his source, Irwin in a letter of 1874 to Benjamin Cox of
Weston-Super-Mare, his *Fidus Achates* in matters Masonic and
occult, stated that he had in fact met with the Fratres Lucis in
Paris and that fifteen years earlier there had been only
twenty-seven members in the whole world; he added that 'all
members were bound to keep [their] immediate Chiefs posted
of all [their] movements'. Surprisingly, or perhaps not so, this
links in with the Crowned Angel's comments to Hockley when
questioned about Freemasonry; presumably the Society in
France, referred to therein, was the Fratres Lucis.

How often, if ever, the Fratres Lucis met is not known. It has
all the apperance of being another Order, organized by Irwin
and MacKenzie, which existed in great detail on paper, was

extensively discussed by letter, but was never actually worked. The only proven members were F. G. Irwin, K. R. H. MacKenzie, Benjamin Cox, and Hockley. W. Wynn Westcott appears to have attempted to join but was refused. Capt. E. J. Langford Garstin (a member of a successor Order to the Golden Dawn), writing to the late Gerald Yorke in 1950, explained that 'Hockley, MacKenzie and Irwin all disliked and mistrusted S. A. [Sapere Aude, Westcott's Golden Dawn motto], which is why he was refused admission to the Fratres Lucis.'[14] Perhaps this refusal was the spur to Westcott concocting the Golden Dawn. In the extant Irwin letters Hockley never refers to the Fratres Lucis, which seems a little odd unless there are letters missing from the sequence. The evidence for his membership comes in a letter from Benjamin Cox to Irwin on 15 December 1885 in which he laments '. . . I was very sorry to hear of the death of Bro. Hockley. There is now one member less of the Order of ⊓ . . .'

Whatever we may think of Rosicrucianism, Spiritualism or the ocult, it is very clear from his letters, writings, and evidence to the London Dialectical Society that Hockley firmly believed in what he was doing and that he was working in the Rosicrucian tradition. Unlike many of his contemporaries, however, he preserved his critical faculties and distinguished between true followers, charlatans, sensation seekers, and the merely gullible. A firm belief in the potential for good in his crystal experiments did not close his mind to the equal potential for misuse and evil. It was this belief that deterred him from experimenting with other magical ceremonials. As he pointed out to Herbert Irwin, the danger in magical operations lay in the errors brought about by not taking the time essential to make careful preparations. Successful and danger-free magical operations required not only great knowledge of the occult but also the freedom of time and action available only to those free of the necessity of working for a living. Magical operations were certainly not for the dabbler.

The claims that Hockley was a progenitor, member, and even author of the rituals of the Golden Dawn remain unproven (but see Part 2). There is little doubt that the Golden Dawn came from the fertile brain of Dr W. Wynn Westcott. Conveniently for Westcott, Hockley, MacKenzie, Eliphas Lévi, and the Revd A. F. A. Woodford were all dead by 1888 when the Golden Dawn began to emerge. My own opinion is that Hockley, having avoided contact with the group practice of magical rituals, would have also avoided the Golden Dawn, the more so in his last few years when illness and exhaustion plagued him. That he might have had an indirect effect on the Golden Dawn is more plausible. He would have at least known of Westcott through orthodox Masonic channels, and more probably through his connection with MacKenzie, Irwin, and the members of the Societas Rosicruciana in Anglia. There may also have been a link through the residence of both Westcott and the Everitts at Hendon, because Hockley appears often to have visited the latter. Westcott may have had access to Hockley's library during his lifetime and may have acquired some of his manuscripts after his death. The only plausible connection between Hockley and the Golden Dawn would be that Westcott (or Mathers) based the original cypher manuscript and rituals of the Golden Dawn on material culled from Hockley's manuscripts.

NOTES

1 The copy of *Uranoscopia* had been given to him by Denley on 5 January 1833 and is now in the Library of the Wellcome Institute for the History of Medicine.

2 Letter to Herbert Irwin.

3 Denley is the 'Dr D . . .' referred to by Bulwer Lytton in the introduction to his novel *Zanoni*. The evidence for Hockley's having worked for him comes in *The Great Secret and its unfoldment in Occultism . . . by a Church of England Clergyman* [Revd C. M. Davies] (London, 1895), and the Redway catalogue of Walter Moseley's Library, item No. 308.

4 *The Great Secret . . .*, pp. 112-14.

5 His obituary appears in the issue of *Light* for 28 November 1885.

6 William Eglinton, Spiritualist medium who specialized in physical manifestations, particularly the appearance of messages on slates.

7 The account was published in *The Rosicrucian* for May 1873 as *Philosophical and Cabbalistic Magic*.

8 A. E. Waite, *The Brotherhood of the Rosy Cross* (London, 1924), p. 569.

9 Redway, *List of Books chiefly from the Library of the late Frederick Hockley, Esq.* [c. 1887].

10 Redway, *A Catalogue of a Portion of the Valuable Library of the late Walter Moseley Esq.* [1889].

11 Information from 1851 Census Return.

12 Her death was announced in the *Croydon Chronicle* for 2 October 1858.

13 See R. A. Gilbert's notes on the manuscripts (pp. 26–9). Bacstrom's original certificate and diary later belonged to the Theosophical Society but were destroyed in a fire towards the end of the last century.

14 Information quoted from Ellic Howe's *The Magicians of the Golden Dawn* (1972, reprinted 1985).

2

SECRET WRITING: THE MAGICAL MANUSCRIPTS OF FREDERICK HOCKLEY

FREDERICK HOCKLEY first made known the existence of his crystal-gazing manuscripts in 1869, when he gave evidence before the Committee of the London Dialectical Society during their investigation into Spiritualism. He told them that 'I have thirty volumns, [sic] containing twelve-thousand answers received in this way [i.e. via the crystal and mirror] which I keep carefully under lock and key.'[1] What remained unknown was that in addition to the crystal-gazing records he had transcribed large numbers of manuscripts on alchemy, divination, the Qabalah, ceremonial magic, and Rosicrucianism; many of them illustrated with exquisite coloured and illuminated drawings, and all neatly rubricated. He also possessed a fine library of printed books on the occult, a library which leading spiritualists hoped would be preserved intact after his death.[2] Both manuscripts and printed books were acquired, however, by the enterprising occult publisher, George Redway, and ultimately dispersed by way of a catalogue prepared by his young and underpaid assistant, Arthur Machen.[3]

Machen enjoyed his work hugely, and added to the catalogue a delightful advertising puff in the form of a pastiche on the *Adventures of Don Quixote*.[4] In this 'grand and diverting scrutiny made by the Priest and the Barber in the Library in York Street' Hockley's manuscripts are described: the barber finds 'a whole nest of curious books, and all engrossed by hand, and painted and adorned with figures, but as easy to read as print' (p. 8), but the priest turns away from them when he discovers inserted in a copy of *The Key of Solomon the King*, 'a Relation of an Interview with a Spirit, showing how a man conjured a demon to appear and how they spoke together' (p. 9). It is tempting to think of this manuscript as being carried off by MacGregor Mathers—he *did* translate and edit the *Key* for Redway—but there is no proof, and it remains one of four of the twenty-three manuscripts catalogued that cannot now be accounted for.

Whether or not Mathers ever acquired any of the manuscripts, he would certainly have known of them and recognized their importance long before Hockley's death, for he was an active member of the *Societas Rosicruciana in Anglia* (of which Hockley was also a member), and it was in the Society's journal that Hockley had given an account of his work with magic crystals and magic mirrors, complete with a reference to his manuscript of the *Key of Solomon*.[5] In addition to Mathers, two other prominent members of the SRIA, W. Wynn Westcott, its Secretary, and W. R. Woodman, its Supreme Magus, were deeply concerned with the subject matter of Hockley's manuscripts, although they do not seem to have acquired any of them—a somewhat surprising circumstance, for the manuscripts would have been invaluable in the systematization of occult practices that was an essential part of the work of the Hermetic Order of the Golden Dawn, the magical Order that these three masonic Rosicrucians created in 1887.

Other students of the occult were more fortunate. Many of the manuscripts had been borrowed and copied during Hockley's lifetime by his friend F. G. Irwin; others were purchased from Redway by W. B. Moseley, a more practical magician than Hockley, for 'whereas Hockley appears to have been content with employing clairvoyant subjects, skryers in crystals and persons who could be passed into the magnetic trance, Moseley is said to have tried more dangerous paths'.[6] From Moseley some of these also passed to Irwin after Moseley's death in 1888—a death which may or may not have been hastened by his occult practices.[7]

Three of the manuscripts that Irwin did not obtain, *The Journal of a Rosicrucian Philosopher*, *Crystallomancy* and *Collectanea Chemica*, came into the hands of A. E. Waite, who quoted extensively from the first two in his early works and published a part of the third in his series of alchemical reprints.[8] The *Journal* is by far the most important of these, for it includes the remarkable account of the 'Admission of Dr. Bacstrom into the Society of the Rosy Cross by the Count du Chazal at the Island of Mauritius 1794' and thus provides evidence for the existence of a Rosicrucian Order of some kind in England during the early years of the nineteenth century.

Waite published the text of Bacstrom's 'Admission' in *The*

Real History of the Rosicrucians (1887, pp. 409–14) and discussed both the manuscript and its implications at length in his later book, *The Brotherhood of the Rosy Cross* (1924, pp. 549–60). In *The Occult Sciences* (1891, pp. 103–8) he gave a précis of Hockley's *Crystallomancy* manuscript, acknowledging the source, and used a diagram from the same text as an illustration in *The Book of Black Magic* (1898, plate X). The final manuscript Waite published in 1893 under its own title of *Collectanea Chemica*, saying of it in his prefatory note: 'The Hermetic Tracts comprised in this volume are printed from a quarto manuscript (itself a transcript from an older but now untraceable work) belonging to the late Mr. Frederick Hockley' (p. 7). He might have added that he omitted some two-thirds of the treatises in Hockley's manuscript, printing only the six that were best known to students of alchemy and including only one that was not to be found in the printed edition of 1684.

Within the Hermetic Order of the Golden Dawn, Waite's compatriots doubtless approved of his caution in withholding alchemical texts from the public, for they were anxious to ensure that the hermetic sciences remained secret to all save themselves. Two, at least, of the Order's alchemical enthusiasts—Florence Farr and the Revd W. A. Ayton—certainly had access to some of Hockley's manuscripts and made transcripts from them, while Waite recorded in his diary Percy Bullock's acquisition of *The Journal of a Rosicrucian Philosopher*: 'I saw at the house of L.O. [i.e. Levavi Oculos, Bullock's motto in the Order], who has acquired it recently, the old Hockley ms. from which I described the obligation of Dr. Sigismund Bacstrom in my history of the Rosicrucians.'[9] Bullock, however, was interested far more in the purely alchemical part of the manuscript.

But the Golden Dawn was destined to be short-lived and with its demise was lost the only real hope of preserving a substantial number of Hockley's manuscripts. Today, a total of twenty-eight manuscripts survives, together with a collection of five transcripts by Hockley's friend H. D. Lea and the Irwin transcripts from the crystal-gazing manuscripts.[10] These last are the most tantalizing of all, for they include Hockley's account of his seer's (Emma Leigh) vision of the explorer Richard Burton on his journey to Mecca in 1853. When Burton returned to England he came to see Hockley, who told him of the vision: 'He assured me it was correct in every particular and attached his name to the acount I had written down at the time, to certify that it was true.'[11] If the original could be found it would provide one of the most remarkable instances of proven clairvoyance ever recorded.

A further ten manuscripts recorded in Redway's catalogues cannot now be traced, including three that appear to be from the 'thirty volumns containing twelve-thousand answers'. If they were part of that series, the remaining twenty-four volumes have vanished utterly—even their titles being unknown—together with an unknown number of manuscripts on magic and related subjects, which might have included something referred to obliquely by Waite in *The Brotherhood of the Rosy Cross*. While discussing F. G. Irwin's assocation with the projected 'Order of the Rosy Cross' in the early 1870s, Waite implies that an unnamed group connected with the Bristol College of the SRIA may have been the ultimate source of the Golden Dawn cipher manuscripts.[12] In his original text, as it appears in the galley proofs of the book, he is more precise, naming Irwin specifically as the author of the texts he describes and suggesting that 'he had a hand in manufacturing the Warrants of another Secret Order or Association of Occult Students to which there are occasional allusions in the Transactions of the *Soc. Ros.*'—i.e. the Hermetic Order of the Golden Dawn.

Westcott's copy of the cipher manuscript is not in an identifiable hand, but if the cipher rituals, or their prototype, were the work of Irwin, it is highly probable that Hockley not only transcribed them but helped to inspire them. It is further possible that such a transcript could have come into Westcott's hands between 1878 and 1880 when he was working on Martinist and Rosicrucian rites during his 'Magical Retirement' at Hendon—where Hockley came to visit Mrs Everitt, the Spiritualist Medium. There is, perhaps, only flimsy evidence to support such a conjecture, but it would provide a fitting tribute to the memory of Frederick Hockley if we were obliged to see him not only as the ultimate source of the Golden Dawn's Enochian Magic, but as an unwitting assistant in the creation of the Order itself.

R. A. GILBERT

CHRONOLOGICAL HANDLIST OF IDENTIFIABLE HOCKLEY
MANUSCRIPTS

There are only thirty-eight manuscripts that can be positively
identified as being the work of Frederick Hockley, most of
which are transcriptions of older texts, while six are records of
scrying and two are what might be termed 'occult commonplace
books'. All save nine of them were included in one or other of
the two Redway catalogues to include Hockley material (*List of
books chiefly from the library of the late Frederick Hockley* (1887),
and *Catalogue of . . . the Library of the late Walter Moseley* (1889),
while ten of the manuscripts catalogued by Redway have since
disappeared.

In the following list, catalogue numbers from the Hockley (H)
or Moseley (M) catalogues are given where applicable, in
brackets; an asterisk indicates that the manuscript cannot now
be located. Twelve of the extant manuscripts are in institutional
libraries and sixteen in private collections, but for obvious
reasons their locations are not given here.

Dated manuscripts

1825 Habai, containing the nature and offices of Spirits,
Mystic Incantations . . . extracted from scarce and valuable
works.

1828 Magia de Profundis seu Clavicula Solomonis Regis et
Theurgia Goetia. With drawings of characters, seals, pentacles etc. (H102)*

1829 Occult Spells (Talismanic Magic). (H112)

1829 Journal of a Rosicrucian Philosopher from April 30th to
June 15th 1797, containing the Process of the Philosopher's
Stone. By an Alchemist.

1832 Book of the Offices and Orders of Spirits; transcribed
from a folio MS. written by T. Porter, 1583 [and] Keys of
Rabbi Solomon, transcribed from a MS translation into
French, and thence into English by Dr Sibley, by T. Palmer.
(H101)

1833 Collection of Horoscopes of Alchemists, Astrologers
and Occult Philosophers. (H121)*

1833 Journal of a Rosicrucian Philosopher . . . [as 1829], [and]
Copy of the Admission of Dr. Bacstrom into the Society of
the Rosy Cross by the Count du Chazal at the Island of
Mauritius 1794. (H108)

1833   Musaeum Hermeticum et Artis Cabalisticae. [A large commonplace book, with additions subsequent to Hockley's death.]

1834   Wheel of Wisdom, with key and directions for use in magical operations. [and] Experiment of one T.W. with the Spirits Birto, Agares, Baalpharos and Vassago. Transcribed from the autograph of Dr. Sibley. [and] Fragment of a translation of a very rare German MS concerning Divine Magic. [and] Dr Pistor, Introduction to the Theory of Cabala. (H115)

1836   The Wheel of Wisdom . . . [as 1834, first text only].

1838   The Book of Solomon's called the Pauline Art, transcribed by Fred. Hockley.

1839   Ars Notoria: the Notary Art of Solomon, translated by R. Turner, 1656. Transcribed with additions. (H98)

1839   Mr. Yardley's Process communicated to him by Mr Garden of London in 1716 transcribed from an autograph letter of Dr S. Bacstrom to Mr Hand in 1804. (H100)*

1839   Book of True Magic Science, formerly in the possession of Dr Barlow and by him defaced. Given to me by Mr Jms. Palmer. (M308)*

1841   Book of the Cabala, i.e. Lemoth or of names written in French by Lenain translated by Geo. Sheppard transcribed by Mr Hockley. (H107) [A similar manuscript appears as M295, but it is undated and it is not clear whether it is transcribed by Hockley, although it was in his library.]

1842   Collectanea Chemica, a collection of rare and curious Treatises on Hermetic Science, illustrated by Extracts, Commentaries, Parallel Passages, Explanatory Notes and numerous drawings. (H96)

1849   Aureum Seculum Redivivum: the Golden Age Revived by Henricus Madathanus, transcribed from the rare edition printed at Frankfurt in 1677. (H99)

1849   Coelum Reseratum Chymicum translated into English by Mr Hockley. (H123)* [The original manuscript, from which this translation was made, appears as H122. It was a German text, illustrated, and dated 1712.]

1854   Clavis Arcana Magica. (H118)

1854   Metaphysical and Spiritual Philosophy; or the connection with and influence over material bodies by Spirit.

Revealed by the Crowned Angel of the Seventh Sphere, through the medium of the Magic Mirror, Miss Emma Louisa Leigh being Speculatrix. 3 volumes. (M312)***

(1855) Metaphysical and Spiritual Philosophy (in two parts). Rough transcript. (H120) [Dated by Redway although no date appears in the manuscript, which appears to be a corrected copy of part of M312.]

1855 Cartomancy. (H114)

1857 Metaphysical and Spiritual Philosophy, a series of discourses delivered through the Medium of a Magic Mirror by the Spirit Eltesmo. (H119)

1858 E.L.L. MS (relating to the Invoking of Eltesmo in regard to the Seeress E. L. Leigh). (H117)

Undated manuscripts
Almadel, 'Key of Solomon the King', the Fourth Book, transcribed from the original MS by Mr Hockley. (H104)

Dr Bacstrom F.R.C. [Letter] [and] The Hidden Sense of Hadamah.

Cabalistic numerals in squares. (H103)

Cabala [Hebrew title] [From the publisher James Burns, with a printed label advertising Hockley's crystals and mirrors for sale.]

Book of the Cabalistic Art, that is to say, of Hidden Theology and Philosophy, by Dr John Pistor. (M302)*

Book of Spirits, Bael, Agares, Marbas etc. (H116)

Crystallomancy, or the Art of Invoking Spirits by the Crystal. [Two copies of this manuscript are extant.]

Magical MSS comprising: Of Intelligences and Spirits, The Method of Invoking the Dead or Raising the Spirit of a departed Person, An Epitome of the Angelican World, Ruben's Latin Manuscript.

Dr Rudd's Nine Hierarchies of Angels, how to bring a visible appearance of them into a Beryll glass. Also Clavis Angelicae containing the 18 great Calls and Celestial Invocations of the Table of Enoch. [Two copies of this manuscript are extant.]

The Schemham-maphora or Seventy-two Mystical Verses of the Psalms of David used by the Antient Rabbies when invoking by the Urim and Thummim. Transcribed from Reuchlin by Fred. Hockley. [Another copy of this manuscript is recorded as M297* but it has since disappeared.]

NOTES

1 *Report on Spiritualism of the Committee of the London Dialectical Society, together with the evidence, oral and written, and a selection from the correspondence* (1871), p. 184.

2 See the Obituary of Hockley in *Light*, Vol. 5, No. 256, 28 November 1885, p. 585.

3 *List of Books chiefly from the Library of the late Frederick Hockley, Esq., consisting of important works relating to the Occult Sciences, both in print and manuscript* . . ., George Redway (1887). Machen described his experiences with Redway in *Things Near and Far* (1923), pp. 15–17 and 25–6.

4 *A Chapter from the Book called The Ingenious Gentleman Don Quijote de la Mancha which by some mischance has not till now been printed* (1887).

5 'Evenings with the Indwellers of the World of Spirits, Being a Paper read at a meeting of the Bristol Rosicrucian College', in *The Rosicrucian and Masonic Record*, New Series, No. 6, (1 April 1877), pp. 223–30.

6 A. E. Waite, *The Brotherhood of the Rosy Cross* (1924), p. 569.

7 Ibid., p. 569. Waite says of Moseley: 'I have been told that his health was injured seriously by the use of drugs for occult purposes.'

8 The *Journal* was published, as a facsimile, at Bristol in 1970. The alchemical texts appeared as *Collectanea Chemica: being certain select Treatises on Alchemy and Hermetic Medicine* (1893).

9 A. E. Waite, unpublished diary, *Annus Mirabilis Redivivus*, entry for 26 March 1903.

10 The Lea transcripts are in the library of the Wellcome Institute; Irwin's transcripts are in the library of the United Grand Lodge of England, at Freemasons' Hall.

11 *Report on Spiritualism*, op. cit., p. 185.

12. A. E. Waite, *The Brotherhood of the Rosy Cross*, pp. 570–81.

3
HOCKLEY'S LETTERS TO THE IRWINS

MAJOR FRANCIS GEORGE IRWIN (1823–98), like Hockley, had a public and a private *persona*. The public *persona* was that of a career soldier: enlisting in the Sappers and Miners in 1842, serving in Gibraltar, Malta, and Devonport and rising to the rank of sergeant. Probably through the patronage of Major-General Gore Munbee, in 1868 Irwin secured the post of Adjutant to the 1st Gloucestershire Engineer Volunteer Corps at Bristol, with the rank of Captain. The private *persona* was that of an avid searcher after arcane knowledge. An enthusiastic Freemason, he joined every Masonic Order existing in England and was one of a small group who revived and introduced other Masonic Orders. A collector of Masonic and occult literature, like Hockley he copied and translated many rare manuscripts and printed volumes, and scoured bookshops and catalogues to add to his collection.

An interest in Spiritualism led him to crystal-scrying using his son Herbert as seer. There is a suggestion, however, in Hockley's letters that the results the Irwins achieved perhaps owed more to imagination and wide reading than to contact with spirits. Herbert Irwin (d. 1879) appears to have shown early promise of a good intellect but was highly strung and, like many late Victorians, died at an early age from an overdose of laudanum which he was taking to calm his nerves after failing his examinations as a medical student. F. G. Irwin was crushed by his son's death and never really recovered from it. Whilst continuing his voluminous correspondence he completely withdrew from public and Masonic life. His few forays into the world were to attend seances at which he attempted to reach Herbert's spirit. All the books added to his collection after Herbert's death contain not only Irwin's book plate but also an *In Memoriam* plate to Herbert.

I   167 Liverpool Road, Islington
18 January 1872

Dear Sir and Brother,
    My friend Mr Everitt [1] has just informed me you are in town
and knowing from Bro. Hughan[2] that you are a collector in
Occult Studies as well as Masonry I shall be pleased if you will
do me the honour of a call on Saturday next any time afer 5.30
to take a cup of tea and have a gossip with old authors on queer
subjects. I shall be alone—
                and remain most fraternally yours,
                Fred Hockley G.S.L.[3] P.M. No. 8[4]

1 The husband of Mrs Everitt (1825–1915) one of the most
renowned mediums specializing in physical mediumship and direct
writing. Everitt was a tailor in Pentonville and they began holding
seances in 1855. Mrs Everitt's mediumship was called into question in
1867 but she was vindicated (see *Spiritual Magazine*, May and June
1869).
  2 William James Hughan (1841–1911), the noted Masonic historian
and author. One of the founders of the Quatuor Coronati Lodge No.
2076, the research lodge which established the authentic or scientific
school of Masonic history, he was also an early member of the Societas
Rosicruciana in Anglia and contributed to early issues of the
Rosicrucian Magazine.
  3 Grand Stewards Lodge, of which Hockley was Secretary.
  4 Past Master of British Lodge No. 8, the lodge in which he had
been initiated.

2   167 Liverpool Road, Islington, N.
February 1872

My Dear Sir,
    I take the earliest opportunity of replying to your favors of the
4th and 8th inst. notwithstanding my being very unwell my time
so taken up that I can scarcely get one night a week to myself,
and my correspondence is sadly in arrear.
    I will answer the last note first. Mr Chevallier's[1] Crystal is one
of Burns'[2] egg shaped 'Glass Receptacles' as they were
accurately termed in contradistinction to 'Crystals' which are
made of natural rock crystal and beryl. All the so-called
'Crystals' I have seen at Burns being made of common glass are
sheared and are very fatiguing to the eyes and indeed if much

used would very seriously affect them—even with good 'seers' I would not advise you to buy it (of course this is confidential). My two factitious Crystals are made of powdered Rock Crystal with Brass, the late Earl Stanhope[3] gave Mr Slater[4] the Optician 4gns. each for them. They were made expressly for me, but tho' great lenses they are by no means comparable to the real article—my others are Rock Crystals. You see Dr Dee's and a magnificent Crystal from Japan with a [hexagram] in gold on it in Case No. 37 at the British Museum.

Mr Chevallier would not lecture on Crystal Seeing which he asserted was all fancy & imagination. One evening he and Dr Danso[5] came down to my place & after looking more than half an hour very intently, the Crystal getting fogged and suffused with red lines which he attributed to the strain on his optic nerves. I begged him to leave off as I was afraid he would strain his eyes. Whilst Dr D. and I were talking about the book Chev. had just published C. said that the Crystal appeared full of sea water rushing about, and presently a fish swimming and darting about—Dr D. asked 'Isn't that imagination' to which Chevallier replied 'Imagination no, how can it be imagination. I can distinguish the white line down the dorsal fin, it is a species of carp.' After a little while he had a vision of a human form lying in the sand at the bottom of the water with a thin light vapory form rising from its head and [*illegible*] as it were being drawn back again into the body and in the air above the water two winged spirits making a strenuous effort to relieve and assist its departure, this was repeated several times, at last he counted 1.2.3.4.5. then said several times 'five times has the spirit tried to escape and the two spirits came down to assist it and then it was quite drawn down again'. Here Mr C.'s. eyes became so painful that he was obliged to desist & of course all he could say was that it was perfectly marvellous & he should never have believed it had he not seen it himself.

I have been long promising Mr Shorter[6] an article for his Spiritual Magazine but as I don't get a night in a month at home it makes sorry progress. I showed you a common chemical ☽ holding about 2 quarts of water priced 2/6, you can easily get one at Bristol. It is excellent for scrying if persons have the facility—but when next you come to town I hope we shall have a longer gossip on the subject.

I went on Saturday to Millards and I return your catalogue and also another just published with a few additional articles. As it was his 2 o'clock day he was just closing so I shall have to go another day and have a look at all his books. Millard's prices are very high but the Accountant says 'a thing is worth what it will fetch'. If his Arcandam[7] is a good copy it is worth 10/- as it is a rare black letter on Arabian Astrology but obsolete as far as our modern practice extends—my copy cost me 12/6 some 30 years since. His Agrippa[8] is far too dear. I see out of the catalogue you sent me I have got about £60 worth of his books, you will see I have marked mine with little dots.

Millard is an odd fish to deal with and of very few words, but telling him I have been nearly 50 years a collector and naming some of his old customers and acquaintances we got quite amicable. I then learned that his crystal ball is a 'standing dish' in his catalogue & when he has one ordered he sends to my friend Slater who charges him £1-11-6 a piece, and then sells them at 2-2-0. The 'Key' Millard sold me was taken out of Barrett—but of course I will supply you with a very excellent formula as given to me by Chev. expressly for the instruction of my friends. As I said before Slater's crystal balls are very superior to the big egg-shaped article & if you make up your mind to have one I will get him to make it if he will let me have it at £1-11-6, which I have no doubt he will.

As to the Rosicrucian College, I little dreamed that when my attention was drawn to the Secret Lodge in the East (from which resulted the revelation from the Spanish Monk I read to you) that I should become a member of the Rosicrucian College in the near West, but I should be pleased to join if you would do me the honour of proposing me & I have no doubt Bro. Hughan will (sight unseen) have faith enough to second your nomination—pray send me word what the fees are & I will send a P[ostal] O[rder] by return of post and trust some fine morning to wake up and find myself an Invisible one.[9]

Having so far trespassed on your fraternal patience—and writing by candlelight does not improve my calligraphy—allow me to remain Most Fraternally yours,

Fred Hockley

I will send the German Catalogue & Millard's tomorrow.

1 Possibly J. O. Chevallier, author of *Experience in Spiritualism by a late member of Mr. Home's Atheneum* (London, 1867). He gave evidence to the Special Committee on Spiritualism of the London Dialectical Society in 1869.

2 James Burns, Spiritualist publisher. Secretary, Progressive Spiritualism, 1867. Published *Human Nature* (1867, in opposition to

the *Spiritualist Magazine*), the weekly *The Medium*, and *Day Book*.

3 As Hockley refers to him as the late Lord Stanhope, this can only be Philip Henry, 4th Earl of Stanhope (1781–1855). An FRS and FSA, he interested himself in the case of Caspar Hauser, the wolf-boy, and paid for his maintenance until the boy died in 1833.

4 Unidentified.

5 Unidentified.

6 Thomas Shorter: member, Committee of the London Spiritualist Union, 1859. Author of *Confessions of a Truth Seeker* (London, 1859). Editor of *The Spiritualist Magazine*.

7 Arcandam: *The most Excellent, Profitable and Pleasant Booke of the Famous Doctor and expert Astrologean Arcandam, or Alcandrain, to find the Fatal Destiny, Constellation, Complexion &c. newly turned out of French into our Vulgar Tongue, by W. Warde. Curious old Woodcuts-Black Letter* (London, 1617). The work had appeared in Latin editions in Paris in 1542 and 1555. The English edition was reprinted in 1626, 1630, 1652, 1670, etc., all in Roman letter with the curious woodcuts of the Zodiac.

8 Cornelius Agrippa von Nettesheim (1486–1585), scholar, linguist and diplomat who numbered Erasmus and Collet among his correspondents. He regarded astrology as the foundation of all occult studies. His *De Occulte Philosophia* (translated into English as *Three Books of Occult Philosophy*, 1651) has been described by R. A. Gilbert as 'a compendium of natural magic and the spiritual magic of Renaissance Hermeticism filled with Cabalistic theory, Astrology, Geomancy and the occult virtues of numbers, and was to have an incalculable effect and influence on occult studies for the next three centuries.' The spurious *Fourth Book* appeared in English in 1655 and gained currency by Barrett's plagiarism of it in *The Magus*.

9 Hockley obviously retained his sanity and sense of humour with regard to matters Rosicrucian, but it is doubtful if the serious-minded Irwin would have appreciated this paragraph!

[Sheet of queries included with letter of February 1872]

Queries [by Irwin]

Replies [by Hockley]

1. Will you kindly tell me where to get a book for newspaper extracts?

Partridge & Co. Stationers, 192 Fleet St., EC, when I bought the one I showed you they said they would letter the book any way I wanted or leave it unlettered—5/6d.

2. I enquired at [illegible] for German catalogue but could not get it—you promised to lend me yours.

I enclose the German Catalogue which I intend to bind as it will be in this country a rare book.

3. Have you got No. 48 of Zoist?

I went to Wheldons in Paternoster Row and found to both our annoyance he had all up to No. 46 and have commissioned them to look after No. 48.

4. In what vols. of Zoist will I find your letters?

Vol. 4, 306; Vol. 7, 250; Vol. 8, 55; Vol. 13, 391.

5. Is Arcandam's most pleasant book etc. worth 10/-?

A clean copy of Arcandam is well worth 10/- my copy cost me 12/6 30 years since. It is a very scarce black letter on Arabian Astrology, but obsolete from present practice.

6. A crystal ball size of orange at £2.2.0 would you advise me to purchase?

See my letter.

7. Have you met with a book called Nimrod said to be full of occult science?

'Nimrod' a sporting work in 2 vols. is the only one I know of—I never heard of any book on Occult Science with such a title either printed or MS.

8. Do you know of any works on Freemasonry or Alchemy for sale?

I will send you down per post any catalogue I may have with any things in on these subjects whenever I get one. I buy very little now—indeed my health is so uncertain that I often determine to sell my own collection.

3   167 Liverpool Rd., N.
                                        10 March 1872

Dear Bro. Irwin,

I have this evening seized the opportunity of replying to your favor of the 21st Feb. and also to our mutual friend Bro. Hughan's [1] letter of the 1st of March. I exceedingly regret the delay but it seems almost impossible for me to have an evening at home to myself—and absent friends.

I was really astonished when taking up your note to reply I saw how long my answer had been deferred—altho' exceedingly unwell I have been incessantly engaged out of town and at home, and my correspondence is deplorably in arrear, nevertheless I feel assured neither you nor Bro. Hughan will attribute my long silence to any want of politeness or respect.

I presume you duly received my note in relation to Mr C.'s Crystal [2] and Millards Catalogue but your favor does not refer to it—I am gratified by hearing your collection increases although unfortunately I make many rash Vows—to buy no more—but my bibliomania has become hopelessly confirmed, chronic, and my Library goes on increasing.

I am obliged by the MS [3] which I return by this post, and will borrow, when the days are longer, for writing so late at night (it is now past one) tires my eyes and also affects the brain—of course I pledge my obligation [4] to conceal whatever is entrusted to me. I enclose a P[ostal] O[rder] for 7/6 and beg you will let me know the registration fees and certificate [5] cost that I may forthwith send a P[ostal] O[rder] for the amount.

Our friend Mrs Everitt [6] has been very unwell—the lady is now at Norwich for a fortnight to refrain from sittings and to recoup her health and lost strength.

Have you introduced Spiritualism to the notice of the FRC. [7] If conducted in order it should be their chief object of investigation—across the threshold—Eternal.

When may I expect the pleasure of another gossip? With kindest regards. I remain dear Bro. Irwin, Most fraternally yours.

1 See Note 2 of Letter 2 (February 1872).

2 See Letter 2.

3 From the commentary I would assume that Irwin had loaned Hockley some SRIA ritual MSS.

4 i.e. by his various masonic oaths (Obligations).

5 For his election as a member of the Bristol College SRIA.

6 See note 1 of Letter 1 (18 January 1872).

7 Fratres Rosae Crucis; i.e. members of the Bristol College SRIA.

4   167 Liverpool Road, Islington, N.
                                              16 March 1872

Most Worshipful Chief Adept,[1]

I have the pleasure of acknowledging the receipt of your esteemed favor telling me that I have been unanimously elected a member of the Weston-Super-Mare & Bristol College of Rosicrucians.

Not being personally known to the Brethren, I cannot but feel that the honour they have done me, upon your recommendation, is a proof not of my qualifications but of the esteen and respect in which you M[ost] W[orshipful] Brother are held by the members of the College.

It is true that when I was Exalted into the Supreme Degree of R[oyal] A[rch] M[ason], after giving due proofs of my proficiency, I was informed by the M[ost] E[xcellent] Z[erubabel] that my humility was a sure indication of merit, and that he was convinced I was qualified to discharge the duties of the most important stations, but these offices being filled I was merely employed to dig and delve, and was in due time promoted to the office of Scribe.[2]

In the Society to which I now have the gratification of being admitted I find myself exalted[3] to the VII° or Grade of Adeptus Exemplus, a post of honour which notwithstanding the assurance of the M[ost] E[xcellent] Z[erubabel] I am afraid I shall but very inadequately fill.

Accepting that office, I beg you will M.W. Chief Adept, accept my grateful acknowledgement and be kind enough to convey to the Officers and Brethren my best thanks with the assurance that I shall at all times be most happy to render them any assistance in my power when extending their researches into the hidden mysteries of nature and science.

I have the honour to remain M.W. Chief Adept,
        Every fraternally yours,
            Fred Hockley Sec.G.S.L., P.M. No. 8, 1167, R.A.[4]

1 Irwin's title as head of the Bristol College SRIA, which in its first

years met at Weston-Super-Mare, before removal to Irwin's residence in Bristol.

2 The Royal Arch is a Masonic Order which, in England, is administratively linked to the Craft and is regarded as the completion of the Master Mason's degree. The M.E.Z. is one of the three presiding Officers of a Royal Arch Chapter. The whole paragraph is a play on a quotation from the Royal Arch ritual which Irwin would easily have recognized.

3 Hockley was indeed *Exalted*. He had never been formally initiated into or taken any of the degrees of the SRIA!

4 Secretary of the Grand Stewards Lodge, Past Master of the British Lodge No. 8, member of Alnwick Lodge No. 1167, Royal Arch Mason.

5   167 Liverpool Road, N.
19 March 1872

Dear Bro. Irwin,

Thanks for your kind note, which crossed mine to you. When I got to Croydon I found I had left out "Hamlet"—in my hurry in London to catch my train. I had posted the letter before I had obt[aine]d the P[ostal] O[rder].

I now enclose it and when I hear from you I will send the other in haste. Most fraternally yours.

6   3 Raymond Buildings, Grays Inn, W.C.
17 June 1872

Dear Bro. Irwin,

On Thursday I had the double pleasure of receiving a letter from you and our esteemed Bro. Hughan—in which Bro. Hughan says 'I am longing to hear from friend Irwin and hope he is better'.

I have been continually thinking about you as for the last 2 or 3 months I have been waking between 4 and 5, latterly unable to sleep afterwards and occasionally not sleeping at all—but with me when I do sleep it is 'like a top' so that I get the full benefit.

One night at my Lodge a Bro. mentioned that he suffered from want of sleep—another replied 'You have the remedy in your own hands, don't drink tea at all'—my complaining friend is like myself an addict and devoted lover of the forbidden beverage—whether he has followed the suggestion I do not know but I left off at once—drinking cocoa in the morning and coffee in milk in the evening—and to assist matters I drink a pint of 6d ale, mild not bitter, with my bread and butter for supper just before going to bed, and this last week I have slept as well as I could wish.

I must admit that during this deprivation I have after business been in a seeming indolent state unwilling to read and still less to write—but these long wearying days when candle light comes one feels too idle to do anything, but I have been, ever since I had the pleasure of seeing you here, exceedingly unwell and taking powerful medicines—in fact like the glow worm 'trimmed my lamp and stayed at home' all the winter.

In your case the symptoms are much more serious. You are acting of course under medical advice but if you come to London I hope you will consult Adolphe Didier[1] the Somnambulist. Some years ago he gave me a marvellous instance of his remarkable faculty and quite upset the assurance of 3 M.Ds to my fears of apoplexy, or rather paralysis.

We also have a Mr Ashman[2] who has performed some excellent cases as a 'healing Medium' and I should like you to see him—yours becomes a more alarming case because the loss of 'nature's soft music' for so long a period must & will affect the brain. For a whole year after my poor wife's sad death I laid awake with unclosed eyes 1 night, half the next I dozed, the third night I slept soundly, the 4th night awake, and so repeated for more than 1 year but it brought me a severe pressure in the right of the brain & from that, more than 20 years ago, I have never recovered.

On the 8th July next I anticipate having my visit to Northumberland on business—for 3 weeks—an entire relaxation in a bracing atmosphere—after that if I take my holidays at all, of which I am rather doubtful, I shall stay at the Baths on the Green opposite the Cathedral—Bristol—and then I shall be able to have an occasional gossip with you.

I have not had the pleasure of seeing Bro. Hughan here yet, so live in the hope of a pleasant meeting and that I shall hear better news as to your health. I remain most faithfully & fraternally yours.

1 Adolphe Didier, and his brother Alexis, came to England from France in the 1840s. Adolphe practised healing by Mesmerism, Alexis

practised clairvoyance, possibly fraudulently.
  2 Unidentified.

7   3 Raymond Buildings, Greys Inn, W.C.
                                                  1 July 1872

Dear Bro. Irwin,
  I have been having my rooms painted and papered and my
landlady has seized the opportunity to alter my bed due East &
West because 'it spoils the look of the room' but on my return
from Alnwick I shall shock her desires by altering it back again.
  It is best for all persons to sleep with their heads as near due
North as possible—but with very electric persons, whether
negative or positive, it is of the utmost consequence and I
speedily felt the difference by waking heavy & giddy &
restless—for altho' I only get 5 hours sleep I have a very sound
doze & could get up quite refreshed—but your case is
unfortunately very different & you must not lose the slightest
chance of alteration. It is also a most excellent plan to have the
bedstead resting on 4 pieces of glass like piano stands—or 4 flat
pieces such as the sky lights that are let into the floors of
outhouses & cellars. You can place a little piece of felt or leather
between the bedstead and the glass—and the *bedhead* must be
kept away from the walls and you are then isolated from the
magnetic currents and 2/6 could pay the expense.
  Of course Medical Men pooh-pooh the matter as rubbish—
but it is none the less true. By this post I have dropped our Bro.
Hughan[1] a note of thanks for his excellent reprints—it is
excellently got up and a marvel of cheapness for a work the sale
of which is so precarious. He writes that he is coming to town
but I leave on business for Alnwick on the 8th inst. for 21 days
so I hope he will be able to delay his visit till I get back. When I
have the pleasure of seeing you here again I shall have my books
in good order as I have another book case at my home today &
then I shall arrange the whole.
  I regret to add that Mrs Everitt[2] is very unwell and has been
so some months, a trip to the country did her much good, but
Miss Nesbit[3] who resides with her has been very ill and is now
going home to Glasgow. This necessarily tends to make her
worse but I hope as Mrs Everitt expects her new house at
Hendon will be very shortly completed & the entire change of
air & scene will restore her to health.

I will not longer tire your patience but trusting I may have the pleasure of receiving better news of your health allow me to remain Most fraternally yours.

Address from 8th to 29th July 'Northumberland Arms, Alnwick, Northumberland'.

1 See note 2 of Letter 1 (18 January 1872).

2 See note 1 of Letter 1.

3 Untraced.

8   9 September 1872

My dear Sir,

I am aghast at my delay in answering your favour of the 1st inst. but I have been engaged out much against my will. I cannot get away from our village[1] this year tho' I had wished to do so, as some of my friends have received great benefit from the treatment at the Baths in the square opposite your Cathedral, where I hoped to have a quiet stay, as hurrying from pillar to post as I did last year, sent me home worse than when I started and a fortnight there would have enabled me to pass all the time you could possibly spare in your company. I must however defer that pleasure till next summer.

My trip to Alnwick did me a great deal of good, as I and my friends stayed in doors every day after dinner and played Bezique till bedtime. I am indeed grateful to hear 'Nature's soft music' has once again come to your aid—for inability to sleep is a much to be dreaded malady—more especially so with an active brain and I hope your 'October' [illegible] will carry you well on through winter.

If I am ashamed at delaying my answer so long I am quite disgusted with our Bro. Hughan's[2] having so recently been in town and leaving without coming to see me. I am grievously disappointed of a long coveted pleasure—and wish the heel of my boot at this moment was on his favourite corn. I've been betrayed and he shall know it.

I am pleased to hear you are increasing your Library and equally sorry to say I cannot leave off increasing my own. I was at Grand Lodge on Wednesday and it was over in an hour. Bro. Binckes,[3] Wm. Carpenter,[4] Boyd[5] and several others adjourned to the depths below—and then learned from Bro. Carpenter that he had been 'converted' to spiritualism against his will. He told me the article in the Freemason[6] had been intended for the Rosicrucian.[7] Bro. C is coming to see me tomorrow evening (Tuesday) for the first time.

Not having seen my friend Mrs Everitt[8] for the last two months I ran down on Saturday to Hendon to inspect the house they have just had built which I am much pleased with & looking over her album I spied your Masonic Carte Visite [photograph], need I add that there is precisely the same sized gap in my album which I am most desirous of filling.

I gave them your kind remembrances which they requested me to reciprocate and added they should be delighted to see us both down there for a sitting at your first available opportunity. The change of air and occupation has much benefitted Mrs E. and there was great need of it.

Now thanking you most fraternally for your kind invitation and assuring you how much I regret my inability of being in Bristol this year allow me to remain with kindest regards Most fraternally yours.

1 Ironic reference to London.

2 See Note 2 of Letter 1 (18 January 1872).

3 Frederick Binckes (?–1904), one of the most prominent English Freemasons of the second half of the nineteenth century. He was Grand Secretary of the Grand Lodge of Mark Master Masons 1861–88; Secretary of the Royal Masonic Institution for Boys 1861–90; and a member of many other Orders, including the Metropolitan College SRIA.

4 William Carpenter (1797–1874). A man of no formal education, he worked for Lackington the bookseller, whom he left to devote his life to writing. As a political reformer, he wrote extensively on politics and theology and edited various journals and newspapers. A Freemason, he was made a Rosicrucian by J. O. Haye in 1857 in the original Societas Rosicruciana in Scotia. An early member of the SRIA he reached the VIII degree and at the time of his death was Master-General elect of the Metropolitan College. Irwin made him a member of the Bristol College, for which he wrote a paper as well as a being a regular contributor to *The Freemason* and *The Rosicrucian*.

5 John Boyd (1809–78), a well-known and immensely popular London Freemason of his day who did much work for the three Masonic Charitable Institutions and was appointed Grand Pursuivant of the United Grand Lodge of England in 1872. Took the Zelator Grade in the Metropolitan College SRIA on 14 January 1869 but although a regular attender did not progress further.

6 *Freemason* Vol. 5, No. 181 (29 August 1872): 'Spirit Agency. Eminent Rosicrucians—Jerome Cardan', by William Carpenter.

7 i.e. the *Rosicrucian Magazine.*

8 *See* Note 1 of Letter 1.

9   168 Liverpool Rd., N.
                                                     3 February 1873

My dear Bro. Irwin,

Many, many thanks for awakening me out of my almost hopeless leter writing lethargy which has oppressed me all winter. The continuous downfall of rain and consequent heavy atmosphere has completely paralysed me and I have returned home every evening so fatigued I find that the pressure on my brain has become so overpowering[1] that I appear to have dozed away all my evenings in listless, thoughtless reading and just at the worst our esteemed Bro. Hughan sent me a copy of a trial (not copied from the Times!) Hockley v. Hughan in which our Bro. vainly tried to show that the Veida was dead against me, although I obtained all the damages I claimed! but perhaps Bro. Hughan has some Celtic blood in his veins and didn't know on which side he was fighting for though I allow he honourably paid the damages (*a carte visite* [photograph] of himself) which so much pleased my landlady that I am under a promise when I go to Truro to have one taken of myself like it (barring the whiskers!)[2]

Unfortunately altho' I was highly amused at the one sided view taken by the reporter, no doubt bribed, I could not help chuckling at the care with which I intended to smash his reporter, Counsel, Jury and Judge—yet whenever I essayed to write a line my head swam and I was afraid spasms would supervene which with me recur instantly. In fact my life this winter has been a truly unenviable one[.] I have not visited one of my friends & passed my Xmas day at home and alone—but should this bright cold weather last I shall soon enjoy better health and spirits.

Now I think I have bored you enough about myself but such is the strange nature of mental maladies that now you have caused me to write this letter I shall feel a great load off my mind, and a letter to our good Bro. Hughan both posted together—so now for further business.

Before I received your last favor I had come to the conlusion
that something unpleasant must have occurred in reference to
my being admitted a member of your R.C. Brotherhood[3] as I
have not been applied to for my fees or subscription or received
my diploma and I am now much concerned to find from your
last letter that you had written (date not mentioned) to me
enclosing my certificate, this I have never received, and I shall
be much obliged by your letter to know the date and whether
you addressed it to me here or to my offices 3 Raymond
Buildings, Grays Inn, that I might enquire about it. As I am one
who doesn't believe in the oft made cry of a letter being lost in
the post, I have lately been assured by two of my friends that
they had sent a letter to me at my office but which I never
received and there may be others, and when you reply please to
let me know the fees and arrears.[4]

I am always pleased to hear of my friends increasing their
collections, tho' I always regret adding to my own! which I do
but sparingly. How is it you do not recognise my calligraphy in
Bumstead's Catalogue, I only bought one book Crollius's
philosophy reformed for 1659,[5] a scarce book but a very good
copy price 9/-.

I do not precisely understand your reference to receiving
instructions from 9 Sages, is it by rapping or writing
mediumship—if so Thos. Norton[6] and Eiraneus Philalethes[7]
ought to be valuable communicants—by the bye has there been
a photograph of Thos. Norton's house in St Peter's Churchyard
in 1490 which he built for himself—which 30 years ago was
called The Mint and now used I believe as an Infirmary[?]. It's a
fine old building—I have got a small wood-cut which the
publisher tore out of a Bristol guide to please a lady friend of
mine who was seeking one for me. I suppose he had a liquerish
tooth for she is a very pretty woman.

NB don't forget to secure (when you have the chance) an 8vo
published by Old Lackington in 1814 'Lives of the Adepts' &
reprinted the following year 1815 as 'The Lives of the
Alchemical Philosophers'[8] a most interesting work with lives
and extracts from their works and a catalogue of 700 works.

Your correspondents are a singular mixture. Thos. Vaughan[9]
was I have no doubt a very truthful, sincere writer altho' his
alchemy is questionable and his attacking so learned a man as
Dr Henry Moore [*sic*] absurd—John Heydon[10] was a downright
imposter, every good thing in his books 'isn't hissen' after
opining 'that marrying was the greatest folly in the world' he

married Culpeper's[11] widow and succeeded to his business, his great good fortune was being committed to the Tower as a printer, where as was wittingly said 'he was better provided for than he had ever been in his life!' he died in an obscure Court in Tower Hill where Lord Clarendon[12] says the Duke of Buckingham[13] often consulted him.

Bro. Elias Ashmole[14] was a world wide celebrity, a great favourite of King Charles, his Chemicum Britannicum in 4to[15] is invaluable & it is a great loss that he did not live to publish the fine companion to it as he intended. I presume you have his life by Burman.[16] 'In alchemy he knew enough to hold his tongue but not enough to speak'.

Arthur Dee[17] was the son of Dr John Dee,[18] his only work is the Chemica by Ashmole 8vo 1650, which I suppose you have, which is one of the interlocutors in that book he says he often saw the projection made.

Everard[19] was a Doctor of Divinity and Chaplain to an Earl—in whose home being short of 'baccy' he smoked the bell pulls in his study—he translated a book of Paracelsus—but his chief work was 'Panacea or a Universal Medicine by the wonderful virtue of tobacco' 8vo. 1659 with his portrait in his study smoking a pipe.

Thos. Norton[20] was the author of the ordinal and a friend of Canynge[21] who built Redcliffe Church—also an alchemist.

I don't remember the anonymous Elias unless it was Helvetius'[22] visitor who made a projection before him and gave him a piece of the gold.

J. A. Comenius's Natural Philosophy reformed, 1651[23] I have forgotten. I remember Denley[24] had it therefore I must have read it.

All Eiraneus Philalethes[25] works are preeminently esteemed but George Starkey[26] was the queerest fish of the lot: a common soldier, astrologer, conjuror, alchemist and if John Partridge[27] speaks truly a 'hang dog fellow' but he certainly was clever.

With regard to the Cabala I never heard of a rudimentary work on the subject, I have the great gem of all the Arte Cabalistica[28] a huge Italian folio of about 100 pages containing all the best writers upon the subject but very little concerning numbers but as John Heydon[29] is your interlocutor I presume his numbers allude to the letters of the Hebrew & Greek alphabets and corresponding letters also adopted to the Latin by which you take out the letters of your name, Father, Mother, House etc. a very antient practice given by Heydon in Book 2

page 8 of his Holy Guide,[30] fudged from Agrippa's Occult
Philos. Book 2 page 30.[31] I have many different forms of same
two MSS and it is a curious subject, I would go into it if I had
time and were not so precious old.

I hope this summer to do a fortnight quietly somewhere for I
found travelling about from pillar to post did me more harm
than good and with the double temptation of trying the Baths
and having some long gossips upon our favourite studies you
may depend that Bristol will be the place but I hope to see you
before then.

When you write let me know how you sleep, I trust it has
improved, for the last few weeks I have slept so little that I have
been obliged to leave off my tea altogether and that is a dreadful
affliction to me.

I enclose our meetings[32] and hope to meet you there the first
opportunity so put them in your pocket book and remember
your promise.

My letter has turned out to such an inconsiderable length that
I must promise not to transgress in future, I have got to write to
Bro. Hughan and it is now past 10 pm and with kindest regards,
I remain, Yours most fraternally.

1 Hockley was to be constantly troubled for the remainder of his life
by headaches and pressure on the brain.

2 This appears to be a humorous comment on some form of
'argument by letter' between Hockley and Hughan, and the latter's
rather extravagant whiskers!

3 Rosicrucian Brotherhood.

4 Correspondence between Irwin and Benjamin Cox, Treasurer of
the Bristol College SRIA, shows the latter to have been lax in his duty;
subscriptions were allowed to go years into arrears.

5 George Bumstead, bookseller, 12 King William Street, Strand.
Oswald Croll (d. 1609). Hockley is presumably referring to H.
Pinnell's *Philosophy reformed and improved in four profound tractates . . .
by O.C.* (1657).

6 Thomas Norton (flourished *c.*1477), M.P. for Bristol 1436;
Ambassador for and member of Privy Chamber of Edward IV. An
alchemist and writer of alchemical tracts. His MS the *Ordinal of
Alchemy* (1477) is notable as having the earliest use of the term 'Free
Mason'.

7 Eiraneus Philalethes: pseudonym used by a seventeenth century
alchemist whose identity remains unknown. He claimed to have

discovered the Philosopher's Stone in 1645. His writings were published 1654–84.

8 The author of the two editions is unknown. They consist of potted lives of alchemists, 'A selection of the most celebrated treatises on the theory and practice of the Hermetic Art', and an interesting if inaccurate booklist. They were hastily re-edited and added to by A. E. Waite for his edition of 1888, a work whose existence he probably regretted in later years.

9 See note 5 of Letter 18 (12 August 1874).

10 John Heydon (*c.*1667), English astrologer and alchemist. Published works on Rosicrucianism although claiming *not* to be a 'Frater of the Rosie Cross'. Imprisoned for two years for incorrectly predicting Cromwell's death!

11 Nicholas Culpeper (1616–54), English physician, herbalist and astrologer. His *Herbal* was edited and reprinted by Ebenezer Sibley in 1798.

12 Edward Hyde, 1st Earl of Clarendon (1609–74), a leading Royalist and historian of the English Civil War. His daughter, Anne Hyde, married the Duke of York (later King James II).

13 George Villiers, Duke of Buckingham. Royalist supporter imprisoned in the Tower 1658–9. The *Dictionary of National Biography* states he was a 'Dabbler in chemistry'.

14 Elias Ashmole (1617–92), English antiquary, astrologer, alchemist and Rosicrucian. His collections formed the basis of the Ashmolean Museum, Oxford. His diary records his initiation into Freemasonry at Warrington on 16 October 1646, the earliest reference so far traced to a speculative initiation in England. The coincidence of his being a Rosicrucian and a Freemason gave impetus to the now discredited theory that Freemasonry was born out of Rosicrucianism.

15 Ashmole's *Theatrum Chemicum Britannicum* (1651) is probably the most important collection of alchemical tracts published in England.

16 Charles Burman's *Memoirs of the life of that learned Antiquary, Elias Ashmole* (1717).

17 Arthur Dee (1579–1657), son of Dr John Dee, alchemist, astrologer and unlicensed medical practitioner. Author of the Rosicrucian *Fasciculus Chemica,* (1631).

18 Dr John Dee (1527–1608), the most celebrated of English astrologers. A mathematician by training he practised crystallomancy with Albert Laski and invoked spirits with Edward Kelly. He headed a fraternity, dissolved in 1589, to seek the Philosopher's Stone and invoke Angels. Wrote *A Treatise of the Rosie Crucian Secrets.*

19 Dr John Everard (*c.*1575–*c.*1650), divine and mystic, translator of

the *Pimander of Hermes Trismegistus* and the works of Paracelsus.

20 See note 5 above.

21 William Canynges (?1399–1474), five times Mayor of Bristol; M.P. for Bristol 1451 and 1455; rebuilt St Mary Redcliffe, Bristol, and the College at Westbury where he became a monk in 1467 and Dean in 1469

22 John Frederick Helvetius (d. 1709), alchemist. On 27 December 1666 he received a mysterious visitor whom he claimed showed him the Philosopher's Stone. He believed the stranger to be Artist Elias, the Prophet of Alchemy, whose coming had been foretold by Paracelsus. See A. E. Waite, *The Secret Tradition in Alchemy* (1926), pp. 307 ff.

23 Johannes Amos Comenius (1592–1671), scholar and educational reformer. Member of the Moravian Brethren: Pastor (1614); Elder (1632); Bishop of Lissa, Poland (1648). Influenced by the mystical writings of Boehme.

24 John Denley was a bookseller in Catherine Street, Covent Garden, from whom Hockley purchased books and occult MSS from early in his career. Denley had purchased Sibley's papers and library in 1799 and had assisted Barrett with *The Magus*. Barrett made no acknowledgement of Denley's assistance but the latter had his revenge by buying up very cheaply all the unbound sheets of *The Magus*.

25 See Note 6 above.

26 John Starkey (*d.* 1665), born Bermuda, educated at Harvard and practised medicine in the American settlements, where he came into contact with Eiraneus Philalethes (see note 7 above). He was in England by 1650 and published medical tracts and a preface to *The Marrow of Alchemy* by Eiraneus Philopenus Philalethes (1654).

27 John Partridge (1644–1715), originally a shoemaker, became a publisher of astrological almanacs from 1678, the most popular being *Merlinus Liberatus*, which first appeared in 1680.

28 Probably Reuchlin, *De Arte Cabalistica* (1517).

29 See note 9 above.

30 John Heydon's *The Holy Guide leading the way to the wonder of the world (a complete Physitian)* . . . *with Rosie Crucian medicines* (London, 1662).

31 See note 8 of Letter 2.

32 Presumably Hockley had supplied Irwin with the meeting dates of British Lodge No. 8 and the Grand Stewards Lodge.

10   167 Liverpool Road, N.
                                       10 March 1873

Dear Bro. Irwin,
    Your last favor of the 7th inst. has fortunately come to hand, I
return your envelope as it explains the miscarriage of your
former missive and points a moral 'that whilst we allow our
minds to delve into the Occult and hidden mysteries of nature
and science' or 'cross the threshold of the mysterious world of
spirits' we must not be unmindful of those little hieroglyphics on
brass which distinguish our humble dwellings in this subluminary
world. No. 168 is between 2 or 3 hundred yards from 167 on
the opposite side of the road, and is in another delivery.
    I thank you very much for your kind note on the certificate,[1]
but as I am out of reach of your immediate wrath, I am bold
enough to think that you are very perverse. You do not mention
any fee or dues. I have never belonged to any society without
paying the full amount as other members & so far as my limited
ability extends endeavoured to do my share of the work, but as I
perceive in the by laws only one scale of fees I enclose a P[ostal]
O[rder] for 10/- for joining fee and subscriptions 1872 & 1873
& presume I must apply to Bro. Wenworth Little[2] with respect
to the Metropolitan dues and my obtaining the back numbers of
the Rosicrucian[3] that I may learn what has been laid before the
Society.
    You do not mention the date you intend holding a Consistory
or Convocation of the Order that I may, if time permits, prepare
a few papers, 'Evenings with Indwellers of the World of Spirits'
commencing with the Spanish Monk which a long time since I
had promised the Spiritualist Magazine.[4]
    With regard to K.R.H.M.[5] I would write to you in a few days
as I am sore pressed for time at present.
    I have many duplicates but where to find them is another
matter. I hope this summer to get my books in good order.
    I will enquire of Mrs Burns[6] about Mrs Jackson's Society[7] but
I have been gradually dropping most of my Spiritualist
acquaintance it entails upon me such a loss of time and a
constant borrowing and consequent spoilage and loss of books
that I have got heartily tired, especially as my health is bad.
    With reference to the other matter I will write in a few days
time but am anxious to send this to prevent any future loss of
your esteemed favors.
    Our good kind Bro. Hughan[8] unfortunately called upon me

most unexpectedly and his stay was very short. I missed many things I wanted to show him, besides my collection is very poor in his consuming passion, Masonry. So that my Dulcinea's had few charms for him however I was delighted to see him altho' I was depriving some more worthy brother of the pleasure of his company. I sincerely hope as the weather & season improve he will get up his strength for altho' both mentally & bodily active he looked to me sadly lacking in stamina.

I made up my mind to be in Bristol for 2 or 3 weeks and get renovated at Bartholomew's Baths. With kindest regards, Most fraternally yours.

1 His certificate as a member of the Bristol College SRIA. The certificate was designed by Benjamin Cox of Weston-Super-Mare, the mainstay of the Bristol College and, later, a member of the Fratres Lucis.

2 Robert Wentworth Little (1839–78). Originally educated for the Church, he entered the Civil Service but left in 1862 to become a Clerk in the Grand Secretary's Office at Freemason's Hall, leaving in 1872 to become Secretary of the Royal Masonic Institution for Girls. A most enthusiastic Freemason he 'revived' a number of Masonic Orders and in 1866 was the founder and first Supreme Magus of the SRIA. Editor of *The Rosicrucian* 1868–78 and of early issues of the weekly *Freemason*.

3 *The Rosicrucian Magazine.*

4 It never appeared in the *Spiritualist Magazine* but was published, without permission, in the *Rosicrucian.*

5 Kenneth Robert Henderson MacKenzie, for whom see the introduction to the next section.

6 See note 2 of Letter 2.

7 Unidentified.

8 See note 2 of Letter 1.

11   167 Liverpool Road, N.
                                            28 March 1873

My dear Bro. Irwin,

I am again groaning in Spirit, in fact ripening into a cross, crabby, grumbling, irritable old fellow—but what can a man do when the usual repository of his brain feels like one warm mass of putty, cerebrum and cerebellum utterly ignored—and finds there is no use mesmerically rubbing his skin as every organ except [illegible] refuses to be excited phrenologically. When I get the Spanish monk[1] or other papers I must precede it with a short explanatory introduction to render the subject intelligible as well as interesting, but at present I am exceedingly unwell & so much pressed with ghostly correspondence which refuses to be exorcised except by long formulas that it is utterly impossible for me to get the article ready for this month though I hope to do so for the next.

I have the utmost reluctance to even refer to Mr Kenneth MacKenzie,[2] I made his acquaintance about fifteen years ago. I found him then a very young man who had been educated in Germany, possessed a thorough knowledge of German & French & his translations have been highly praised by the press, exceedingly desirous of investigating the Occult Sciences, & when sober one of the most companionable persons I ever met. Unfortunately his intemperate habits compelled me 3 different times to break off our friendship after 6 or 7 years endurance & since then he has once so grossly insulted me in a letter that I cannot possibly hold any communication with him. I regret this the more on a/c of his mother who is a most estimable lady & his uncle our esteemed Grand Secretary Bro. Hervey[3] who has long favoured me with his acquaintance.

Of course Mr M's information is derived from his intimate knowledge of German & French, & when you have mastered their difficulties a vastly enlarged field of Occult Science will furnish you with *Original* matter, as well as others (especially on Alchemy). I do not know Mr M's address but a letter thro' Bro. Kenning[4] will doubtless reach him—I saw in the last issue of the Freemason[5] his marriage announced[6]—I very sincerely hope it will be a turning flood in his favour.

It now wants a quarter of twelve so I must conclude & go to bed, & with kindest regards am Most fraternally yours.

1 The subject of his paper *Evenings with Indwellers of the Spirit World.*

2 See introduction to the next section.

3 John Morant Hervey (1805–80) who was Grand Secretary of the United Grand Lodge of England from 1868 until his death.

4 George Kenning. Manufacturer of Masonic regalia and publisher of Masonic books and periodicals including *The Freemason.*

5 *The Freemason* was a weekly Masonic newspaper published from 1869 until 1941 when its premises were bombed. It then appeared intermittently until finally ceasing publication in 1951.

6 Hockley was here mistaken. MacKenzie's marriage had taken place the previous June.

12 South Western Pottery, Parkstone, Poole, Dorset
19 August 1873

My dear Bro. Irwin,
I have by this day's post sent off the Monk's appearance in the Crystal[1] and a very great load is now off my mind. I have been so thoroughly prostrated the last 5 months on reaching home that I have been alike unable to read or write or see my friends, my only relief has been my pleasant Wednesday evenings for which I have been indebted to my good Bro. Walter Spencer[2] & the kind attentions of his amicable little wife, and the pressure on my brain has been so unusually severe on attempting to write in the Evening that I have been afraid of paralysis coming on.

I have made arrangements & determined to be in Bristol in July for the Baths, as I believe my stay there for 2 or 3 weeks is the only chance of relieving me & I need not say that I am almost fretfully anxious to get there—but a client begged me to stay in Town till his business was sorted—and now I have to make a set of accounts for a very old client who has gone 6 years in arrears and I shall be located here for 5 or 6 weeks at least. I had determined to let my friend, a PM of Amity Lodge,[3] drive me over to Blandford to attend the Prov.G. Lodge[4] but I am too unwell.

I came here last week & commenced the MS I had hoped to send you a copy in my old style bound for your Library but at present I am quite incapable. I indeed regret being obliged to send such a horrid rough copy but writing by candle light—with treacle—by no means improves my calligraphy. I hope our Bro. who will kindly read the paper for me will read it over to himself—I brought down with me the MS containing the life of Capt. Anderson[5] & the bottle imp—to accompany this but I will not delay this longer. I have for years promised them to Mr Shorter & I want to get them into the Spiritual Magazine before I publish my C.A.[7] notes.

As for our much valued Bro. Hughan[8] I am altogether in arrears. I must write to him tomorrow night to beg his forgiveness—but I find my head is getting very bad—& must conclude with the kindest regards to yourself, and Mr Herbert,[9] I remain, Yours fraternally.

1 Presumably refers to his *Evenings with Indwellers* paper.
2 Walter Spencer. A member of the family of Masonic regalia manufacturers in Great Queen Street, London. A member of

the Bristol and Metropolitan Colleges of the SRIA he printed a vituperative note on the SRIA in his 1880 catalogue of Masonic regalia and furniture. Well known in Spiritualist circles.

3 The Lodge of Amity No. 137, Poole.

4 The Provincial Grand Lodge of Dorset. Masonically, England and Wales are divided into Provinces, based roughly on the old counties, headed by a Provincial Grand Master appointed by the Grand Master to superintend all the Lodges within the Province.

5 One of Hockley's contacts in the crystal. See the extracts from his Crystal MSS.

6 See note 6 of Letter 2.

7 Crowned Angel of the Seventh Sphere, the Guardian Spirit of Hockley's crystal.

8 See note 2 of Letter 1.

9 Herbert, son of F. G. Irwin, who was himself to become a correspondent of Hockley.

13   South Western Pottery, Parkstone, Poole, Dorset
                                              6 September 1873

My dear Bro. Irwin,

I hope you have received the long delayed MS for the 26th ult.[1] and were able to decipher the introduction. Unfortunately I was suffering so much with my head I could hardly keep my mind on the subject.

Bro. Walter Spencer[2] tells me he also sent you a paper for the meeting. I am going to the 'village'[3] on Saturday 13th returning here on the following Saturday, when I expect to be engaged for some weeks longer.

If it will not inconvenience you I shall be glad to have the Rosicrucian numbers[4] when I reach town, as I can bring them down here and churn them over.

While in town I hope to go twice to see Manfred at the Princess—it is a monologue I am never tired of reading and as I have seen Denvill the first time it was produced on stage—and Phelps when it was magnificently produced at Drury Lane—I hope to see it at the Princess as I do not think it will run long—but to me it is an enthralling piece of elocution and scenic display.

Trusting you are quite well—with kindest regards to yourself and Mr Herbert, I remain, Most fraternally yours.

1 The MS of *Evenings with Indwellers* for the Bristol College SRIA.

2 See note 2 of Letter 12.

3 i.e. London.

4 *The Rosicrucian Magazine*, issued by the Metropolitan College SRIA.

14   167 Liverpool Road North
                                                    25 November 1873

My dear Bro. Irwin,

Your favor has grieviously afflicted me—I feel positive upon receiving intimation from me that your kind present had arrived. I not only acknowledged its safe arrival, but reminded you that I had not received any assurance that my paper[1] forwarded from Poole had come to your hands, your present note in fact being the first intimation on that score.

I had been detained in Poole from 12th August to the 7th November with the exception of one week, and the labour had been so great and my poor brain is so worried that fearing paralysis I came home and had the books[2] sent up after me to be finished, which tomorrow I shall attempt.

Unhappily I find constantly that those things I earnestly desire to do, hardly have been done—so that if any of my friends affirm a thing I am obliged to acquiesce—I do intend however if I get safely thro' this horrid job I will not undertake such another on any account.

I have been so mentally prostrated that I continually determine to part with all my books & furniture and only last Wednesday mentioned to Bro. Walter Spencer[3] that if I do so I would return to you your kind and esteemed present. Unfortunately also for the last 8 weeks I have been unable to sleep more than 4 hours a night and to me who requires so much—that is most distressing—tea of course I have entirely given up.[4]

I am afraid from the hurried circumstances under which I copied the Monk's[5] account you found the paper rather incoherent—it is given in the colloquial manner as my seer expressed herself on spiritual relations. I prefer being able to affirm 'it is exactly as I received it'.

As for our good Bro. Hughan[6] and other kind friends, I feel bewildered when I think how remiss I have been in correspondence.

I will not further bother you with my reiterated grievances but trust you will attribute any future shortcomings of mine to its real cause. With kindest regards allow me to remain, Most fraternally yours.

1 *Evenings with Indwellers.*

2 Hockley was apparently assisting a friend with a pottery business in Poole to sort out his accounts. See Letter 11.

3 See note 2 of Letter 11.

4 See also Letter 6.

5 i.e. *Evenings with Indwellers.*

6 See note 2 of Letter 1.

15   167 Liverpool Road N.
                                          18 June 1874
                                          11 p.m.

My dear Bro. Irwin,

I have long been wistfully meditating writing to you, but I have been utterly unable, ever since we met I am never out of pain—indeed yesterday morning walking to the office my chest became so painful that had not my neck burst out in perspiration I should have fainted in the street. Fortunately a cab came up into which I was helped & driven to my office, unfortunately it comes on with most severity in the Evening & by the time I reach home I am thoroughly exhausted, unfit for anything, read only with difficulty, forgetting what I have read.

My doctor tonight says I live too loose. I must eat more & take stimulants—but my horoscope has for a long time been grievously afflicted & the long continued □ of ♄ & ♅ to each other & Squaring of so many of my Radical planets' places accounts for all my perplexity in private affairs & business & the state of my health—to add to my distress I cannot sleep after I once awake, which of late varies between 2,3,4, & 5 o'clock so that I am almost knocked up.

I have also just lost my dear friend and partner Mr. Begbie after 32 years of the closest & kindest connection. We buried him on the 10th Inst.[1]

I have not written a line in my diary or towards the history of the Grand Stewards Lodge[2] since you were in town. I dropped *all* our friends except our good Bro. Spencer[3] & his kind little wife.

Now dear Bro. Irwin as I like to write to both at the same time I have written a copy of the above to our esteemed Bro. the P[a]st Grand Warden of England!!! Long may he live to enjoy his well earned honours—truly a reward of merit.[4]

The cuttings from a printed Catalogue. No. 1 Solomon's Clavis—[5] exquisitely done by a profess! is a very old friend of mine. I have Denley's catalogue for 1822 before me with the identical copy marked £20. When Dr Ṣibley died in 1799 he left his MSS as an heirloom to his nephew who within a month sold them all to Denley and I made my copy of his.[6]

The Complete book of Magic Science is I presume from its title one of my particular babes for at Denley's suggestion I made up the MS from other sources & made him several copies one after another.

And the 3rd 'Very Rare MS' The Grand Oracle of Heaven is I presume by old Dr Parkins of Gonerly near Lincoln.[7] I have a MS (I believe the same) by me if I knew where to put my hand upon it but at present my rooms are all in confusion. I have had my back room white washed & papered & my book shelves taken down & my front room new carpeted and the book cases cleaned & all the books turned up and dusted so at present I am in a hopeless mess.

A Mr Fryar[8] has copied the MSS correctly—they are worth the money he charges—30/- 15/- & 25/-. He sent me a copy of his sixpence pamphlet on Crystal work but in it they are all worked by planetary spirits—they are to me objectionable.

4 and 5 can only be judged by actual inspection—the little Key of Solomon may only contain a portion of the original MS.[9]

Of course it will always be a great pleasure to me to aid you in any way in your purchases & I shall be very glad to inspect [remainder of letter missing]

1 Hockley's two business partners have proved elusive.

2 It would appear he was preparing a history of the Grand Stewards Lodge. It was never published and the Lodge records contain no mention of a MS.

3 See note 2 of Letter 12.

4 W. J. Hughan, who had been appointed Past Junior Grand Warden of the Grand Lodge of Mark Master Masons of England in 1872.

5 *Clavicula Salomonis:* variously referred to as the Key of Solomon, Key of Rabbi Solomon and the Rath Solomon. A magical and

Qabalistic MS for raising spirits. Legend has its source as Hebrew MSS of the time of Solomon; the majority of the earliest known MSS are in French. An English translation by S. L. MacGregor Mathers was published in 1889, based on a Latin codex in the British Museum.

6 Ebenezer Sibley (1752–99), astrologer, 'doctor', and Freemason. His printed works on astrology and occult sciences did much to revive the subjects in England and paved the way for Barrett's *The Magus*. Hockley copied a number of Sibley's MSS from Denley's collection.

7 John Parkins, astrologer and author of *The Universal Fortune Teller* (1810) and *The Book of Miracles, or Celestial Museum* ..., (1817). Apparently referred to himself as the Grand Ambassador of Heaven!

8 Probably Robert Fryar of Bath, a bookseller, printer of occult works and importer of Tarot cards.

9 The *Legemeton* or *Lesser Key of Solomon*, a collection, in four sections, of rituals for raising spirits, some of a very dubious nature.

16   3 Raymond Buildings, Grays Inn, W.C.
                                      19 June 1874

Dear Bro. Irwin,

I received your note and cheque but my letter written last night was in the post, so I could not get it back. I am sorry you sent the cheque but at any other time you wish me to do anything in London for you I will pay whatever it may be, you can then settle with me afterwards.

You do not mention whether the MSS are copies of printed catalogues or the originals—I hope the Miss Cooper is not the daughter of Mrs Cooper[1] at Norwood for Mrs Cooper is a most impossible Spiritualist who has long threatened me with a visit*—however I won't buy if the books are not quite worth the money. I look forward to seeing Herbert[2] with much pleasure. I want a long talk with him on the use and abuse of Spiritualism.[3]

With kindest regards to both I remain, Most fraternally yours.

Burn this note

1 Unidentified.

2 Hockley apparently developed an avuncular affection for Herbert Irwin.

3 It would appear that Herbert was doing too many experiments with the crystal, the implication being that he was using it as we would today use the telephone.

17   167 Liverpool Road N.
                                              24 June 1874

Mr dear Bro. Irwin,
    I was much pleased at receiving your note, and have written
by this post (pillar) to ask our good friend Bro. W. Spencer[1] to
join & as you are on the spot possibly you will come together. I
shall be at home by half past five. I have not seen our friends at
No. 26[2] for an age. Yours faithfully.
Mr Herbert Irwin.

    1 See note 2 of Letter 12.
    2 Possibly the Everitts, who had introduced Hockley to Irwin.

18   167 Liverpool Road, N.
                                              31 July 1874

Mr dear Herbert,
    The Fairies have restored my lamented book all safe much to
my gratification.
    I am afraid you have hurried yourself too much to have made
a good copy, which it richly deserves. I will send you down a
copy of the Almadel[1] and then the MS is perfect. I intend to
insert it in my little MS and then have it rebound as it is very
dingy—& it will then stand a better chance of being taken care
of when I am across the threshold.
    I will be in Bristol the very first opportunity I can seize. If you
send the exact size and pattern you wish the cross to be made I
will get it cut by a Book Binder's tool cutter.[2]
    I am much obliged by the reply to 'Livre des Esprits'[3] and will
have it bound to match the indices.
    The MS of Vaughan's has interested me exceedingly—it is
strange coming from such a source that nothing they tell is *new*,
you see the curious experiment of the two parallel lines had
actually been printed by Dupotet in the little rough MS I lent
you. I shall be delighted to read the Count's[4] account of
Vaughan's work.
    I never tried the experiments with Warytes mentioned in the
Zoist.[5]
    You did not send Cuss'[6] letter and when I write again I will
return his note that you left with me when in London.

I don't remember if you have the Key of Rabbi Solomon's[7]—
if not when you come to town I can lend you mine.

You do not mention whether I am to send the MS by book
post or rail, I think the post is best—let me know. I am rather
better than I have been but still very unwell.

I am going to a friend's on Saturday & I am back on Tuesday
& on the 10 August I hope to be in Northumberland & with
kindest regards remain, Most fraternally yours.

1 The 'Almadel' is the fourth part of the *Legemeton* or Lesser Key of
Solomon. A. E. Waite characterized the *Legemeton* as a mixture of
black and white magical rituals for invoking what he termed 'four
choirs of spirits', some of a very dubious nature. Despite claims of a
Hebrew origin, the earliest known MSS of the Almadel are French.

2 The Irwins bound and decorated their own books. The collection
contains a number of printed and MS volumes, the bindings of which
are decorated with symbolic tooling including a cross, presumably the
result of this offer.

3 Presumably Allan Kardec's *Livre des Esprits*.

4 With his son Herbert as seer, F. G. Irwin regularly invoked the
spirit of Joseph Balsamo, Count Cagliostro, the notorious charlatan
and purveyor of pseudo-Masonic degrees, who apparently passed
commentaries and 'additions' to the published works of departed
Rosicrucians.

5 Unidentified.

6 Unidentified.

7 See note 5 of Letter 15.

19   White Swan, Alnwick, Northumberland
                                               12 August 1874

Dear Bro. Irwin,
     On Saturday last I sent in a box your two MSS and also the
Key of Rabbi Solomon[1] & a little MS copy of some of my MSS
made by an old friend of mine—now guess on!

I am sorry that Herbert hurried himself over the King
Solomon as the seals in that MS are done with the utmost
precision from two different MSS. It would have been quite
enough to let me know the MS was in his hands.

The Rath Solomon sent may be depended upon for the
accuracy of the Talismans etc. The other MS contains the
admission of Bacstrom into the Society of FRC translated from

his autograph copy now in my possession & I will send you another MS with Anecdotes of the Comte de Chazal by Bacstrom.[2] I could not find it on Sunday. The MS Yardleys Process is a very curious MS highly esteemed. *I have never seen it printed* & is well worth Herbert copying. The Diary is merely curious. I do not remember where I got the original.

Your two MSS are very curious and very interesting—it is astonishing to me that our Invisible Friends do not give us anything *valuable and new*.[3] The Book of Seth—as stated in the MS—is vastly like a plagiarism upon the Scriptures & the lives of Constant [illegible]—being so very unwell & overworked at my office I have not compared it with the 'Book of Enoch' published by Bishop Lawrence[4] & others I have but hope to do so at another opportunity when you can furnish me with the MS.

Vaughan's[5] work coming from the source it does is much more perplexing. He does not give us any of his Metaphysical explorations—as he printed either in Theologizing Alchemy or Alchemizing Theology—but a disquisition on Magic which he never published anything of the sort—and his magnetic experiments are 'obvious plagiaries' from Dupotet[6] (I don't know whether Bro. Vaughan is looking over my shoulder or not, if so I beg his pardon for writing it—but think so all the same). I had hoped to have compared his Recipes with Salmon, Culpeper and Blagrave[7] but did not wish to detain the MS as I was leaving London so soon—but when you come to town we can talk the subject over.

There is a recipe on the properties of the plant Rue I know you will allow Herbert to copy out for me as I wish (after comparing it with Salmon) to try it—although I read it over several times my mind gets too confused to remember it and I promise you on my obligation that I did not copy a word or figure out of either of your MSS.

I hope this will find Herbert all right & that he has not overworked himself for his examinations—it is vexatious that Spirit intercourse weakens us physically—and the Crystal sadly tries the Seer's eyes if much used—unless carefully guarded against.

I shall be here about 3 weeks & intend taking a day or two going home to see Lincoln and Ely Cathedrals and Cambridge—my partner is going on to Bury & will not be back in Town till early October & then I think of coming down to Bristol for a day or two of which I will give you due notice. I am writing this at 11 o'clock by gas light and must conclude with kindest regards & best wishes to yourself & Herbert. Most fraternally yours.

1 See note 5 of Letter 15.

2 Bacstrom had been initiated into a Rosicrucian Order by the Comte de Chazal in Mauritius in 1794. The certificate and *Anecdotes* referred to here have recently been reproduced in facsimile by R. A. Gilbert. The original certificate has been lost, but was shown by Hockley at a SRIA meeting and published in *The Rosicrucian*.

3 Hockley had presumably been reading MSS supplied to the Irwins by one of the Spirits called up in their Crystal. He may be having a slight dig because the Irwin's crystal contact appears to be able only to give them information which has already appeared elsewhere.

4 It is not clear but it would appear that the *Book of Seth* was dictated to the Irwins through the crystal. According to Josephus' *History of the Jews*, Seth (3767 BC) was the first astrologer. The apocryphal Book of Enoch was an important source for occultists as it listed the names of the Archangels and fallen angels and gives the legend of the sons of heaven coming to earth, marrying mortals and teaching them charms, enchantments, herbalism, and astrology.

5 Thomas Vaughan (1622–66), English Rosicrucian who used the pseudonym Eugenius Philalethes. His translation of the *Fama* and *Confessio* appeared in 1652. His writings provoked an angry response in print from the Cambridge Platonist Henry More (1586–1661) using the pseudonym Alazanomastix Philalethes.

6. Hockley presumably refers to J. Dupotet, *La Magie devoileé* (Paris, 1852). The Irwins certainly had a clever spirit if he could plagiarize the works of a nineteenth-century author to provide reputedly new information from a seventeenth-century writer!

7 William Salmon, *Botonologia—the English Herbal or History of Plants* (1710); Nicholas Culpeper, *The English Physitian* (1652); Joseph Blagrave, *Supplement or Enlargement to Mr. Nich. Culpeper's English Physitian* (1655), or possibly his *Astrological Practice of Physick* (1689).

20   167 Liverpool Road N.
                                            24 September 1874

My dear Bro. Irwin,

   In my last letter when I returned your MSS I mentioned I was going to Northumberland hoping I might in some measure restore my over-troubled system. I went on 10 Aug. and was getting 'All serene' when on 23rd I was attacked with Diarrhoea which I stopped but staying on my way home at Lincoln to see

the Cathedral I was again attacked the following Sunday—
which I stopped sufficiently to reach home on the Tuesday when
I had a violent relapse accompanied with other painful
concomitants which has kept me confined at home now 3
weeks—but I am all right now so far as that is concerned.

Tuesday was the first day for 3 weeks that I had meat for
dinner & dining with a friend on 'Sir Loin' helped down with a
little brandy and kept down with a little port—I went home quite
rejuveniled [*sic*] & determined to pay off one of the heaviest
debts on my conscience by writing to our esteemed Bro.
Hughan[1] & endeavour to palliate in some measure my apparent
neglect—reserving as I told him the pleasure of writing to you
tonight.

I much regret to learn from you that like myself you have been
suffering so much both bodily and mentally. When the brain
suffers what would otherwise be the greatest pleasure un-
accomptably becomes insurmountable, at least it is so with
me—but I hope and trust we may both be enabled this winter to
enjoy a more frequent communication.

I very much sympathise with Mr Herbert on his mishap in not
passing[2] but the best and the only way to succeed next time is
not to allow himself to dwell upon it but try & strengthen his
system—and his brain will soon recoup itself for a successful
effort.

He is at a critical age & requires great care, growing and
studying hard at the same time would try any system.

It is of course a grievous affliction to lose our spiritual
communications.[3] Still his health is of paramount importance, I
hope he will never let himself be Biologised by any one.

As I mentioned in my note I read your MSS with very great
interest. Being on the eve of leaving London & my books all at
sixes and sevens I could not compare them with Salmon,
Culpeper[4] or other authors on R[osie] C[rucian] Medicines, but
now altho' I have not got my books in order the occult portion is
collected together under different heads and consequently most
readily available. When you are in town bring the R[osi]
C[rucian] MSS up & we will compare notes for altho' I retain a
general idea of the MSS my memory does not serve in
particulars—by the bye I asked you for a copy of the recipe on
the herb Rue. It is only a few lines.

Though I and my partner have decided in future to take
holidays as well as our clerks we have this year been so thrown
out of gear by the illness and decease of our partner & esteemed

friend—with other matters—that I am not likely to do so this year but if spared have made up my mind to a fortnight in Bristol next year, travelling about by myself only does me harm. I therefore look forward with great pleasure in meeting you and Mr Herbert here in Dec. but I am almost certain I shall have occasion to run down to Bristol on business for a couple of days—Saturday to Tuesday about the end of October.

As for the MS Rath Solomon etc. take your time in copying, in your own hands they are as safe as in my own.[5]

As it is not worth your while buying modern Spiritualist works which in a year or so will be at half price or less—I have bought the two last works 'Astounding facts in Spiritualism' (American) and the Mendal by Consul Barker which I will send down if you or Herbert would like to read them or any other book I have.

Now I think I have given Br. Hughan & you a dose which I think you will deem rather more than quantum stuff & I therefore conclude with kindest regards and best wishes, Most fraternally yours.

1. See note 2 of Letter 1.

2 Herbert Irwin was a medical student and had just failed his examinations.

3 Presumably Herbert's illness and general mental state had called a halt to the Irwins' crystal scrying.

4 See Letter 19.

5 See Letter 19.

21   3 Raymonds Buildings, Grays Inn, W.C.
                                        28 October 1874

Dear Bro. Irwin,
    After losing all this week idling about I am only now able to say I intended being in Bristol on Friday—leaving Paddington by the 10.30 train & I must return on Monday. In haste. Yours fraternally.

22   167 Liverpool Road N.
                                        December 1874

My dear Herbert,
    Your kind note is to hand. I shall pass Christmas at

home—Monday 21st Dec. is my lodge night & election of W.M. & Treasurer[1] & we have a good deal to do—but the 23 & 24 I will be at home to see you as a matter of course. What are you going to do on Tues 22nd? I shall be at home—if you are able to come up on that night.

Pray give my kindest regards to your dear Mama and your Father and very best wishes for your success—and a happy Christmas to you all. In great haste, Yours most sincerely.

1 The Master and Treasurer of a Masonic Lodge have to be elected by the members each year. Only in exceptional circumstances may a Master serve for more than two consecutive years.

23   167 Liverpool Road N.
                                                 22 December 1874

My dear Herbert,

I am disappointed at not seeing you this evening—but hope to see you on Wednesday.

I shall be at the Royal Farmers Insurance Office, 3 Norfolk St., Strand all day from 10 to 4 if you wish to see me—if not I hope to see you here as soon after six for tea—if you can make convenient. Faithfully yours.

24   167 Liverpool Road, N.
                                                 22 April 1875

My dear Bro. Irwin,

I began a letter to you shortly after receiving yours but I broke down—last night was the Grand Stewards Lodge so now I have a respite till November. Hitherto I have been worried beyond measure, the members all having the Installation fever[1]—then returned tickets[2]—this evening I am at home but almost knocked up.

I regret exceedingly to hear so bad an account of my dear young friend,[3] he looked very unwell when here but I was in hopes that would pass off on his return home—it must indeed have been a source of great alarm to Mrs Irwin & yourself and I rejoice to learn he is now improving and will I trust thoroly [sic] recover his health, but he will require great care for some time.

I am very pleased to find I shall see you soon—if well enough I intend being at the Installation with 16 other PMs[4] from the Grand Stewards Lodge but I have written this morning to our WM No. 8[5] who is also our Grand Steward of the year to decline a ticket for the Banquet which he had kept for me—as I cannot stand the worry of getting from Kensington to Freemasons' Hall.[6] I suffer so much from neuralgia of the muscles and then racing of the heart that I cannot make the least muscular exertion without great pain—but I must not worry my friends with my complaints—but look forward to the great pleasure of seeing you here & making the most of it.

With kindest regards & best wishes to Mrs Irwin & Herbert I remain, Most fraternally, yours.

1 The Installation of Albert Edward, Prince of Wales (later King Edward VII) as Grand Master of the United Grand Lodge of England on 28 April 1875.

2 Hockley as Secretary of the Grand Stewards Lodge would have had much work to do as the Grand Stewards, since 1728, have been responsible for the arrangements for the Annual Grand Festival and Installations of new Grand Masters.

3 Herbert Irwin had a weak constitution and was often ill.

4 Past Masters.

5 Worshipful Master of British Lodge No. 8, in which Hockley had been initiated.

6 As accommodation at Freemasons' Hall was limited, the Installation of the Prince of Wales took place in the Royal Albert Hall, Kensington Gore, but the Banquet which followed was a more limited affair in the Grand Hall of the Freemasons' Tavern.

25   3 Raymond Buildings, Grays Inn, W.C.

12 May 1875

Dear Bro. Irwin,

The books[1] arrived safe yesterday but I could not open them as a friend came in & stayed till evening—talking nonsense. I will pack up the next three vols. & thank you very much for letting me have them in town. I wish the box had been a little larger, you will have to get a small screw driver as it is so much better to screw the box than knocking it to pieces unpacking it. I found the other paper of yours when I put my books up—it was laying under your bound books but I forgot it was in a brown paper case—I had shelved it with my MSS.

I have got the Talmud No. of the Review which I will put in also if the box is large enough, it will [illegible] with your other extracts—as to the other contents & queries in your note I will write when I get home this evening.

I have not heard whether I am elected or not at the M.C.[2]
With kindest regards, Fraternally yours.

1 In the areas of both Freemasonry and rejected knowledge students regularly circulated their books and MSS to each other and made wholesale copies or extracts from each other's work.

2 The Metropolitan (i.e. London) College SRIA.

26   3 Raymond Buildings, Gray's Inn, W.C.
                                                          12 May 1875

My dear Madam,[1]
When my esteemed friend Capt. Irwin arrives at 'our village'[2] his time is so short, his engagements so many, and the visits allotted to me so fully occupied that I had no opportunity of writing to you to request your acceptance of the picture I entrusted to his charge.

The painting is by my highly respected friend Mr Henry Bielfield[3] and represents an incident in my Crystal experiences. The book given by the Angel to the kneeling figure is a treatise upon Metaphysical and Spiritual philosophy with which I was afterwards favoured and am now preparing for publication & trust I shall have the pleasure of sending a copy for your acceptance.[4]

I was much pained at hearing my young friend Mr Herbert had been so seriously unwell but under the best of nurses, a loving Mother, I doubt not he will soon recover & with kindest regards to him and best compliments to yourself allow me to remain,
dear Madam, Most faithfully yours.

1 F. G. Irwin's wife, who appears to have shared her husband and son's interest in Spiritualism.

2 Hockley's ironical term for London.

3 Unidentified.

4 The MS came into the possession of Walter Moseley and is listed in Redway's catalogue of Moseley's Library (1889) as follows: 'Metaphyiscal and Spiritual Philosophy; or, the connection with and influence over material bodies by Spirit. Revealed by the Crowned Angel of the Seventh Sphere through the medium of the magic mirror, Miss Emma Louisa Leigh being Speculatrix, 1854. 3 vols., 4to. This is presumably the work Hockley refers to in his letter of 13 May 1875 as

being prepared for publication. As far as can be traced it was never published.

27   13 May 1875

Dear Bro. Irwin,
  I have sent off by Passenger Train Vols. 7. 8. 9. of the Crystal MS & 3 or 4 pamphlets. The Quarterly Censer Talmud must come at another time.
  When you open the box take out the little newspaper first then the two blue pamphlets.
  My MSS not being indexed I have been looking through them till my head aches & I am so unwell I get worse instead of better—I feel at the present moment too insipid to do anything.
  You cannot judge of the C.A.'s theology until I have got out my manuscript for publication.[1]
  The Evan's[2] glass was made thus: a square top of wood with a hole in the middle   then a piece for the bottom without any hole—upon this last piece is spread a piece of fine thin white silk—I think they call it [illegible] or some such queer name & upon that a piece of plain thick glass.
  Then I made it square by putting 4 brass rods which fitted into the corners of the top and bottom pieces thus   . Of course you see here the sides open & therefore to make it dark inside I put a piece of leather all round & thus it becomes a box with leather sides & only one hole in the top—but were I to make another I should cut differently. I would have a square box of the same size made with a loose bottom—the top with two holes the width of my eyes with sockets like an opera glass and then there would be no occasion to flatten a ladies nose or bring on strabismus.
  I could then cover the bottom of the box with the white silk place the glass on it and fasten it in place. Then I could consecrate the Mirror and all would be complete. In these matters so much depends upon their being manufactured by the exegist [?] who uses them. Of course there is no hole in the glass—that is on the bottom with the white silk under it.
  I have just found the place in my MS but I must refer to the rough book taken at the time. I will also work out the ring matter and let you know.
  I never could learn anything of Capt. Anderson[3] but for a great annoyance he became my favourite companion in the

C[rystal] MS—reference to the Crimea. I presume was only [illegible] to Selina—you will see more of him in the following vols.

I see you meant Runnelly [illegible] of the R[osi] C[rucian] books—but I have packed up the books. Of course I am writing on Wednesday night tho' my letter is dated tomorrow— but the box is too small. I am afraid it will be the next time & I send down only two vols. of my MSS and I must now go to bed—I have been much worse the last 2 or 3 days—with kind regards, fraternally yours.

1 Presumably a reference to the Crowned Angel's *magnum opus* which never appeared in print and the MS of which is lost.

2 Evans was a popular medium who specialized in slate writing produced either directly onto slate or glass covered slate sealed into a box.

3 See extracts from the Crystal MSS quoted on pp. 109–28.

28   167 Liverpool Road
                                         18 May 1875

Dear Bro. Irwin,
I returned the card merely to save you the trouble of writing another—no charge was made here.

The box would only contain my 3 vols. and your MS—the pamphlets were put in to fill but I could not have put in the R[osi] C[rucian] MS but surely you don't intend copying what is already in print—'Silence after clamour'.

The questions in my diaries have no direct connection with the Book I received from the C.A.[1] When I commenced the diary my views were Unitarian with Jesus as an inspired Man—but from the C.A.'s teaching they were suddenly changed to a ∴ God——the Divine birth of Jesus and their Holy Spirit (or influence)—but the Trinity as held by priests of the Athenasian Creed I do not and cannot understand and I have determined to dwell no more upon it and in this I am supported by my learned friend Bro. Dresser. The Immaculate Conception & Divine Birth of Jesus as a matter of belief has to me no difficulty. Of course you will perceive my questions & can ask any of your communicants the same—but the two standpoints are not the same. The C.A's work is Metaphysical and Spiritual Philosophy or the Connection with Influence over material bodies by Spirits & opens with the following syllogism 'where there is life, there also is spirit. In all things created there is life therefore in all things there exists spirit.' It was given to me in 3 parts but I am condensing it into one.[2]

I cannot but laugh to myself at the fever heat you work up in Spiritualism—I could have gone on for 20 years communicating with Anderson or any one else without attempting to find out their position in life if they themselves declined telling me. You will see I tried to obtain it from Anderson himself and I truly believe I saw him and his sister at the London Bridge Station the night he said he saw me there—only a very small portion of what passed between me and Anderson has been recorded by me because we used to [illegible] with him in Lord Ashburton's Park in the [illegible] & consequently did not keep any record.

Lord Stanhope[4] made several attempts—but failed to find out his whereabouts—but one very singular relation he would apear to be a son of The Queen of Spain—it is in the Magic MS with the 'Hand of Glory'—I do not know in what volume.

I am sorry to say that I get worse rather than otherwise & I have been indoors ever since Saturday and I cannot walk nor can I ride on the Tram or Omnibus—but as usual it is past 11 & I must go to bed & with kindest regards to Mrs Irwin and yourself I remain, fraternally yours.

1 Hockley's spirit, the Crowned Angel.

2 See Note 4 of Letter 26.

3 Captain Anderson was a spirit Hockley had contact with in the crystal. He had apparently been killed in the Crimean War. It would appear that the Irwins had also contacted him. See the excerpts from Hockley's Crystal MS pp. 109–28.

4 See note 3 of Letter 2.

29   167 Liverpool Road, N.
                                                              2 July 1875

My dear Herbert,

I must apologise for not acknowledging the safe receipt of your books and regret now to hear that you have been so ill & trust now that you are convalescent you will strictly attend to your doctor's advice & bless your lucky stars in having so good a nurse.

As I rarely read a newspaper I was surprised to see the article on the medium which however contains very little—'M.A.

OXON'[1] must be very wrath with the scamp and I expect to find a longer account in this month's Human Nature. I presume we need not try to [illegible] the 50 faithful at 30/- a piece just yet.

Mr Spencer gave me a cat. of his Masonic sale[2] but I do not think I shall attend as there are many books I should like to have—but I am so utterly unwell and suffer so much pain—that I have no desire to increase my collection, in fact my books are literally becoming a nuisance to me for want of room to stow them in—my place is always in a litter and altho' in pain I have wasted several evenings trying to put them in decent order for I can never find anything I want without an hour's hunt.

I wish you had mentioned when Constant[3] died & the papers that attended to him—I am glad you are adding to your 'gems' as Cagliostro's[4] must be very scarce—there will be some which will be knocked down at Spencer's sale.

I came home so thoroughly knocked up—& these horrid long days, all twilight, prevent me doing any thing and I have not been able to answer your worthy Papa's letter yet and must now conclude with best compliments to Mrs Irwin & best regards to yourself, faithfully yours.

1 Revd William Stainton Moses (1839–92), clergyman, teacher and private tutor, Freemason. Introduced to Spiritualism in 1872, he developed his own mediumistic powers. Author of books on Spiritualism and contributor to *Light, Human Nature*, and *The Spiritualist*. Founder member British National Association of Spiritualists. Member of the Council of the Psychological Society. Member of Society of Psychical Research. President, London Spiritual Alliance, 1884–92.

2 Richard Spencer (1800–76) was a manufacturer of Masonic regalia and publisher of Masonic books from his premises opposite Freemasons' Hall, Great Queen Street. His collection of Masonic and occult books and MSS was probably the finest private collection of its day in England and was the subject of the catalogue referred to here by Hockley. It was offered as a collection to the United Grand Lodge of England for their Library but they would not pay the price. It was dispersed by auction, much of the choice material going to American collections.

3 Alphonse-Louis Constant (i.e. Eliphas Lévi) died on 31 May 1875.

4 Count Alessandro Cagliostro, the assumed name of Giuseppe Balsamo (1743–95) an Italian adventurer who claimed to have been initiated into Freemasonry and various occult orders by the Comte de St-Germain. He practised an Egyptian Rite, a mixture of pseudo-

Freemasonry, alchemy and occultism. Hockley is possibly referring to
The Life of Cagliostro, printed by Hookham (1787).

30   [No address]
                                                    22 July 1875

My dear Herbert,
Considering the excessive bad weather and the critical state of
your health I think you are fortunate in only catching a severe
cold—unfortunately you may not yet have experienced all its evil
effects—I trust you will get well over it and not plan such visits
again, if you truly wish to remain on this side of the 'Threshold'.
With regard to the case you allude to you have made a great
muddle—can you suppose notwithstanding your pathological
investigations that the learned physician who told me the
particulars of the case & attended her, & other numerous
medical friends could not tell whether it arose from such a
'common occurence' in practice as you refer to or otherwise—the
matter remained quite inexplicable—I regret having mentioned
the circumstance—but pray do not talk about it for the young
lady's sake. I do not know whether she is now alive or not. It was
a sad affliction for her family, both her father and uncle were.
officers in the Army.
Do not be at trouble about writing about Eliphas Lévi.[1] I will
write to my Mr Shorter (Thomas Breviour)[2] and he will give me
the particulars.
You do not mention the name of the Masonic work Mr Cooke
intends to reprint.[3]
I do not know which you mean by the two vols of MS
scraps—but I must decline lending my diaries and private MSS.
On my own part I can only say that I am not the slightest
degree better for all my doctoring—to walk or make the slightest
muscular exertion I come home knocked up—although kept a
close prisoner.
On Monday 2nd August I am going to Alnwick for 3 weeks
and as the weather has been fine in the North I hope the entire
change of air & living will in some measure release me.
With kindest regards to Mrs Irwin & your father believe me,
Yours faithfully and fraternally.

1 See Letter 29.
2 Editor of *The Spiritualist*.
3 Matthew Cooke was a curious figure: musician, journalist,

professional researcher and copyist of MSS in the British Museum and other libraries. A member of numerous Masonic orders, he quarrelled with many people. He applied to the Grand Lodge for financial aid in 1880, after which he disappears from the records.

31   Royal Hotel, College Green, Bristol
                                   Sunday, 10 October 1875

Dear Brother Irwin,
   I arrived here on Saturday at 6 p.m. but I am so exceedingly unwell and unable to get about that I remained indoors all day today except walking to the Baths to see Mr Bartholomé & I have engaged to be there at ½ past 10 tomorrow morning— intending to take my first Turkish bath & if it does me good I shall stay a week or ten days for I cannot keep on as I am at present without imminent danger of a sudden collapse for I feel a very little more will hit me out of life altogether. I shall of course be very glad to see you and Mr Herbert here any time in the afternoon—tho' I don't know yet the time I am to take the bath. I have brought the papers you kindly sent me & when I get well [illegible] I hope to have a gossip over the contents. It is to me perfectly ludicrous to read the astounding almost second-hand knowledge that is now being passed off as original but we can have a laugh together when we meet.
   Brother Spencer came to see me and read the paper to me.[1] Have you yet received [illegible] or paper [illegible] know the work I will get a copy also.
   I hope Mrs Irwin is quite well and has become converted and trust I shall soon be well enough to pay my respects to her, & with kind regards I remain, Faithfully and fraternally yours.

   1 An untitled paper given by Spencer to the Bristol College SRIA, a rather confused statement on the history of occultism, Rosicrucianism and the search for the Philosopher's Stone.

32   3 Raymond Buildings, Grays Inn, W.C.
                                        8 March 1876

Dear Bro. Irwin,
   I rejoice I am so soon to see you. I shall be in the restaurant (down below) at the Freemasons' Tavern[1] on Thursday at ½ past 4 to get a [illegible].

Of course I shall keep Friday evening sacred for you, but that we can talk about on Thursday. I received your further particulars of your friend's very interesting case of Clairvoyance which interests me much.

Trusting you will have a pleasant journey up, Yours faithfully and fraternally.

1 The Freemasons' Tavern was attached to Freemasons' Hall in Great Queen Street and was used both for refreshment and informal meetings. Its modern counterpart is the Connaught Rooms.

33   3 Raymond Buildings, Grays Inn, W.C.

22 June 1877

My dear Herbert,

Your letter came to hand just as I was sitting on the floor for the first time this two years pulling out my books in search of some MSS I want to separate. I did it two evenings but it did my side such pain I have not been able to continue the job yet.

Your letter would indeed have been welcome if it had contained better news. I am indeed very sorry tho' not surprised at your having been so unwell—I hope your proposed change will do you good, strengthen your nerves and put some 'go' in.

My getting out of Collar seems hopeless at present as I cannot leave either my partner or my business in the lurch but I am always in pain and last night put on a stiff mustard plaster which has relieved my side.

I am going to stay here until September unless I am lucky enough to get suitable apartments—I am advertising—but with my abominable load of books moving is no joke.

I am much obliged by the Catalogue. I shall try & find out the deceased Gentleman's name—I have no doubt that the Rotalo is Sibley's[1] copy as with it is [illegible] work in MS which he also copied. I regret much not having known of it in time.

Reading thro' your note now I see your note about the Human Nature.[2] I intended to get it down & read it but unluckily it quite passed out of my mind—but I will look at it when I get home & will write you again. Fortunately we have just turned the longest day, I am tired of them if too dark to read or write or too light to burn up Candles & the evenings lost—but I will attend to it when I get home.

I am much obliged by your kind Mama's remembrances &

beg you will tender my kindest regards to her—but when I shall reach Bristol is at present obscure & with kindest fraternal regards to your father & yourself believe me both faithfully and fraternally yours.

My head is so cluttered I quite forgot to ask: Will you kindly let me know by return of post if you can—how many leaves there are in the *second* part of the longer German RC work—including the title—I lent my copy much against my *stomach* to an old friend & it came back last night, I think a leaf short.

1 Sibley's *Rotalo* is a MS scrapbook or commonplace book now in the Library of the Wellcome Institute.

2 A Spiritualist periodical edited by James Burns (see note 2 of Letter 2).

34   3 Raymond Buildings, Gray's Inn, W.C.
                                                   24 June 1877

My dear Herbert,
    I am obliged by your very prompt reply to my note, it must have been my mistake in first collating the work—as my copy has the same number of plates as yours—it enables me to write to Mr Moseley[1] to apologise before he leaves London on Tuesday.
    Re-reading your letter this morning I found that I had entirely overlooked 'next Wednesday' you intend going to Paris. I have been in so much pain I have not been able to get up to Puttock & Simpsons but will let you know if I obtain the deceased Collector's[2] name. I wish you had said what was the number of 'The World' which mentions Lord Houghton's[3] name. I must try and brush up my memory about the Theosophic Society MN alludes to—not the one of which Cap. 'Webb' was a member but the former which met at Hoxton. Oddly enough my old Schoolmaster at Hoxton was a member [and] his name was Webb. He was very fond of Astrology & occult science & also Bishop the Master at Sir John Cass' School on Church Row as I learned afterwards from Mr Jno. Denley the Bookseller. I was only eight years old when I left Mr Webb's school.
    If I can find my old Catalogue of cuttings tonight when I get home I will send you the name of two very scarce French books & their authors & dates—you may have the luck to pick them up.

One was Trithemius in French[4] 4to & the other Lenaine on the Cabala, we have nothing like it in English & the Hebrew in the German books are very incorrectly printed. I saw the Monk of course in the R[osie] C[rucian] and was vexed[5]—it had been put in without consulting me first.

Have you not selected a bad time to go to Paris—I have been told and often read that it is insufferably hot in summer months, however you must take care & not expose yourself to the chance of sun stroke. I only wish that I could have a month with you this year—I am fire proof against hot weather—& I should like to poke our noses together over the old Book stalls on the Quays if they are there still.

I am in a horrid lot of trouble about my moving—I have heard of nothing to suit me but must do so before Michaelmas—my books are a horrid nuisance and I must get rid of a lot (not occult) they get so horrid dusty in the London smoke if they are not kept in a bookcase, and even there they are bad enough, but I am always in pain and have no heart to move about or do any thing after business is over. Let me know where to address you when you get to 'Paradise'—and with kind regards believe me, Yours faithfully and fraternally.

Now act like a Philosopher and take care of yourself!

1 Walter Moseley of Builduas Park. He had been initiated into Freemasonry in Apollo University Lodge No. 357, Oxford, when a student at Trinity College, but although remaining a member for the remainder of his life he was not an active Freemason. He appears to have been more interested in practical magic. On his death his collection was bought by Redway and included a number of Hockley MSS, including the Crowned Angel's *magnum opus*.

2 See Letter 2.

3 Richard Monckton Milnes, 1st Baron Houghton (1809–85), politician, dilettante writer, and literary editor. Collector of books and MSS and Founder of Philobiblon Society, whose *Transactions* he edited.

4 See note 2 of Letter 35.

5 MacKenzie had published Hockley's paper *Evenings with Indwellers of the Spirit World* in *The Rosicrucian* without permission.

35   167 Liverpool Road, N.
                                          26 June 1877

My dear Herbert,

I enclose the titles of two books which are very desirable. I
have got Lenain[1]—but the Trithemius[2] I have parted with many
years since. I have five editions of Trithemius in Latin. If you
could get a clean copy 4to of the French I would give a guinea
for it—if you do not want it for yourself. The binding would be
of no consequence—let me know your address so soon as you
have got a permanent one.

I wish I was going with you, though you might desire a more
lively companion, but I am in such pain when up—& worried by
any work and being so hopelessly unsettled as to my obtaining
suitable lodgings that I really get too idle or rather weary to do
anything after I get home—but I must turn over a new leaf and
hope when you come back—like a giant refreshed—I may be
able to say in some measure 'Richard's himself again'. Now take
care of yourself & let me hear from you as soon as you can—till
when I remain. Yours faithfully and fraternally.

1 Lenain, *La science cabalistique* (Amiens, 1823). Lenain was
described as a 'Franc-maçon hermetique', probably a member of one
of the numerous French quasi-Masonic orders which were a mixture
of Freemasonry and various strains of occultism.

2 *Polygraphie et universelle escriture cabalistique de M. J. Trithème,
traduit par Gabriel de Collange* (Paris, 1561). John Trithemius of
Spanheim had been educated at Basle University and taught magic,
alchemy, and astrology to Paracelsus (Theophrastus Bombastus von
Hohenheim).

36   167 Liverpool Road, N.
                                          13 August 1877

My dear Herbert,

I am just starting by the 10.30 a.m. for Alnwick where I shall
be for 3 weeks & then must return straight home to remove to
my new domicile. My books are the greatest plague to me & I
must part with a good many as I have at my new place no room
for another book case, besides I have made up my mind if I am
not better this time next year to sell my furniture, books etc. and
set myself in as small a compass as possible—I am going to

Alnwick in very low spirits, my pain is so continuous—I have closed nearly all my business. I have returned the books so far as I could get at them—but I have doubtless others which are at the back of my books—& as the books are all being cleaned (in my absence) they will pass through my hands and I can pick out any with your father's name in them & send them down—but clear out I must.

I was in hopes of hearing from you as soon as you returned as I was much alarmed at you being in Paris alone whilst subject to fainting. I hope & trust to hear better news of your health—addressed to me at the White Swan Hotel, Alnwick—do let me have a note soon.

Pray give my kindest regards to your Mama & fraternally so to your Father & I hope to hear they are both well. In haste, Most faithfully and fraternally yours.

I expect to be back on 3rd Sept.

37   3 Raymond Buildings, Gray's Inn, W.C.
                                              26 September 1877

Dear Bro. Woodman,[1]
Your favor arrived on the Eve of my moving to a fresh domicile & the worry with first sending my books, over 2,000 volumes unpacked, & pulling down my bookcases & other matters one week, and my furniture the next, & too ill to do any thing but look on have prevented my answering your note before this and my being in business away from my own office I am unable to write private letters, I must beg you kindly to forgive the delay.

I am sorry to hear you have been personally troubled by Mr Hubert Noyes[2]—mine was only by correspondence which fortunately I nipped in the bud.

I received a post card written all over with closely lined verbiage of the most extravagant assertions and astounding declarations of his position and knowledge of occult science, jumbled together with the most absurd notions evidently due to a disordered brain. Fortunately the two letters I sent to him closed our communications.

I afterwards learned from a friend that he had been confined to a lunatic asylum, a few weeks after he was brought before a London Magistrate for annoying & demanding money on account of an alleged debt [illegible] due from a person who brought him to court—and he was bound over to keep the peace & especially to refrain from using the first [illegible] for his semulous [?] charges—you will perceive he is a man to be vigorously & thoro'ly [*sic*] discarded.

I have enclosed my address tho' at present more like Robinson Crusoe in his cave than a sedate Rosicrucian—my books are all put in their cases higgledy piggledy—according to sizes instead of subjects—& with my bad side will take a long time to put in their former order—but whenever you have an hour or so to spare when in London to talk over old books & queer subjects I shall be delighted to see you—I do a little Spiritualism 'with a spoon'—to our great comfort if not edification & with kindest regards & esteem. Most faithfully and fraternally.

1 Dr William Robert Woodman (1828–91), medical practitioner in Stoke Newington until 1871 when he inherited a considerable horticultural estate in Exeter. A prominent Freemason, he had a knowledge of Hebrew, Cabala, astrology, Egyptology, alchemy, and the Tarot. Secretary-General SRIA 1868–76; Senior Substitute Magus 1877, and Supreme Magus 1878–91. With W. W. Westcott and S. L. Mathers he was one of the founding Chiefs of the Order of the Golden Dawn.

2 Unidentified.

38   3 Raymond Buildings, Gray's Inn, W.C.
                                           28 September 1877

Dear Bro. Irwin,

For the last three weeks I have been & still remain in a perfect muddle. I have changed my residence, & first had to send off my books & cases & the following week my furniture—being utterly helpless as far as doing any thing myself & obliged to depend on others and the wearisome process of putting down carpets, putting up blinds & curtains, & my books piled up all over the room & even now only placed away according to size and not subject—& my incessant pains when moving about—& worried in my business matters—I have been unable to attend to my private affairs & you will if you know my sufferings readily excuse any delay in answering your favor—my head becomes so intolerable the moment I have to think on any irksome subject or figures.

Upon reading your kind favor whatever unpleasantness may have arisen in my mind—let me at once say it is now dispelled, blotted out ('not with an Angel's tear') and utterly oblivious— not to be thought of or mentioned in future by either. I hope you will say Amen.[1]

Saturday week 13th October is my birthday (69) and I hope by that time to have all my things arranged (except those horrid indispensable books) and fit to be seen. I like my new place very much & my landlord is a Bro. Mason, tho' very recent, and the place is very pleasant—unfortunately I cannot yet make arrangements for leaving my business but I have a Chancery Suit Accounts to complete & that I hope will be ended shortly and thus I must determine my future when I hope to leave off my incessant grumbling and groaning.

When are you likely to be in London? Our Grand Stewards Lodge meetings are on the third Wednesdays in November, January, March and April—January is our Installation. It is always held at the Freemasons' Tavern & our time is ½ past five, as I am Secretary I of course am always there.

I must now beg you will give my kindest regards to Mrs Irwin and my hope that the lady is quite well, as for Mr Herbert I will drop him a note shortly & remain with kindest regards, Most fraternally and faithfully.

1 It would appear from this that some unpleasantness had passed between Hockley and Irwin—possibly a misunderstanding over Irwin making copies from the crystal MSS.

39   4 Richmond Terrace, Clapham Road, S.W.

5 October 1877

My dear Herbert,

Here I have been 3 weeks and have not yet got up my curtains, and as for my books, being utterly unable to do anything towards the moving all I could say was get them in according to sizes and this my factotum did to the letter and every work almost is in the wrong book case. However I have got the bound books in the front rows, tho' not in order and the back books 5 or 600 on the floor still to be started. I must make up my mind to send another lot to the slaughterers—Religious & General—but after all I am afraid I shall be obliged to get a new book case which I don't like having spent so much in removing—new carpets, dyeing of curtains, new fenders and gas fittings and brightening up my picture frames—I am quite aghast at my extravagance in my old age (next Saturday week, the 13th, I begin my 70th year—you will perhaps tell your Mama I am getting into my second childhood).

Nevertheless I am sure you will be pleased at the change I have made. My sitting rooms are all in one, no folding doors, & 32 feet long. And we have a nice shrubbery at the back between houses, altogether I am delighted with the place. 'Come and see.'

Now my dear Herbert have you any idea when I shall have the pleasure of seeing you here—I was grieved to hear that you have not recovered your health as could be wished since you left Paris, and now the cold weather is coming on you must take great care of yourself, and above all you must take to wearing *flannel vests*, after the first few days it will be a wonderful comfort to you and prevent most of the little attacks, catching colds etc. which in the long run end in asthma or bronchial afflictions.

Considering the delicate state of your health I should rejoice at hearing you had given up the medical profession, which above all other professions to excel in necessitates the most laborious continuance of mental exertions, continual study and anxiety & requires a very strong constitution or otherwise the brainwork utterly enfeebles the physical system.

In a mercantile or public office when the office hours are over (however comparatively hard the work) you are freed for the rest of the day and there are no difficulties in leaving your duties, they are gradual—and then your mind is at rest, do think it over. Your health and happiness is to your father and Mama of far more consequence than any thing else can be & the expense they have so lovingly born would be felt of as little consequence compared to your future health, welfare & happiness and the severe training you have gone through in your medical study would be most serviceable in any other occupation in life which may fall to your lot, I am well and thoroly [*sic*] aware how hard it is to give up the results of hard work & long cherished aspirations but health & vigour is the paramount object of existence, your physical frame would soon recruit its lost energies—do not worry your mind but make a bold resolve at once, an honourable living is open to a young man in any line of life he may assume & far better to be an Alderman with good fat turtle belly than Hamlet's lean Apothecary—let me hear your mind on the subject & if you do not come to see me I will come

& see you—with my best wishes for your health & happiness and my kindest regards to your dear Mama, believe me, faithfully & fraternally yours.

40 [No address]
19 June 1878

My dear Herbert,
I am up to my eyes in a mess, I suddenly have to move tomorrow, Thursday, and I am worried almost to death. I have been very ill ever since I saw you.
Pass my kindest regards to your Mother and most fraternally to your worthy father. In haste, Yours ever truly.

41 87 Fentiman Road, Clapham Road, S.W.
29 July 1878

Dear Herbert,
I received your two letters but I have been so ill in constant pain & the worry of moving suddenly with all my books & papers & unable to do anything myself—I have been kept almost off my head my vast store of books are all right but might as well be in Jericho as here, that is if I want to find a particular one, & I have been all the week hunting for my Catalogue & at last found it down in a box room tied up in a brown paper parcel with some old book covers. When I shall get them in order goodness knows for I have no inclination to do anything when once I sit down my head is so heavy that I cannot think of any thing & writing letters is the most irksome job of all.
You are very fortunate in having secured a copy of the 'Hermetic Mystery'. My friend has sent me word there are only 25 copies extant.[1] He sent me also a MS catalogue received from Mr Halse of 40 Addiscombe Rd, Kensington,—modestly asking 10/10/- for a copy and requested if I did not buy it to forward the Catalogue to Miss Leigh Hunt[2] as my friend Mr Wallace[3] was anxious to obtain a copy—the Author is not willing to republish it—and certainly not in full—which of course I sent not wishing to give such a fancy price. However he kindly offers to lend me his copy again at any time. The Author is, and also his wife, a Spiritualist of the high church type and like Vaughan a mystic rather than a material Alchemist—he is or has been a

clergyman of the Church of England.

They live at Newcastle on Tyne & if I had not been so unwell & unable to collect my thoughts on the subject I would have asked him to give me an introduction as I am passing thro' next Monday to Northumberland.

I have read the preface or introduction, I forgot which, of Madame Blavatsky's work.[4] It is certainly very interesting being a compilation, or rather a pillaging, from lots of Authors—or what I should say 'a selection of the notes contained in the works' of learned English writers & therefore already translated & so passed off as original extracts from Greek, Latin and foreign works—'and consequently a proof of her extensive and varied learning'-*for many of the learned translated passages were perfectly familiar to me*—still the book is valuable & rather useful as a selection on Spiritual matters otherwise spread in many volumes but I am too unwell to tax my brains where I had read them but looking thro' the Contents of the Chapters she appears to bring up the common matters over & over again, but what I have read has not given me a single new idea that is in any way tangible only the incessant chatter about what they have seen done by others & [illegible] profess to be able to do the same wonders themselves.

Certainly it cannot be expected that any one will pass their lives & spend their money in travelling to & fro purchasing magical secrets, mystic rites and sacrifices—and then give it to the world at 30 bobs a piece[5]—but rather as Capt. Olcott[6] said in the Spiritualist, which highly tickled my fancy, 'If you don't believe what we tell you we saw, go to India & see for yourself'.

I wrote a note to your father thinking he might be coming to Town before I leave London—I shall go North next Saturday & as usual stay 3 weeks, but it is very hard work—but I expect that my Gas will be turned off in a moment or two & I must close with my best compliments to your Mama, I remain, Faithfully & fraternally yours.

1 Mrs Mary Anne South Atwood, *A suggestive inquiry into the Hermetic mystery with a dissertation on the more celebrated of the Alchemical Philosophers being an attempt towards the recovery of the antient experiment of nature* (1850). Mrs Atwood's father, Thomas South, suppressed the work and it was not re-issued until 1918. R. A. Gilbert describes it as 'the most remarkable contribution of the nineteenth century to the problem of the interpretation of alchemy, and a book of the very greatest rarity ... [which] set out to explain alchemy as a science of the

soul by which the adept sought Divine Union by way of Illumination gained in an exalted form of mesmeric trance.'

2 Unidentified.

3 Unidentified.

4 Helena Petrovna Blavatsky (1831–91). Born in Russia, later became an American citizen. Widely travelled; an avid reader of occult, mystical, and religious works, she founded, with Col. Olcott, the Theosophical Society in New York in 1877. She also dabbled in Spiritualism but on at least three occasions her seances were exposed as mechanical trickery.

5 I.e. thirty shillings, now one pound and fifty pence.

6 Colonel Henry Steele Olcott (d.1906), American co-founder of the Theosophical Society with Madame Blavatsky.

42   [Undated memorandum to Herbert Irwin]

A. I never worked with the Almadel[1]—if practicable it would be very astonishing—but none of these things can be satisfactorily accomplished except by those who are independent and Perfect Masters of their own time—those who have to get their living by daily toil of whatever kind had better eschew all thought of it—but I have reason to believe it can be done—and were I out of business I would try it.

B. Tycho Brahe's Magic Calendar[2] is contained in the large quarto you have seen at my place with the engraved plates mounted—with references to Agrippa, Barrett &c. I decline lending this to any one. All that can be learned about Tycho Brahe is to be found in biog. dictionaries but I never saw any reference to his occult studies—of course in his day all Astronomers & Math[ematicians] believed in Astrology and Magic.

C. Dr Sigismund Bacstrom[3] died very poor but still to the day of his death engaged on the Great Work in a street leading off of the Commercial Road. I cannot at present find the year, I have seen it somewhere—nor do I know if any account of him was given in Alex Tilloch's Philosophical Magazine[4] for the year of his death—but they were old friends. Bacstrom was the author and A. Tilloch the commentator of my 17 vols of Hermetic Science.

D. With respect to my diaries which I was unwilling to lend, I have your father's promise that *he will not copy any thing but what relates to Cagliostro.* There is nothing relating to Vaughan or any of those who write thro' you.[5]

E. I did not copy a word out of your R[osi] C[rucian] MSS.

F. I will send a MS copy of the Anecdotes of Bacstrom[6] down in the box when I get it back.

G. Comte de Gabalis[7] is a curious book—& rather scarce—in the form of a dialogue. It is generally stated to have been written by the Abbe Villary [?]. It appeared in the Italian 'La Chiave del Cabinetto' by G. Borro in 1 vol. 12mo. Cologne 1681 & in French as 'Le Comte de Gablis on entretiens les sciences secretes' 12 mo. Paris, 1671 & in 1715. In English 'Comte de Gabalis being a history of the Rosicrucian doctrine of Spirits', 4to. 1714 (this is rare), and in 12mo. Comte de Gabalis or the extravagant mysteries of the Cabalists expressed in five pleasant discourses on the Secret Sciences, 1680.
    Borri was confined in the Church of St Augustine for life by the Pope for magic and heresy and died in 1695. Lemprier's [i.e. Lemprière's] dictionary gives a sketch of his life—of course thro' Catholic spectacles.

H. The editor of the MS catalogues name was Blanchard but I know nothing of him.

I. The MS on Cartomancy was written by me from various sources—and I very much regret having lost the rough copy of it many years ago.

J. I don't know any work in herbs except Astrological herbals such as Culpeper, Maynard or Salmon.[8]

1 See note 1 of Letter 18.

2 Tycho Brahe (1546–1601), Danish nobleman and astronomer. Educated at the Universities of Copenhagen and Leipzig, where he came under the influence of Copernicus and Johann Möller (Regiomontanus). Later he went to Bohemia and for the last two years of his life worked on alchemy and astrology with Johannes Keppler. Brahe gave astrological interpretations of astronomical effects. A firm believer in astrology, he stated it was 'not a delusive science when kept within bounds and not abused by ignorant people'.

3 See introduction and letters.

4 Alexander Tilloch (1759–1825), formerly Tulloch, editor of

scientific journals. Interested in Mesmerism and alchemy. Friend of Bacstrom and of the poet William Blake. His correspondence with Bacstrom was reputedly in the possession of Madame Blavatsky and the Theosophists in the 1890s.

5 The Irwins were granted a great favour as Hockley normally refused to loan his Crystal MSS. Cagliostro was the main spirit raised by the Irwins in their scrying experiments.

6 See note 2 of Letter 19.

7 *Comte de Gabalis* was written by Abbé Montfaucon de Villars and first published in Paris in 1670. The hero of the novel meets the Comte de Gabalis, a German Qabalist, who teaches him the doctrine of elemental spirits, adding a new dimension by describing the meeting of elemental spirits and mortals. The novel was not associated with Rosicrucianism until two English translations appeared in 1680.

8 Nicholas Culpeper, *The English Physitian* (1652) characterized as astrological botany derived from Aristotle. William Salmon, *Botonologia*, (1710). Maynard is untraced.

43   [No address]
                                                              [Undated]

My Dear Bro. Irwin,
  To save delay I return the MS Catalogue. I had 13 vols. of the lot. I do not wish to increase by stock of merely curious books when high priced. I am very unwell indeed—I find tonight my letter too long to send but will finish it on Sunday next.
  With kind regards to Mrs Irwin, yourself and Herbert. Yours fraternally.

4

EXTRACTS CONCERNING HOCKLEY FROM THE MACKENZIE-IRWIN CORRESPONDENCE

[KENNETH ROBERT HENDERSON MACKENZIE (1833–86) was the son of a physician. Spending his early years in Vienna he showed promise as a linguist and writer, but one that was never realized. At seventeen his translations from the German were praised and he was contributing regularly to *Notes and Queries*. By his early twenties he had achieved membership of the Ethnographical Society, the Royal Asiatic Society, and the Royal Society of Antiquaries. A love of the bottle, bogus claims to academic titles, an irascible nature and a veritable passion for mystery lost him many good friends. Hockley possibly came into contact with MacKenzie when the latter was publishing, at his own expense, *The Biological Review* (1858–59), a journal devoted to Mesmerism and fringe medicine. Hockley appears to have adopted MacKenzie as an occult pupil. It was to Hockley that MacKenzie rushed after his visit to Eliphas Lévi. The relationship was soured by MacKenzie's intemperance and severed completely because of some unknown offence perpetrated by MacKenzie. They were brought together by Irwin and an uneasy peace ensued. MacKenzie is remembered today, if at all, as compiler of the *Royal Masonic Cyclopaedia* (1875–7), a remarkable compilation of translations, plagiarisms and pure imagination.]

1874 12 Oct.   ... Circumstances have, I am sorry to say, intervened to estrange me much against my own desire from Bro. Hockley, who in my opinion is the most profound Occult student in this country and who has preserved his results in an admirable form so as to be easy of reference. I confess I often miss my old friend, with whom I was too long intimate and to whom I am indebted for the most valuable part of my knowledge on these subjects.[1]

1874 23 Oct.	I am glad to hear of Bro. Hockley thro' you—there is no one knows more of our favourite Occult subjects than he. Can you be a peace-maker between us as I am willing to say and do anything to that purpose.
1874 7 Nov.	As to Bro. Hockley I assure you that I am greatly obliged to you—such a man cannot be spared from amongst us, and we all know how ready he is to aid and advance our common studies . . .
1875 1 March	Capt. Morrison I know was not a Mason but used frequently to mention his connection with an Order which he called the Order of the Swastika but which Bro. Hockley humorously familiarised to the Order of the Swashtub! I meant nothing disrespectful of Capt. Morrison's attainments. He was an excellent Astrologer although not so good or deep as Hockley whom I still believe to be the profoundest man in England. I must deplore my estrangement from him but I fear there is no chance of our meeting again. My respect for him remains, however, unaltered and will so continue . . .[2]
1875 7 April	[MacKenzie had been discussing problems within the Metropolitan College SRIA] . . . I find that Frater Hockley is proposed as a joining member of the Met. Coll. and if he is not disposed to be friendly with me, it would be an additional reason for my departure. However we shall see . . .
1875 22 April	[MacKenzie has been discussing the possible publication of a Rosicrucian periodical]. I do not think even if Bro. Hockley should prove to be favourably disposed towards me, that he would do more than back up such a matter with a contribution, and perhaps some aid from his store of knowledge . . .[3]
1875 3 May	I am exceedingly sorry to find Bro. Hockley so bitter against me . . .
1875 17 May	I am very glad Bro. Hockley has lent you his MSS and given his sanction to what you name.

If ever there was anyone on this earth I loved and respected and still love and respect it is Bro. Hockley. I will do so through good report and evil report and trust that things may ultimately turn round.

1875 11 June   Let Frater Hockley now he is a member of the Metropolitan College supply my place. I voted his admission previous to my resignation acting thus on Masonic principles to the last. I feel no great animosity against him, and he is as you know well qualified—perhaps the most qualified—to instruct my Rosicrucian Fratres. But it would not be a pleasant thing for either of us to be forced into hypocrisy at the Convocations of the Society.

1875 16 June   I never thought of Bro. Hockley taking such a position as Assistant Secretary-General. My meaning was that he might perhaps open some of his store of learning to the Society and raise the character of the magazine . . .[4]

1877 5 March   I return herewith your catalogue, as far as I am concerned I cannot just now afford to buy. I think you were quite right in consulting Hockley, there is no man in Great Britain or Ireland better qualified to judge.[5]

1877 16 Dec.   Do you hear anything of Bro. Hockley? Bro. Ayton asked me about him but I could tell him nothing. Do you know a Bro. Walter Moseley living somewhere in Wales who 'affects the Occult'? I never saw him but Hockley knew him at one time but they had some sort of difference. I think he annoyed Hockley by copying some MSS which H. did not wish him to know the contents of. It was a long time ago.[6]

1878 25 Jan.   I have been working at Astrology a good deal lately. The new Raphael does not seem up to much. Hockley was Raphael once, he told me . . . I always regret the loss of Hockley and retain an affectionate regard for that friendship which once existed. Perhaps when earthly ideas depart from us it may again flourish, but that is in the hands of En Soph alone.[7]

1878 2 Nov. You will be exceedingly pleased to know that I have this morning had a long and friendly letter from Bro. Hockley inviting me to the Grand Stewards Lodge on the 20th. As long since as last April he told my Mother that he was anxious to be reconciled with me, and I therefore wrote a short note to him in May last. My note with the address he had mislaid but finding it a day or two since he has written. I am very glad of this as our very long and close friendship made the estrangement more painful. I have no doubt that I have to thank you and some other mutual friends for bringing about the solution of a great difficulty.

1878 27 Nov. Our friend Hockley tells me that he is going to retire from business at Christmas and then he will be at leisure to attend to literary matters.

1879 19 Feb. I have had a note from Bro. Hockley and we were to have you to see him but he was taken ill.

1879 28 Feb. I do not much expect that the R Cn [*The Rosicrucian*] will benefit much at Bro. Hockley's hands. He seems to be too ill to be able to copy out much from his store. I wrote to him on Monday last for the first time since my illness but as I have had no reply I suppose he continues ill.

1879 3 May I can't make Hockley out at all and like yourself shall give up any attempts about him. He must please himself. He always was peculiar, however I bear him no enmity.[8]

1879 30 May I too have heard from Hockley. When he has settled in his new abode we are to see him.

1880 11 Jan. My poor Uncle Hervey remains in the same sad condition and so does our friend Hockley. I had a sad letter from him last week—the first he had written me since last July.[9]

1883 26 Feb. I saw Hockley about a fortnight ago—to me he seemed in better health, but is sadly troubled at not being able to get any communication from his wife—however he was cheerful and we conferred on some of our subjects for a short time. I did not stay long for fear of exhausting him and perhaps bringing on a sleepless night for him.

1883 24 Aug.　　Regarding the Society of eight . . . I fear Bro. Hockley is too advanced in years to join.[10]

1883 16 Sept.　　Yesterday came a letter from Bro. Hockley whom I wish to interest in the Society of Eight. He is again on the move with all his Library. He has been ill. I am sorry he is so uneasy but I know he has a series of harpies around him and perhaps he may avoid some of these. He always says now that I am his oldest living friend and that is so for I have known him thirty-two years—a long time. I only wish I had a tithe of his Occult knowledge.

1884 18 Feb.　　I saw our dear old friend Bro. Hockley on Saturday last and was with him nearly four hours. He talked most kindly about poor Herbert [Irwin] and bade me say when I wrote to you that a seeress has lately been in communication and said that Herbert appeared and was at last happy . . . P. S. Hockley is moving somewhere but I don't know where yet.[11]

1885 20 Nov.　　I was very upset by Bro. Hockley's short and fatal illness which ended with his departure on the 10th. I much fear I shall never hear anything more as to what becomes of the books, mirrors, Crystals and MSS.[12]

1 MacKenzie had been a pupil and friend of Hockley but had abused their friendship in some manner and his intemperate drinking habits had not helped their relationship. Hockley's reaction to attempts by Irwin to bring about a reconciliation will be found in his letter to Irwin of 28 March 1873 (Letter 11).

2 Captain R. J. Morrison, R.N. (Rtd). (1795–1874), characterized by Ellic Howe as 'a well-known astrologer and promoter of dud companies'. Using the pseudonym Zadkiel he published an annual prophetic almanac. For further information see Christopher Cooke, *Curiosities of Occult Literature* (London, 1863) and Ellic Howe, *Urania's*

Children: The Strange World of the Astrologers (London, 1967), re-issued as *Astrology and the Third Reich* (Aquarian Press, Wellingborough, 1984).

3 MacKenzie appears to have been attempting to set up a rival to the SRIA's *Rosicrucian Magazine*, to which he had been a contributor. Perhaps the latter was not prepared to publish the more occult material in which MacKenzie *et al.* were interested.

4 Irwin had misunderstood MacKenzie's letter of 11 June, believing MacKenzie to have suggested that Hockley should take his place as Assistant Secretary-General of the SRIA, whereas MacKenzie was simply suggesting that Hockley should take his place as a *member* of the Metropolitan College.

5 Irwin appears to have been incapable of making up his own mind about what to purchase from booksellers and regularly sent catalogues to other interested parties for advice.

6 The Revd William Alexander Ayton, Vicar of Chacombe, who was an early member of the Golden Dawn and a practising Alchemist. A collection of his letters have been edited by Ellic Howe in the same series as this volume (*The Alchemist of the Golden Dawn*, 1985).

7 MacKenzie is wrong here. Ellic Howe has identified all those who used the Raphael pseudonym to publish the prophetic almanac.

8 MacKenzie and Irwin are both being unfair to Hockley. Once again he was on the move to new rooms, in constant pain and unable rather than unwilling to answer letters.

9 John Morant Hervey, Grand Secretary of the United Grand Lodge of England 1865–80.

10 The Society of Eight was a stillborn attempt by MacKenzie to form a group for the study of alchemy. Prospective members were F. G. Irwin, John Yarker, the Revd W. A. Ayton, and Frederick Holland. The idea never really caught fire and had fizzled out by November 1885.

11 After the death of Herbert Irwin on 8 January 1879, his father was bereft and continually tried to contact his spirit and entreated all his Spiritualist friends to do the same.

12 MacKenzie was wrong because he was a beneficiary under Hockley's will, being left 19 guineas. The will specified that all Hockley's books were to be sold.

5

HOCKLEY'S EVIDENCE TO THE LONDON DIALECTICAL SOCIETY

[Hockley gave verbal evidence to the London Dialectical Society's special Committee on Spiritualism on Tuesday 8 June 1869. It was printed on pp. 184–187 of the Report on Spiritualism published by the LDS in 1871.]

Mr Hockley, the next witness, spoke as follows:

'I have been a spiritualist for 45 years, and have had considerable experience. This is a crystal encircled with a silver ring, as a proper crystal should be. It was formerly the custom to engrave the four names of God in Hebrew on this ring. I knew a lady who was an admirable seeress, and obtained some splendid answers by means of crystals. The person who has the power of seeing, notices first a kind of mist in the centre of the crystal and then the message or answer appears in a kind of printed character. There was no hesitation, and she spoke it all off as though she was reading a book, and as soon as she had uttered the words she saw, they melted away and fresh ones took their place. I have 30 volumns [sic], containing upwards of 12,000 answers received in this way, which I keep carefully under lock and key. A crystal, if properly used, should be dedicated to a spirit. Some time ago I was introduced to Lieutenant Burton by Earl Stanhope, and he wished me to get him a crystal, with a spirit attached. I also gave him a black mirror as well, and he used that in the same manner as you would a crystal. You invoke the person whom you wish to appear, and the seer looks in and describes all, and puts questions and receives answers. Lieutenant Burton was greatly pleased and went away. One day my seeress called him into the mirror. She plainly recognized him, although dressed as an Arab and sunburnt, and described what he was doing. He was quarrelling with a party of Bedouins in

Arabia, and speaking energetically to them in Arabic. An old man at last pulled out his dagger and the Lieutenant his revolver, when up rode a horseman and separated them. A long time afterwards Lieutenant Burton came to me, and I told him what she had seen, and read the particulars. He assured me it was correct in every particular and attached his name to the account I had written down at the time, to certify that it was true. These books are locked up and nobody can see them; and sometimes, if I repeat some previous question which has escaped my memory, I am referred to the book in which it has been previously answered. The seers are generally of the female sex, and it is impossible to tell by their personal appearance whether they have the gift or not. I once knew a seeress that weighed 19 stone. The only way to tell whether a person is a seer is by trying. Two persons occasionally see the same thing at the same time. On one occasion a lady was looking into the crystal, and when the mist divided she saw her husband in conversation with a lady, a friend of hers, and then a boy made his appearance. A friend looked over her shoulder as she had put it down to rest her eyes and saw precisely the same thing. Although I have had a crystal since 1824, I have never seen anything myself. My seeress was perfectly in a normal condition, and in full exercise of all her faculties, and used to give answers to metaphysical and other difficult questions, which she could not possibly understand. I have nearly 1000 volumes on occult sciences. I do not think it has anything to do with mesmerism. I put a crystal in the hands of a spiritualist, and she became quite rigid, and I had to make a pass before she could see. Some ladies would look five minutes, others ten minutes, and others fifteen, before they saw anything, but if it appeared to them foggy it has merely to be developed. The words appear on the mirror the same as they do in a crystal. The girl sits in front and you ask a question. The answer appears on the glass more in printing than writing, and as she repeats the words they disappear. Only the girl sees the writing on the mirror. Gentlemen come to me and say, 'I want to see my guardian spirit.' The girl sees and describes the appearance. It appears in the same form as in life. I have sometimes come in the mirror in spite of myself—my double I should call it,—to my annoyance. She would say, 'You are in the glass now,' I would say, 'How am I dressed,' and she would reply, 'As you are now,' or 'As you were last week,' as the case might be; and then would follow a dialogue, my spirit or double talking to the seeress, while it has also been in the glass. White's Life of Swedenborg embodies my views as to this.'

A MEMBER: 'This is surely something more than a double, there would then be three. I do not understand this.'

MR HOCKLEY: 'There is a great deal more in this than you can understand. I do not believe that I have two spirits, but one soul, a body and an atmospheric spirit apart from my body, and that my spirit is not in me now but with my soul, and that it will form the covering of my soul in the future state, but that it may even now occasionally be visible to others. On one occasion a man appeared in the small crystal with a book before him, and she saw it was splendidly done but too small to read. I gave her a powerful reading glass and she could then read it, for the glass increased the size.'

MR SERJEANT COX: 'Are you of opinion that this is in any way connected with spirits?'

MR HOCKLEY: 'Yes.'

MR SERJEANT COX: 'You think the spirits appear in the glass.'

MR HOCKLEY: 'I have no means of telling whether the spirits are there. I believe it is a spiritual manifestation, because I receive answers to questions which the seeress could not fabricate.'

MR SERJEANT COX: 'Is there any evidence that the things seen are objective and not subjective?'

MR HOCKLEY: 'Yes, the book I alluded to, which was too small to read; when I got the glass the seeress could read it.'

MR ATKINSON: 'A book was seen; was it a real book, or do you suppose it was the spirit of the book in the glass?'

MR HOCKLEY: 'Yes, I suppose it was; why shouldn't I believe there is a spirit to everything? I believe that if I, or any human being, had forged a man's cheque and then burnt that cheque, it could have been seen by my seeress?'

MR SERJEANT COX: 'Supposing she had never heard anything about it?'

MR HOCKLEY: 'It would have been the same.'

MR SERJEANT COX: 'Do you think the spirit is in the glass, or in the mind of the seer?'

MR HOCKLEY: 'I have no means of forming an opinion.'

MR SERJEANT COX: 'Then why do you believe that spirits have anything to do with the matter?'

MR HOCKLEY: 'Because she speaks Hebrew and languages of which she knows nothing, and because, moreover, events that are taking place at the very hour can be brought up and the circumstances of their occurrences accurately described.'

DR EDMUNDS: 'You believe it is spiritual, because nothing else will account for it; if I had a cheque in my pocket now, could a seer read it?'

MR HOCKLEY: 'No.'

MR ATKINSON: 'It could be done.'

MR HOCKLEY: 'Cruikshank and others have had a wrangle about the spirit's clothes; did anybody read in Scripture of a spirit appearing without clothes? It is no good twisting words into fantastical notions, if you want to get at truth.'

Books and Crystals, &c., were produced and the proceedings terminated.

6

THE BURTON EPISODE

[Copied by F. G. Irwin from Hockley's MS into his own Rosicrucian commonplace book, now in the Library at Freemasons' Hall. The whereabouts of Hockley's Crystal MS containing the original is not known.]

Called R. F. Burton.

Now it is light I see some sand—all sand—now I see some camels one is lying down, the other two standing up there's a black boy with a tremendous rough wig—he looks like a negro laying down. There's a tall dark man with a black beard and moustaches, and no hair he's quite clean shaved, he looks so funny, he's got some sort of a white dress and trowsers on, and something wound round his waist loosly tied at the side—and something like a knife but no sheath, stuck in something coming from the girdle, it hangs from the girdle—he looks quite white against the black boy, he's got a head of hair there's no mistake about that.

It's getting plain, there's sand coming behind them, and a clump of trees more like dried thyme, there are tents, they are very low not peaked—they look as though you would be obliged to crawl in—the tree, if it is a tree, looks like a bunch of dried thyme sticking up above a tent.

Now there's two or three dressed like the other who are lying flat down upon their faces, there's one smoking, he is standing up—none of them have any hair, the one standing up is dressed in a yellow and white striped dress and rather greyish blue around the bottom, they are comical looking figures. Now there's one gone up to the first—I don't think he's Mr Burton though he has such black hair and eyes—the other is a nasty looking old man—he does show his teeth so—he's all action— he looks like a monkey—going to eat him—it is Mr Burton—the old man keeps on spitting—he looks so spiteful—Mr Burton only smiles.

Now the boy has jumped up, I don't know hardly what shape he is. I never saw such a droll boy he looks almost a dwarf.

The one that is smoking would be good looking if he had some hair—the black boy has gone up to him and laid hold of his pipe and took it out of his mouth—now they seem quarrelling there's two or three more round them.

Now there's such a beautiful house come up, and a man with a turban at the side of it—he's the only one with a turban on—they all seem quarrelling—the old man seems exactly as though he was going to eat the others—he has a grey beard and moustaches and a wide mouth—but such white teeth for an old man—now it is going—it's all gone.

I quite recognise the correctness of this vision, the old grey man the negro like boy and the quarrel about the pipe; this is easily ascertained by a reference to my 'Pilgrimage'.

(signed) Richd. F. Burton

The circumstances happened Sept. 4, 1853.

The above is extracted from Crystal MS Vol. 4, pages 124–5 in the blank page. Lieut. Burton wrote the above certificate.

7

CRYSTALIOMANCY, OR THE ART OF INVOCATING SPIRITS BY THE CRYSTAL

[Transcribed from Hockley's original manuscript, acquired by F. G. Irwin and presented to the Library at Freemasons' Hall as part of his Masonic collection.]

The Art of Invocating Spirits by the Crystal was known and practised by the Ancients which all those who read Sacred and profane History may discover, also the Sacred Text contains many instances in which Invocation by the Crystal is alluded to and it is the opinion of many learned and Eminent men that the divine Urim and Thummin of the Holy Scripture was used for a similar purpose as the Crystal is in our day.

Now all those who wish to obtain the assistance of the Good Spirits in the Crystal must lead a Religious Life. Keeping themselves as it were apart from the world. The Invocant must make himself clean and pure, making frequent ablutions and prayers for at least three days before he begins his operations, and let the Moon be increasing. The Invocant may if he choose have one or two wise and discreet persons as companions to assist him in his operations, but he or they must conform to all the rules and forms necessary to be observed in the practise of this Art. He must be true, patient, courageous and have great confidence, taking great care that no part of the Forms, Ceremonies &c. be omitted if he wish to succeed in his operations. For upon the exactness with which these operations are performed depends the accomplishment of his desires. The Invocant may perform at any time of the year if he find the Luminaries in fortunate aspect with fortunate Planets, when the Sun has reached his greatest Northern Declination, is said to be the best time.

Concerning the Room containing the Circle &c.

The Invocant must in order to carry out his work have a small room in a retired part of the house such as an Attic or a low Kitchen might be preferred, made clean and neat having no sumptuous ornaments to divide or distract his attention, also free from the hurry of business and from the prying and curious intruder. The floor must be perfectly clean and even so as to receive the lines of the Circle and the characters to be traced therein. The Circle may then be drawn seven feet in diameter and the Holy Names and Characters written therein according to the following model with Consecrated Chalk or Charcoal. Should the operator not have a pair of compasses of sufficient radius to trace the lines of the Circle, he may use a piece of twine attached to a pin as a centre, and the other end to the Chalk or Charcoal. The Invocant may if he choose in the absence of the above mentioned articles, sprinkle the floor with fine sand and then draw the Circle &c. with the Magic Sword, but the first mentioned method is by far the best, and being the most durable may be so carefully used as to serve in several Operations. The room when not in use must be locked up. The Invocant must be reminded that every operation belonging to the Art must be made during the Moon's Increase.

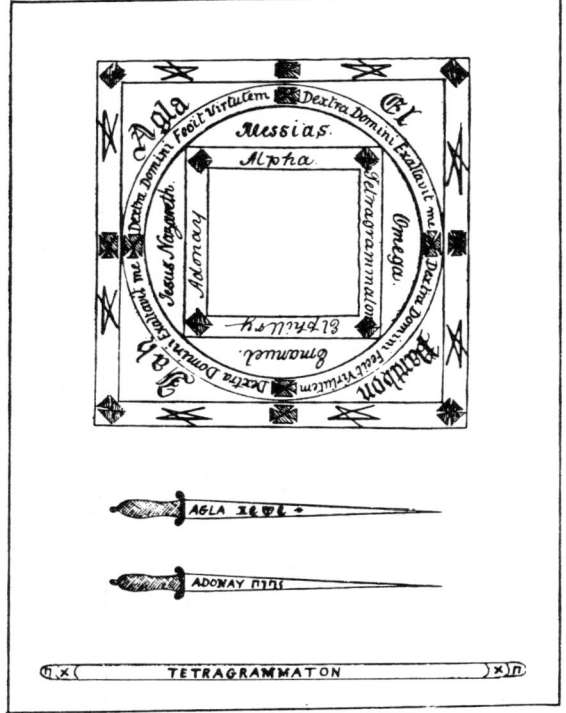

Concerning the Apparatus and Instruments to be used in this Art

The Operator must be provided with a small table covered with a white linen cloth, also a chair which should be placed in the room ready for the operation. Also the necessary apparatus for making a fire (if required) in order to burn the perfume proper to the planet governing the hour in which he would work, likewise a torch and two wax candles placed in gilded or brass candlesticks highly polished and engraved as shewn. The Operator must have a pair of compasses, some twine or thread, a Knife, a penknife, a pair of Scissors, a Magic Sword of pure steel, also a wand of Hazel-wood of a year's growth and a yard in length and engraven as shown.

He must also have a box in which to place these small articles, also some paper or parchment, Pens, Ink, etc.

All these instruments &c. must be entirely new and never before devoted to another purpose. They must be duly consecrated before being used.

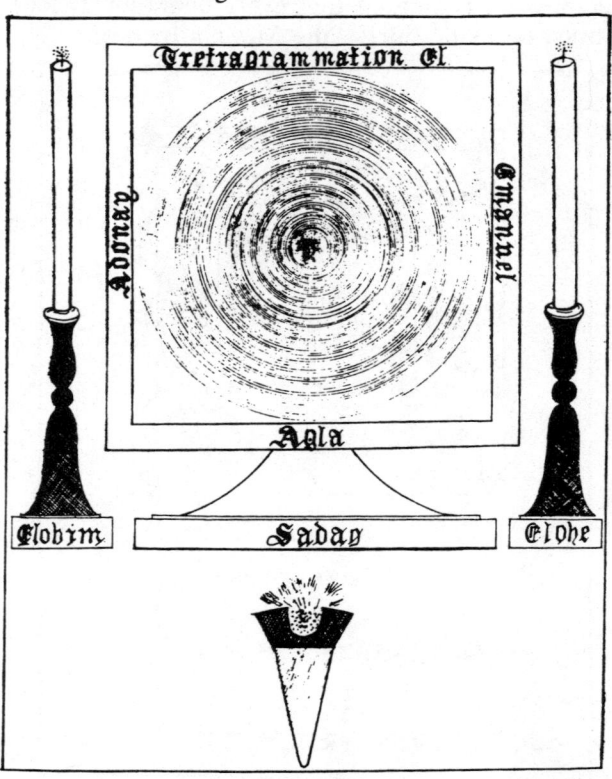

Description of the Crystal

The Invocant must be provided with a Crystal of about nine inches in diameter, or at least the size of a large orange, properly ground and polished so as to be free from specs or spots, it should be inclosed in a frame of Ivory, Ebony, or Box-wood, highly polished. The Holy Names round about it must be written in raised letters of gold. The pedestal to which the frame is fixed may be of any suitable wood properly polished, the name written in the manner aforesaid.

The Crystal, like the other instruments, must be consecrated before being used, and when not in use it ought to be put in a New Box or drawer properly fastened, to be kept free from dust, and not to be exposed to, or handled by, any one, but the Invocant.

Consecration of the Ground

Bless O Lord I beseech Thee this ground and place and drive away all evil and wickedness from this Circle. Sanctify and make it become meet and convenient for thy servant to finish and bring to pass therein all my desires through Our Lord and Saviour, Amen.

Be thou Blessed, Purified, and Consecrated in the Name of the Father, and of the Son, and of the Holy Ghost.

Blessing of the Lights

I bless thee in the Name of the Father, and of the Son, and of the Holy Ghost.

O Holy, Holy, Holy Lord God. Heaven and Earth are full of Thy Glory, before whose face there is a bright shining light forever. Bless now O Lord these creatures of light which thou hast given for the Kindly use of man, that they by Thee being sanctified, may not be put out nor extinguished by the malice, power or filthy darkness of Satan, but may shine forth brightly and lend their assistance to this Holy Work, through Christ our Lord, Amen.

Consecration of the Instruments

O Great God who art the God of Strength and greatly to be feared. Bless O Lord these Instruments that they may be a terror unto the Enemy and therewith I may overcome all phantasms and oppositions of the Devil through thy influence and help of thy Holy and mighty Names. *On Agla, Tetragrammaton*, and in the Cross of Christ our only Lord, Amen.

The Operator must have the seal and Character of the Spirit he would Invoke. Also the Pentacle and Character of the Planet governing the day and hour of the operation, written on Virgin Parchment and duly Consecrated in the aforesaid manner.

Consecration of the Crystal

Eternal God who by thy Wisdom has given and appointed great power in the Characters and other Holy Writings of thy Spirits and hast given unto them that useth them faithfully, power thereby to work many things. Bless now O Lord this Crystal formed, framed, and written by the hand of thine unworthy servant, that being filled with divine Virtue and Influence by thy command O Most Holy God it may show forth its Virtue and power to thy praise and glory through Jesus Christ our Lord, Amen.

(then say)

I Bless and Consecrate this Crystal in the Name of the Father, and of the Son, and of the Holy Ghost.

In Consecrating all the Instruments &c necessary in this Art, the Invocant must repeat the Ceremonies &c while placing his hands upon the different articles with his face turned towards the East, having done that, he may then place before the Circle the table with the Crystal thereon together with a candlestick containing a wax-candle on each side. All being ready the Invocant and his companions (if any) may enter the Circle in the day and hour of Mercury (the Moon increasing) and commence operations by earnestly invoking the Spirit *Vassago*, as an experiment in the following manner.

Invocation &c.

I exorcise, call upon and command the Spirit *Vassago* by and in the Name of the Immense and Everlasting God, *Jehovah, Adonay, Elohim, Agla, El, On, Tetragrammaton,* and by and in the Name of Our Lord and Saviour Jesus Christ, the only Son of the Eternal and True God, Creator of Heaven and Earth and all that is in them *Wipius, Sother, Emanuel Primogenitus, Homonsion Bones, Via Veritas Sapientia Virtus Leof Mediator Agnus Rex Pastor Prophetas Sacerdos Athanatos Paracletus Alpha et Omega* all by these High, Great, Glorious, Royal and Ineffable Names of the Omnipotent God and His only Son our Lord and Saviour Jesus Christ the second Essence of the Glorious Trinity. I exorcise, command, call upon and conjure the Spirit *Vassago* wheresoever thou art (East, West, North or South, or being bound to any one under the compass of the Heavens) that you come immediately from the place of your private abode or residence and appear to me visibly in fair and decent form in this Crystal Stone or Glass. I do again exorcise and powerfully command thee Spirit *Vassago* to come and appear visibly to me in this Crystal Stone or Glass in a fair, solid and decent form. I do again strongly bind and command the Spirit *Vassago* to appear visibly to me in this Crystal Stone or Glass as aforesaid, by the virtue and power of these names by which I can bind all rebellious, obstinate and refractory Spirits, *Alla Carital, Maribal Carion Urion Spyton Lorean, Marmos Agaiou Cados Urou, Astrou Gardeong Tetragrammaton Strallay Spignos Jah On, El Elohim* by all aforesaid I charge and command thee Spirit *Vassago* to make hast[e] and come away and appear visibly to me as aforesaid without any further tarrying or delay in the Name of Him who shall come to judge the Quick and dead and the world by Fire. Amen.

This conjuration after repeated, and the Invocant being patient and constant in his perseverance, and not disheartened nor dismayed by reason of any tedious prolixity or delay, the Spirit will at last appear. Bind him with the Bond of Spirits, and then you may talk with him &c. That this is a true experiment and that the Spirit hath been obliged to the fellowship and service of a Magic Artist heretofore is very certain as may appear by the following Bond or Obligation which the Invocant may if he pleaseth have fairly written on an Abortive and laid before him and discourse with the Spirit concerning it.

Bond of Spirits

I *Vassago* under *Baro*, the King of the West, not compelled commanded or fear but on my own accord and free will especially oblige myself by these presents firmly & faithfully and without deceit to T.W.* to obey at any time and at any place wheresoever and whensoever he shall call upon me personally to appear in this Crystal Stone or Glass and to fulfil his commands truly in all things wherein I can by the virtue of all the Names of God and by virtue wherewith the Sun and Moon were darkened and my Planet and the Celestial characters thereof and principally by this Seal binding most solidly. In witness of which guilty person he commanding I have signed this present obligation with mine own Seal to which I always stick close.

---

*The name of the person who wishes to obtain the Spirit in the Crystal.

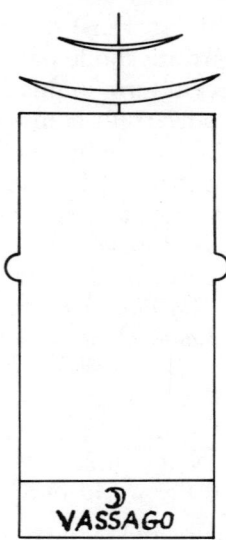

Seal of the Spirit Vassago

After having obtained the desired information &c. of the Spirit the Invocant may license him to depart in the following manner.

License to Depart

Inasmuch as thou comest in peace and quietness and hast answered unto my petition I give humble and hearty thanks unto Almighty God in whose Name I called thee and thou comest, and now thou mayest depart in peace unto thine orders and return unto me again at what time soever I shall call thee by thine Oath, or by thy Name, or by thine Order, or by thine Office which is granted from the Creator, and the power of God be with me and thee and upon the whole issue of God, Amen. Glory be to the Father, and to the Son, and to the Holy Ghost.

As all Aerial Spirits are very powerful and slow in their appearance, so also is their departure and it would be well for the Invocant not to leave the limits of the Circle for a few minutes after the Licence is recited.

8
EXCERPTS FROM THE CRYSTAL MSS

[THE Crystal MSS constituted a diary of Hockley's experiments with the crystal and consecrated mirrors and must have amounted to over a hundred notebooks, the whereabouts of most of which is unknown. As is shown in the letters, Hockley with great reluctance loaned some of the notebooks to F. G. Irwin who, despite solemn promises to the contrary, copied extracts into his own Rosicrucian notebook, from which the following extracts are taken.

The first two extracts are concerned with how the seer received information, the nature of spirits, and the manner of invoking them. The use of the crystal or mirror was essentially a religious experience for Hockley, regardless of the sometimes surprising information he received. The crystal or mirror had to be consecrated to God (see previous section), in Hockley's case the Trinitarian Christian God. On each occasion the crystal was used an invocation had to be made calling on both the Spirit of the Crystal and the protection of God. One of Hockley's invocations survived in a notebook once in the possession of Mr J. Watkins and was copied from there by Gerald Yorke.]

The following Call for the Crystal was given to me on the 10th July 1834 by my friend Mr James Elliott the Astrologer who received it from Mr John Worsdale Snr. of Lincoln the author of the Celestial Philosophy 8 vo; Genethliac Astrology 8vo 1796, Nativity 1819; this Call has been used with great success by him, but my friend Mr Elliott who would be his own Seer, but could never obtain any visions, shortly before his death, gave me the Call and also his Crystal . . .

The Divine Call

Probatum Est F[red] H[ockley]

I humbly desire Thee, O Lord God, my most merciful and loving God, the Giver of all Grace, to permit a Holy Angel of

Thine to manifest unto me so much glory in this Crystal Stone (or glass Receptacle) thus consecrated and charged that I, Thy unworthy servant, may thereby be allowed free access to see in it all those things of which I am desirous of having a perfect and previous knowledge.

O most strong and mighty God without Beginning or End, by Thy clemency and knowledge in all things, I humbly desire Thee to allow a blessed ministering Spirit to make manifest unto me in this Crystal (or Glass) all the desires of my heart so that I may be answered to my satisfaction clearly and fully through Thy worthiness good Lord, who livest and reignest, ever one God, world without end.

O, Holy, patient, merciful and great God and to be worshipped, the Lord of all Wisdom, clear and just, I most humbly and heartily desire Thy holiness and clemency to be extended unto me in Thy permitting a blessed Spirit ever before Thy Throne, to show me all that I require to see in this Crystal (or Glass) which I hold in my hand, that I may, by looking into it, be able to ascertain the answers to my questions. I do now therefore, at this time, most humbly request that . . . . (here state the wish).

To these most humble Petitions and Enquiries thus made known unto Thee by Thy unworthy servant do Thee, O Lord, permit them to be answered and to my comprehension. I humbly implore of Thee, that by Thy aid I may be enabled to bring this Work to perfection. Amen. Amen. Amen.

Having satisfied yourself in these matters with the Crystal or Glass for that time you are to discontinue looking in it, and then repeat the following

Discharge

O Almighty and Everlasting God who art blessed for ever more; I, Thy unworthy servant, in being satisfied in what Thou has condescended to manifest to me at this time, do give Thee humble and hearty thanks and implore Thee to open my understanding more and more in these Divine things, the Mystery of Revelations, when I ask them of Thee in future, that I may glorify Thy most Holy Name. Amen. Amen. Amen.

[Having called down the protection and assistance of God in working the Crystal the next step was to call on the protection of the Guardian Angels. Their names were written in a square on paper then the call was given.]

O ye glorious Angels written in this square [Gabriel, Zamael,

Raphael, Sachiel, Anael, Cassiel, Michael] be ye my co-adjusters and helpers in the Name and by the Power of the Most High God, the fountain of Wisdom who knoweth our necessities before we ask and our ignorance in asking things in our blindness. We dare not ask, yet we beg to have these things through the Virtue of Thy blessed Son the Christos and His Mother. Amen.

And by Alpha and Omega and them that shall come to judge the quick and the dead at the Latter Day of Judgement; that when two or three of us are gathered together whatever we ask for in thy Name, Thou wilt grant it unto us, as this Glass is held in hand through the merits of the Lord Christos, for he was the Truth. So help me God. Amen.

And if it be on Sunday you may say:

I pray by all the powers written on this paper that the Angel of the Sun, Michael, may have power to assist me in seeing things of my desire .... On other days—say the Name of the correct Angel.

[The third excerpt shows Hockley's interest in alchemy and is followed by a longer series of extracts outlining the Crowned Angel's ideas on religion; the Church of England; the Spiritual development of Man; the nature of good and evil, sin and punishment; the development and numbers of Angels; and the duties of a Guardian Spirit. These are followed by an extended allegory on the nature of Good and Evil.

The sequence of the Capt. Anderson extracts is curious. From the letters to Irwin it would appear that they had also contacted Capt. Anderson and from other sources it seems that friends of the Irwins had had similar contact. From the extracts printed here and the other sources it is clear that Capt. Anderson was deliberately used by the various experimenters with the crystal or mirror as a means of establishing the veracity of the various messages they were receiving. It has not proved possible, now, to establish the existence of Capt. Anderson himself, or whether or not the various scryers were able to satisfy themselves as to the truth of their received messages. With Hockley's undoubted faith in the crystal it seems rather surprising that he should have indulged in this testing.]

Crystal MS Vol. 6, pp. 124–6

The writing which is seen in the mirror is done by the Spirit forming the letters in his mind as each word passes through his mind, so they take form of a reality and appear—the Seer who sees and the Spirit through whose mind these ideas pass are for the time one, but they are united by so slight a cord that the least thought jars it, when it is joined the writing appears small and when severed the writing disappears until the bond is again completed—they see with the Spirit's eyes and they read what is impressed upon the Spirit's mind.

Crystal MS Vol. 7, p. 11

The Urim and Thumin was the first means of Divining by the Crystal, its origin was semi-divine, from this all other means of Divining arose, that in the first place gave man a desire to obtain knowledge unknown to others so that as mortals increased in knowledge it became more used, it is the best means by which spiritual knowledge can be used or gained.

It is so closely connected with the spiritual world, that any one using it, with the gift of second sight, can see thro' that into the Spirit world, the Spirits do not actually appear in that—but you look through it and converse with them while moving through their own sphere—in the same way that you make a window in a house to look out into the street—you will stay in your room but if you wish to converse with any one in the street you would speak and common courtesy would oblige them to answer—that is the way with Atmospheric Spirits.

With Guardian Spirits and Spirits of a higher plane it is rather different—wherever they move in the Spiritual world the air which surrounds them is cleared of everything in any degree more gross than themselves.

Thus if an Atmospheric Spirit meet a Heavenly Spirit the Atmospheric Spirit yields to the pressure of air which surrounds the other and retires to let him pass—in this way he visits the Atmosphere, the sphere lower than his own and the Earth without once coming in contact with those below him without he wishes it—so that when he is called on to converse with a person the caller's thoughts will immediately reach him and he appears—aspirating before him all less angelic than his own—whether bodily or spiritual.

Guardian Spirits and those of the highest degree are only seen in the Urim and Thumin, the Crystal, the Glass and the globular vessel of water. Unless a person study long and earnestly the different ways of developing the Urim and Thumin—with human reason for their guide, with truth and with pure intentions to the benefit of their body and soul and to the good of others they can never arrive at any perfection in Divining—they can never place reliance upon it or arrive at the truth, if any one wishes to begin this study I would give him a few directions.

Do not make use of a mediator but firmly yet humbly trust that God will put you in possession of a Guardian Spirit who will show you the visions you may hereafter wish—having done this inspect the Crystal and before asking to see any vision ask the name of your Guardian Spirit and having done this ask to see him and ask him to give you any advice he may think fit in using it, ask him to name the days on which he will appear, and also the days on which you may see other visions—ask him to become the Guardian Spirit of your crystal to prevent any evil spirit from appearing, and to give you timely notice of anything about to happen to you that you may prevent it, or that he may prevent it for you—this done discharge him—he should not be kept more than half an hour at the first meeting.

When you invoke him the next time call 3 times before you ask any questions if after that he does not vanish you may perfectly rely upon him—after the first time you may keep him as long as suits your convenience and his—if he wishes to leave he can do so without discharge—but be careful that you always use a discharge after having finished off a sight.

In invoking Atmospheric spirits or a Spirit of an inferior degree such as those of the ⊙ ⊔ the Atmospheric spirits of being as well as of dead people always use the term if convenient and agreeable at your pleasure, but more particularly of a living person, to a spirit of a higher order or your G[uardian] S[pirit] it is not necessary but above all do not make it any way directly or indirectly an object for gaining money, it may appear to go on well for a few times, you may have the information, and the visions, you wish—but in the end the consequences are lamentable, and they come sooner or later.

When you have become used to the Crystal—full confidence in it—and assured in many ways of the truth of it—then you can use the mirror which is a great deal the best—this is used in the same manner as the Crystal, but from seeing visions so large and life like and from the size of the hole which is made in the Spiritual wall it enables you to come more closely in contact with the Spirits you address.

Of all modes of Divinity this is the easiest and the best, the information is given slowly at first and gradually quicker and quicker until you reach the Grand Height of all human knowledge upon Spiritual matters until you know as much as the human mind can in any way comprehend of what passes beyond its own world.

By the allegorical picture of the City of human habitations, and the wall that surrounds in—I meant the world and its inhabitants—the space above it, the atmosphere, the walls that surround it the bounds of human knowledge unassisted by spiritual aid—and the holes in those walls which so few could reach—the way of attaining the true and the only true method of divining—when there you are still liable to great error unless helped and directed by your Guardian Spirit—the water which surrounds that wall is what is termed by men hell—the space above the atmosphere, and the seven that tower above that the spheres of Happiness.

Crystal MS Vol. 9, p. 135
A drop of water is divided by a stream of electricity into two gases Ox. and Hyd., and by subjecting certain proportions of these gasses to electricity water is produced, may I ask please if pure gold can be separated into its elements as a metalic ☽ or a metalic ♃ or a metalic ☿?

Nothing exists in an unalloyed state, everything is mixed and extracts from this mixture make mixtures of many different kinds. Gold cannot be divided for were this possible ☉ gold might be made of other substances for the substances which make that could be found separate, and were that the case gold might be easily made.

Ancient Alchemists held that ☉ might be reduced to its own △ ☽ ♃ and sophic ☿ from which by a certain process the powder of projection might be made—which combined with other metals in a certain state transmitted them into gold.

There are no objections to a trial but it cannot be done—pure gold has never yet been made, it is a natural production a combination of minerals, and nothing man can do will make it.

May I ask if transmution, or projection of metals as understood by alchemists has ever been done has ♀ or ♄ been turned into ☉? It has not—I depart in peace.

Crystal MS Vol. 7, pp. 114–6
There are no torments that are everlasting. Can any Christian imagine that God, and when I say that I mean the Highest of all Angels, the Disposer of Beings and the Author of Blessings and goodness could consign these creatures that He made with his own hands and moulded after His own fashion—that He would let them taste the blessings of life and allow them to commit crimes in that life and then consign them to the most frightful torments for ever without end—that no space of time known to

God, Angels, or man should in the least relieve them from these frightful torments.

Death is the transition from the corporeal to the spiritual state, but in passing from life into death man only loses his flesh—the mind, faculties and desires are exactly the same as those with which he quitted the Earth, as he loses these faculties so he loses the perception of the things he left and when he has entirely lost sight of them he begins his progress.

Seven propositions.

1. That nature is God's revelation and His laws the only infallible standard of Truth.
2. That man is a progressive being, becoming by a law of his nature better, nobler, and more Godlike, and will in time as a race become pure and righteous.
3. That evil is a relative term and originates in the misuse of things, principals and faculties.
4. That death is the process of transition from the Earthly to the Spiritual life, that by this process the man is separated from his body for ever and in his spiritual form commences his new life, possessing precisely the same mental and moral attributes which he possessed before.
5. That the Spirit entering the Spirit world is drawn by Spiritual attraction to such society as corresponds to his or her mental and moral conditions, similis similibus—and the enjoyment of all is in just proportion to moral and intellectual elevation.
6. That all, even the lowest, on entering the Spirit world may progress—for ever rising higher in the scale and becoming purer and lovelier and grander.

   Observations by the C.A.: They depend upon others for many things, they progress with them, they show each other kindness, they have their differences of opinion concerning things unknown to them, but when they rise they are perfect beings in themselves, they are at peace with all because there is no difference of opinion, they all recognise the same law and they are all governed by the same desires. The bad stop until their punishment is over before they begin to progress—the good progress until they achieve perfection or the 7th Sphere where they remain until the Judgement Day after that we know not what shall be.
7. That men, women and children from the Spirit world may and do communicate with those on Earth and that such communication is full of good to the race.

Remarks by the C.A.: Spirits both good and evil, but more especially the latter, can communicate with man before their gradual rise towards happiness, after that they lose all their knowledge of man and therefore have no desire to communicate with them—when a manifestation is desired by good through undeveloped spirits—Evil spirits alone feel themselves justified in giving man an opportunity for deception and imposture.

The language that is preached from the pulpit by persons of different sects, we will suppose them to be all true Christians—there are true Unitarians of every sect—he tells them that unless they hold exactly the views he preaches they cannot be saved—and that is the one and only way of salvation—such a place as that is enough to drive good Spirits away instead of enticing them, but the time will come when there shall be no Archbishops or Bishops to domineer over poor Curates and Vicars and make them often [blank] views of 1½ hours to a crowded congregation to ask them for some subscription, half of which is put in their own pockets.

Whilst this continuous true religion will never exist on Earth—when all the Clergymen are levelled when they are paid so much equally—and not permitted to rob the people, when they are paid liberally, then they shall not want to do it—then they will preach more to their own feelings and show example at the same time.

Not until the Holy Fathers in God, as they are so proud to style themselves, have their robes and gowns burnt and three parts of their money distributed among the poorer clergy will there by harmony in the Church. Dr Wheatly Archbishop of Dublin is the only exception he is really and truly a good man and a thorough Christian—not in religion alone but in humanity a Christian and in charity a Christian.

I am directed by the C.A. to show you my opinion and firm belief on the essential subject of Salvation.

1. The beliefs and sentiments of Lero [?].
2. I believe in three persons and one God, Father, Son and Holy Ghost, I recognise the Father as Creator and Sole director of the Universe and all the Elements it contains. But his Son, Jesus Christ, is the one most essentially necessary for the salvation of mankind. The Holy Ghost the Comforter—the Spirit emanating from the two combined who together with them form the Supreme Being.

3. I believe a man is rewarded or punished according to his merits or demerits on Earth. That no punishment however great while it lasts is everlasting, but punishment for all sins is shortened and finally ended through the mediation of Jesus Christ, and for the Roman Catholics through the Blessed Virgin. Christ's death upon the Cross and His death only is the means by which mankind is finally saved from destruction.

4. I believe that it is wrong to try to reveal those secrets of futurity which are purposely hidden from man's knowledge—all visible Spiritual communications are ungodly—and that evil Spirits only use the means to deceive man. That Spiritual knowledge which induces man to seek for truth and reveals [blank] opinions which coincide with those given in the Word of God is right and the true way of divining.

5. And finally to state my opinion that the millennium is near at hand, that after that Jesus Christ will appear to those upon Earth and the day of Judgement is at hand. The blessing of one religion will then reign in the world—all will be unity, peace and concord and ready to receive the Blessed Saviour. His coming will truly as said in Isaiah 'shake the nations of the Earth'.

Now instead of the belief used by the Church of England I would substitute this one for it.

There is one God the embodiment of all goodness, all charity, all love, the Creator of the Human race—emanating from Him are the divine qualities—His Influence, His Holy Spirit and His Son.

God has angels in his presence perfect as Himself in purity, in goodness and in truth but unlike Himself either Almighty, All-knowing or All powerful, their capacities are limited, His are boundless.

There is an antagonist to all this good in the shape of an Angel fallen from his high degree—he is the power of evil always at enmity with God, always striving to rule His Creator by gaining man—the greatest of acquisitions—over to him and subservient to his will.

This power of evil so strong it was necessary that God should send into the world, to arm man with a weapon by which he might defeat the power of evil.

This weapon is His word given by His Son to man, in the New Testament, having given that word to man as a sure passport in all afar ages to eternal happiness. He gives to man His mortal body returning as pure in Spirit as when He descended from God.

The two are again one and that Holy Spirit is still the universal influence that is felt in the hearts of those who are willing to be Christian men.

Through the intercession of His Son, God saves those who believe in Him, but through His Own Love and charity to the Creation (the human race) He saves others.

Father and Son were One long before the world was created. For the good of mankind the Son descended to the Earth, took the form of man, and died for Salvation of souls.

Judas Iscariot is not condemned to everlasting misery—he is now the same as the twelve apostles and one of them—he was only the instrument by which the Son of Man was betrayed. It was ordered that he should be so—he (Judas) went out of sight of man and starved himself—destroyed not hanged.

It is His will that mankind should be saved. To effect that he allows us in our different way to inform man according to our degrees of knowledge as we get higher and nearer to him— nothing is wrong that tends to enlighten man in religion—but the knowledge of things which are to come while on Earth, and the knowledge of each other's thoughts and feelings, although not in themselves evil, does not promote the happiness of mankind.

By punishment everlasting is meant they shall never attain the same glory exactly—in the Presence—as those who are right- eous—but God is too merciful and just to commit a man to torments everlasting, for sin which he in a manner could not help—I do not mean by this to justify the sin—but I mean that a man who is led away by the temptation of Evil Spirits—who tries—but tries in vain—to withstand them—under the immedi- ate eye of God and without his stretching forth a hand to save them—God would not punish that man everlastingly.

In any part of His life while upon Earth and before his Ascension he did not lose the form and the feelings of the human body—he was then the Son of Man—He could not live forty days and forty nights without any sustenance. He did not fast during that time—he only took what was necessary to keep the body animated.

Without losing consciousness Jesus Christ was tempted, as many others have been, to sin—for a moment he felt inclined to abandon his object, but the thought of man's salvation and the example he was required to set enabled him to triumph—all Evil was banished from his mind, he then exclaimed 'Thou shalt not tempt the Lord thy God.'

Those who leave Earth in unrepentant sin—the nature, place and duration of their punishment? It is a planet unconnected with any other—there is no fire in it—that would not be a torment to spiritual beings as they could exist in it—but only to flesh—it is a place of punishment which causes a person to act without ceasing the crimes that he committed in life—at the same time having a knowledge and feeling of better things that causes him to loathe the acts he is forced to commit. If murder, gambling, drunkenness or any other vice was his ruling passion he would always be in the state he was in when he left earth—he would be forever acting though loathing the crime. The duration of punishment is longer than from the beginning to the end of the whole world.

Crystal MS Vol. 7, p. 7
Before the earth was made about 2,000 Angels were created, formed in the image of their maker, there was no distinction between them, they were Angels of the highest order. When the Earth was made and the first man it was the intention of the Divine Master that the Angels should have the guardianship of those upon Earth and the whole generation of their offspring.

One of these Angels was expelled from the highest orders for his endeavours to create in the minds of the others to become the rulers entirely of the Earth, in this he succeeded partially, but over the majority he had no influence. He was degraded for this but in no other way punished. He then blasphemed the Most High and cursed the human race. For this he was turned out of the Spheres and left to dwell upon Earth. It was thro' him that the orders of Angels were divided, the holiest were those who would not hearken unto him, these then constituted the Seven Spheres.

The 2nd agreed with him a little, the 3rd more so, they all agreed more and more with him until they came to the first—and they agreed with him at that time almost entirely.

At this time no place of punishment was made, but Eve being created and living with Adam in the Garden of Paradise he thought he could not revenge himself better, on those who expelled him, than by making her eat the forbidden fruit, for that he was turned into the boundless space in which the world was a speck.

Once being there he soon created monsters in the waters under the Earth. He then had no companions in the human form—and so he continued planning the modes of destruction until the birth of Christ.

By that time many had died upon the Earth and Cain was the first he induced to commit sin—he had received their souls into his own hands—at the time of the Birth he had in his dominion about 300 souls, but some time after that passed they increased very rapidly so that up to year 1704 there were 15,000 souls with him—but since that time religion has become more prevalent—not so many mortal crimes have been committed—and what has been done has in a great many cases been reported of, so that at the present time there is not more than 1,675 souls in punishment, considering the number who have died and attained perfect or partial happiness that is not many.

The number of Angels from the Creation of the world down to the birth of Christ was continually increased by many good men who left the Earth and at the time of the birth the number in the whole of the 7 Spheres was 5,500, but of these the Heavenly Host was 1,500, the remaining Spirits of mortals who had inhabited the Earth were either passed the state of bliss and being dormant, as I explained to you before.

Those who were not created and were in the atmosphere awaiting perfection—all these 5,500 Angels were the Guardian Spirits of mortals upon Earth, and as the population increased the number of Angels also increased from those who died.

Since the birth of Christ the number of Angels has so increased that at the present time there are about half the number of Angels as mortals upon Earth—one Guardian Spirit in most cases does for a man, his wife and one child until it is two years—so that when they are single the Guardian spirit has more power than when married, for then the power is divided. There are some cases in which they have separate guardian Spirits.

When mortals arrive at 3rd or 4th Sphere there is no danger of losing their happy state.

A few of the most beautiful animals of every kind are in the Spiritual World—the likeness of animals are in the atmosphere.

There is only one body of Angels which continually increases and they all stay in one place, the highest, but they can descend into each sphere at their pleasure.

There are many kinds of Spirits—Angels are Spirits but every Spirit is not an Angel—there are Planetary Spirits, Atmospheric

Spirits, Wandering Spirits—and Spirits that animate the body. The heavenly hosts are a band of Spirits but they are also ministering Angels.

It is the Atmospheric Spirit that you commune with he gives you an insight into the future and very often unintentionally it is wrong—dreams are not of a high order of Magic neither are they sent for a Divine or a good purpose they are only the means by which a person communicates with his own Atmospheric Spirit, and by him he receives information.

The unknown tongue is a language known to none upon Earth—it is the language sent by God to convey his meaning to the soul of man. The man who understands it himself should pray that he may be able to interpret properly unto others.

You are right everything evil as well as every good comes under the direct knowledge of God and He would not permit any evil to come unless some good were to come from it—the rappings, the appearance of deceased persons on Earth, and the gift of tongues are sent for no actual divine purpose but to convince the outward and bodily sense.

The duties of a Guardian Spirit are: to watch over and protect you from all those evils that would harm you—to keep evil spirits away—and when the purpose for which you were sent on Earth is fulfilled—and your Spirit is prepared to meet its Maker—then will a Guardian Spirit conduct you to your everlasting home—all things are ordered for the best—and man without God would be left to the disposal of the evil ones.

Crystal MS Vol. 6, p. 175
Suppose a City that is thickly populated with human beings, their habitations are in the middle of the city, the city is surrounded with a high wall—the wall towers high above the reach of the mortals who are in that city—and between the wall and the habitations of these mortals there is a dangerous and rocky path—so that no one not accustomed to the road could even reach the wall—he may reach half way and he may reach farther—and he may nearly reach it—but unless he has been accustomed to it and traversed it in lightness and darkness he will not be able to find the wall.

In this wall and at a distance ranging in the length are holes—there are many, many of them, these holes, those who traverse the path are in search of them.

Underneath this city and nearly as high as the loop-holes in the wall is a mass of water—it is dark and deep beyond all compare, and in this water live many monsters—monsters out of number—the entire space covering the city and joining the walls is air that which immediately joins the waters and rises a considerable distance above the level of the waters is inhabited by beings exactly similar to those in the city—they are clothed the same, eat the same, go through the same actions however minute, have the same friends, in fact entirely live over again the life of those in the City but Spiritually.

Although they do thus live the same—and love the same—and to all appearances have the same being—they are spiritual, in fact they are like shadows of those on earth—thrown above them—for even although the colours are the same and the dresses are the same they are still shadowy and transparent.

Immediately over that part of the City which is inhabited by the mortals is a space in which a very different sort of beings live—but not entirely, there they come as a cloud—they pass thro' the space they unite themselves and enter the corporeal body of the mortals below, they know their actions, they do them without the knowledge of these beings, but still they are with them—when they leave a stream of electricity continues between the aerial and corporeal being that unites them—in this way they are united—however far apart, they are joined—so that when one ascends into the space above, or above that, or above that—or again above that—the stream of electricity widens and even becomes stronger, that their thoughts and their feelings—their wishes and their wants can be conveyed to the beings that are above them.

There is one of these beings attracted to nearly every one of those in the city.

Again above that space which is immediately over the city—there is another space that is divided and the two spaces run parallel into the other—this is inhabited by those spirits who had once been upon Earth, with the mortals below—those when they die are conveyed by the electricity—and with the Spiritual being that is attached to them—into the space that is immediately above them, after dwelling there still connected with the Spirit, which does not even then stay with them—but moves upwards and backwards.

These deceased mortals while remaining in this sphere—can see what is going on below and have also memory—but as they are purified in this state, the Guardian Spirit stays longer and more frequently with them—they get more united and as this takes place the faculties are blended by which he has seen and recollected the things below him.

When he has so far purified himself and been purified by his Guardian Spirit, he ascends with him into the space above and there they are more wholly joined together than in the last—there he has but slight recollection of the things which took place when alive and sees them never—after a due course of time, some longer than others, he ascends to the 3rd sphere and then his Guardian Spirit leaves him to ascend further alone.

He so gets purer and purer until at last he obtains eternal happiness—then he is dormant, not sensible of anything that takes place, either around him or elsewhere, he has no faculties and is dead or either asleep bodily or spiritually—I should not say bodily, for by this time all the dross of human nature has left him—but he has still the form of a body, but so beautiful, so small and angelical—he is now the same as one of the Guardian Spirits who never resided in the City—but he is senseless, there to remain until the judgement day.

Those who ascend in this manner from the Earth gradually into the Seven Spheres are those who have died in or approaching to the right path.

Those who have not absolutely committed and died in a great crime—I do not call crimes any of those sins not of great magnitude—I think I have before explained to you in what those crimes consist, or do not consist—they are murder in any way—Blasphemy—violation of oaths by intention—robberies— I mean to say there are crimes which if not reported of at the time of death, will cause destruction. Robbery of all kinds, from downright stealing to systematic swindling—conspiracies to defraud—overthrow or ruin governments or state affairs, which will be in any way injurious to the lives or interest of the people.

The firing or maliciously destroying rooms, homes or other buildings—slandering or spreading evil reports—invocation or calling of evil spirits—knowing them to be so—or making use of anything through their aid a disobedience in principal of God's word—I do not mean to say minor points—such as might be overlooked or misunderstood but those glaring facts which are laid down and so strictly enjoined in the New Testament.

Again I repeat that the minor ones are not of importance in any way.

For these offences there are very few others that are not punished everlastingly and yet so lastingly that to those who bear them, they appear everlasting, until the time cometh that they shall be released from their suffering.

The persons who leave the city that I have described in their manifold wickedness leave it through the holes in the wall they are received with revelry and joy by the inmates of the water—each mortal in the City has one, I do not mean individually but there are the same number—so one may have two or three & one or two of the mortals may have more of the Spirits that inhabit the water attached to them—the revelry and joy that is occasioned at the departure of a mortal into the water is occasioned by the triumph of evil Spirits over the Good Spirits—for although no mortal can leave the world through those holes in the wall—the evil spirits can enter in their form—all the sins by which men are led into these destructive waters is thro' the influence of these spirits.

At the time of birth all men are equal in goodness—it depends upon themselves—their power of opposition, their leaning to the right or the wrong—whether their Guardian Spirit or the evil spirit shall become their possessor.

After those loathsome festivities are over which the rejoicing has occasioned, the mortal is conducted still in the possession of every feeling of the man—possessing the same conscience—more finely pointed than he had on earth, knowing how happy and blissful they are who are left in happiness—and knowing how wrong it is in him—to have done as he has done—his feelings still getting more purified and his sense of wrong truer—he is conducted to place after place—until at length into the 7th that is the worst.

In that he enacts unceasingly the things he is most disgusted with—that which he most abhors, in fact that for which he was excluded the blissful state.

In this way he remains while those who departed life happily are sweetly insensible to all around them until the judgement day—he enacts over and over again the things that he loathes—he wanders about seeking for the society of good men—he wishes for it—and longs for it with a desire unknown to any mortal, but instead of that coming his ears are only assaulted with the yells and groans of those who are doomed to the same punishment themselves.

Return now to those we left upon the Earth. The holes of the walls by which the evil spirits glide in and away—the opening the entire of the top of the City, by which the Guardian Spirits move upwards and downwards through the several spheres, the ministering Angel of Man, is not seen by any of them on Earth—unless they reach those holes in the walls—unless carefully guided there by the powerful and good spirits, and sustained there by a knowledge of the way, in which they ascend there—they are liable to great danger and error, but having arrived there, and once looked through those holes, they obtain whilst still upon Earth a glimpse of the Spiritual world, through that they see and converse with their Guardian Spirit—the Atmospheric Spirits that guard the loop-hole, and are more nearly connected with them or if they wish it with the evil spirits that dwell beneath.

I must again go back further than I have done and explain, the rise and cause of Evil Spirits and the rise and the end of Good Spirits—it will take too long for me to do so this evening—shall you be alone next Tuesday evening?—I will then continue— there are other things connected with it which I will then tell you—

Crystal MSS: Extracts concerning Capt. Anderson
Vol. 7, p. 108: He is so altered, so changed, he's copper coloured, rough—I am afraid you have not been playing at soldiering by your looks. 'It's the weather knock's me up it is not what I do. How are you. If they had begun fighting in the Spring we should have had the war probably ended, with the loss perhaps of not a great many more men than have died of disease. Yes I am all right now thank you.'

Vol. 7, p. 198: Here he is in uniform. 'Thank you I am well as can be expected as the ladies say.' Where are you? 'Within gun shot of Sebastapol.' Were you under arrest a little while ago? 'Being nearly arrested for ever on the 5th at the battle of Inkerman, on the 5th I had advanced on horseback in favour of the Column when some chap singling me out took aim with a revolver. One bullet, perhaps two, went into the chest of the horse—but instead of his falling on his side, as most dead horses do, he fell on his knees or rather fell forward in a heap—the consequence instead of being pitched off and rolling over I continued sitting bolt upright with my legs out on each side, at the same moment two or three bullets whizzed past in the place where my head had been only a moment before. So ludicrous was the aspect I presented and so miraculous was the escape that the men fairly burst out laughing.' Have you got rid of your phantom visitor? 'I have and would 10,000 times rather be in front of one of the Batteries of Sebastopol than alone in my room with an unearthly visitor.' Have you been promoted in the Crimea? 'Not yet, I was promoted so early—when so young.' As this is 28 Nov. [18]55 & we cannot by any possibility receive news from the Crimea for 10 or 12 days cannot you give me the name of some officer killed or wounded within two or three days? 'General Hamilton was wounded on 25 (Hermilan?) one of the family of Hamilton Williams an English Baronet.'

'The next time I appear I shall be able to give you my name—Spanish political affairs which have so long induced me to remain in disguise are now settled—the government of Isabella is settled so far that she is made a constitutional Queen—and I can now return to the Court from which my [blank] is banished.' Selina has not yet seen her future spouse? In the human as well as the spiritual body I presume—? 'Perhaps I shall get bandboxed out here and that will put a stop to all acquaintance.'

'No indeed but I think grandpapa S— will have his name in History as the inventor of a great many spiritual instruments, if he had flourished in the 16th or 17th centuries—he would have been fuggled before he was half his age for wizard.'

'I have not been in England long enough at a time to know all her celebrated characters.'

I am afraid, when in Spain, you will have a chance of a fuzzle? 'No I should not, my mother has too much influence for that.'

Do you think the Allies will take Sebastopol before Xmas? 'No indeed I don't—the fortifications are astounding—there's a great deal of brag about the little we do, but they have, as yet, got the better of us.'

You served them out at Alma and Inkerman? 'Yes when it comes to the direct battle we gain the victory, but we lose so many men in the meantime for our strength.'

I am afraid the troops suffer badly? 'Yes it is very bad, and the weather wretched, we thought a good deal of a shower at Chobbam—here we sleep under a canvas tent when the fog is so thick it completely saturates everything including ourselves—the men are satisfied and thankful for the comforts they do receive.'

Have you any other incident of the war to tell us? 'A great deal of our baggage is still at Constantinople. On the 6th November I started for Constantinople and returned on the 16th.'

What will be done to Lieut. Henderson for mislaying his despatches? 'Discharged, doubtless—and that's all.'

Do you think Messrs. [blank] and [blank] will be tried for cowardice?

'They will not be dismissed, an aide-de-camp of the Duke of Cambridge refused to ride at the Battle of Inkerman from the place where His Royal Highness was to Lord Raglan who was on an eminence on the other side of the field. What do you think was done? It was said nothing at all about—and he was absolutely allowed to call a corporal from the Ranks, mount him and send him with the message to Lord Raglan, when he returned safe he was applauded by the whole set and will be made Sergeant—did you ever hear anything like that.'

Vol. 7 last page: Communication from the C[rowned] A[ngel]. You will be sorry to hear that Mr Anderson was wounded on the 2nd December.

Vol. 8, p. 68: Called Mr Anderson. Dear me how altered he is to be sure. 'Thanks for your kind wishes but health cannot exist here.' Where are you now? 'At Balaclava about to start for home.' Give me your name. 'I will tell you when I leave this place. I have been seriously wounded since I saw you. Very nearly time I think—no imagination can fancy the state we are in.'

To whom do you attribute it?

'The English Government in not supplying the necessities— Lord Raglan in overlooking them. It is perfectly impossible that he (Lord Raglan) could do it (command) I believe also that he is neglectful of his men—he ought to support their wants more urgently than he does, he has a very comfortable place himself and takes care not to leave it in the cold.'

'There is some justice in your remarks, but there are many of the British Aristocracy more competent than Lord Raglan, and there are many officers out here almost in the same condition as the men, and they do not desire better.'

'It is the 27th Jan. with me nothing of importance has happened to my knowledge. I have been ready to start for 3 days. I came there from the Hospital.'

Where were you wounded?

'A Minnic rifle ball in the right side.'

Have you been promoted?

'No but I was given to understand that I might expect it in a short time.'

What ship do you intend to come home in?

'The Hymelin.'

Is she English or French?

'English.'

Do you know the Captain's name?

'I cannot tell you he came out with provisions and stores and will return with the sick and wounded, the Captain who brought her out is ill.'

'I am aware that I am here as an atmospheric spirit and the personification of my body. I know not whether the knowledge is the same but I believe here myself that I am telling you the truth. I am aware that there is no law other than you mention by which you can discover its accuracy but I feel the same here as I should in the body, and I assure you on the honour of a soldier that the ship I have mentioned is an English one and now lying in Balaclava Bay and that, if life remains in me 'till that time, I shall sail in it to Malta, from thence to Marseilles, then to Madrid—the Court—and from thence to London, and I think if you feel any doubt as to whom I am, the best way to satisfy yourself is to ask your Guardian Spirit—I am aware you place great dependence in him, and I am sure you will do me the justice I so much wish. I shall perhaps be in Spain in less than a fortnight you can call me there as often as you please.'

Do you know Lieut. Burton?

'He is not in the Army is he?'

Vol. 9, p. 51: 'I am again before Sebastopol. I have been ill, I wish that I was dead. I have got my crystal here. I have seen you in it several times. I have seen your Guardian Spirit in it—I have seen my own—he has told me very painful things not only to me but to the whole company could they be brought to believe it. I use this crystal as a relief after my work—I see so much death—so much mortality that I return with relief to that which gives me a knowledge of spirits, and a hope and faith in immortality.'

9

PUBLISHED MATERIAL

i
RAISING THE DEVIL

[FIRST printed in the *Spiritualist* (2 July 1880) and reprinted in *Lucifer*, Vol. 6, No. 31 (15 March 1890).]

I had been looking in the crystal one evening for a long time without having a vision. Before I left off, I asked the spirit of the crystal, very earnestly, when I could have a vision, for it was so very wearisome to look and to anticipate, and then be disappointed. This message immediately came:

'Procure a glass vessel a foot deep, flat inside, and six inches square; fill it with water from a fish-pond; let the neck of the vessel be sufficiently large to admit your three fingers. Cut the middle finger of your left hand, and having put a strip of paper round the outside of the middle of the bottle, write with the blood of the finger you have cut, this one name . . . . . Paste this strip of paper round the bottle, and then insert the finger you have cut and two other fingers into the neck, and from it into the water let a drop of blood flow. If you do this, you will see and hear of that which will instruct you in spiritual knowledge, and aid you in all that you desire appertaining to the world.'

Although I thought it could not be good, I did not desire anything evil, and I thought, foolishly, that I could hear, and see, and know what they said, without allowing them to influence me, or without for one moment surrendering myself to their possession. I would not do it again. It was not the power, but the knowledge that I sought. I was at the time in a house with a good many people in it, and, fearing that someone might interrupt me, I locked the door. Before I began I had been obliged to have the glass bottle made to the exact size, and I wrote the name on a vellum band and sealed it on. This I placed on the table, and very soon without any call—I used nothing more than the name on the bottle—the water began to change to a thick, dirty-red liquid, and from this there formed, as the water again became clearer, a spirit more like an animal than even a distorted human figure; it had a tail as long in proportion to its size as is the tail of a mouse to the rest of the animal, and it had peculiarly shaped horns. It increased in size so as to fill the entire bottle, the tips of the horns rising above the water in the neck of the bottle. When I saw its head coming above the water, I thought I should be able to prevent its getting any larger by putting a stopper on the top. I could not find anything to place over it at the moment but a book from the mantelpiece. The instance that I stepped across for the book, the horns of the spirit were visible to me above the bottle. Very quickly you may imagine I was back with the book. I am very strong—as strong, I believe, as most men—I can lift a couple of hundredweight, and now I had occasion to put my strength forth. I tried to press the book on the neck of the bottle with all my might, but I could not move it one inch. My hands and the book in them went up as easily as I could have lifted a baby's hands. I grew desperate. I tore the band off the bottle; I used exorcism. There was no fire in the room, and no light, or I would have immediately burned the band. I could not tear it, and I had no means of destroying it. The spirit all this time was gradually getting out of the bottle.

I could not think what to do. I took the bottle up, threw it down and broke it; the water of course ran all over the carpet, and I thought for a moment that I had got rid of the spirit, but I was mistaken, for from the water, as it lay on the floor, it rose again much larger than before.

I went to the door, but I was afraid to open it; then in an instant I thought he might be only visible to me and not to others, and that if I were with other people he would disappear from me, and I tried the door, but could not open it. I forgot that I had locked it. Again I used the form of dismissal and exorcism, but it was of no use. Having done this, I asked him what he wanted. He asked me to test his power by naming anything I desired, and said that if I found that he gave it me and if I would promise him obedience, he would do the same in all other things.

I resolutely told him that I would not—that had I known he was evil and could escape from the bottle I would not have called him; still he did not leave, and I then felt the place to be insufferable, so oppressive as to be almost suffocating. My eyes seemed to burn, I was getting giddy, and appeared to see instead of the one figure a thousand of all shapes and sizes. I still remained with my hand on the lock; the room became confused and dark for one instant only, then all was light, The evil spirit was gone, and I noticed that every drop of water was gone from the surface of the carpet, and that on the white ground which surrounded the pattern was a single red spot. Although unnerved whilst the spirit was present, I was not the least so the moment it was gone, and, on stooping to pick up the small pieces of bottle, I observed round the red spot a circle containing words. Even then, by an impulse I could not control, I was all on fire to know what those words were, down on my knees I deciphered with much difficulty, '. . . returns blood which is too white for a sacrifice'. The red spot rose above the carpet, the words disappeared, and there only remained a little piece of cold congealed blood: this I removed. In an adjoining room I burnt the band which had been round the bottle, threw away the pieces of bottle, and determined to be more cautious in future.

ii

EVENINGS WITH THE INDWELLERS OF THE WORLD OF SPIRITS

BEING A PAPER READ AT A MEETING OF
THE BRISTOL ROSICRUCIAN COLLEGE

[Published in *The Rosicrucian and Masonic Record*, New Series, No. 6, 1 April, 1877.]

In presenting the following paper for the consideration of our brethren of the R.C., I am, at the risk of seeming tedious, compelled to make some prefatory remarks upon the occasion of this apparition, which occurred unsought and undesired, that I may render the narrative intelligible, and show, moreover, how earnestly and strenuously the earth-bound spirits among the departed strive to enter into communion with mortals, now that the veil which of old could only be penetrated by the adept after a long and laborious formulæ, has, by the widespread practice of Animal Magnetism been effectually rent in twain.

After thirty years' desultory working with crystals and mirrors, I had in 1854, under spiritual instructions, prepared and consecrated a large mirror, dedicated to a spirit known to me as the C.A., for the purpose of receiving visions and responses to metaphysical questions proposed by myself and friends. To this object I devoted my Tuesday evenings, and on these occasions was very reluctant to receive spiritual communications from other sources. But on Tuesday, the 30th December 1856, a friend having sent to me a small rock crystal, for the purpose of identifying it with a much larger crystal purchased by Capt. Morrison at Lady Blessington's sale (in Zadkiel's Almanac, 18—, he gave an account of the visions seen therein, illustrated with woodcuts), as having formed pendants to a chandelier destroyed at the Tuileries during the Revolution of 1830— shortly after each event these pendants were offered to me by a lapidary in London.

This small crystal being on the table without any intention on my part of using it that evening, my seeress casually taking it up, observed, 'The crystal is clouded,' and immediately the vision appeared, as related in the following paper, transcribed precisely as written in my diary.

Being at the time especially engaged in receiving from the C.A. a translation of his 'Essay upon Metaphysical and Spiritual Philosophy' (which I hope to get printed this winter), I could ill spare the time, but consented to receive 'the Monk's MS' at every convenient opportunity. The MS duly appeared in the mirror prepared for its reception, and my seeress copied it first in pencil, and afterwards in colours. Unhappily, my seer's health, and her subsequent death, precluded her from copying more than a small portion of the work, and we had no further verbal communications with the monk than appears in this paper.

The monk appeared afterwards to another seeress I then had, and offered to continue the MS and enable her to copy it. He also appeared very unexpectedly to Mrs Britton—then Emma Hardinge—in a large mirror I had opened for her to look at, and afterwards in the small mirror I had prepared to receive his book originally, but, not having my crystal books here, I do not remember what took place.

I exceedingly regret that I am unable to be with you and produce the book, which I have at last had bound, but I hope soon to be in Bristol and bring the Monk's MS and some other articles which may prove interesting to our members, and, till then, I have the pleasure of remaining,
Most fraternally yours,
QUANTI EST LAPERE, 8°

Croydon
♂ die 30th Decr., 1856
VOL. II, p. 128.

Mr Dresser, having presented me with a small crystal for the purpose of identifying Captain Morrison's crystal as one of the pendants of a crystal chandelier destroyed in the palace of the Tuileries during the Revolution under Charles the Tenth (29th July, 1830), which had this evening arrived and had been laid upon the table, and had not been charged, my seeress, Miss Emma Leigh, taking it up, said: 'It is thick—there is a vision in it.

'There's a pair of compasses and a square. Now the compasses are opening; now there is a point on each end of the square, which has turned sideways. There's a book come underneath—a thick book, bound in rough calf, with thick bands up the back; now there's a man's face, very thin, dark, straight hair quite black, come inside the compasses, and a thin, very thin hand placed upon the book.

'Now the face has come from the inside of the compasses to a small space outside. The hand has opened the book—the book is very beautiful inside; it looks like a picture. There are two figures with wings on each side of a little oval. In the middle of the oval there appear words or figures beautifully coloured.'

This remained some time, and as the hour for using the C.A. mirror was at hand, I tried to dismiss the vision, but it remained. I then placed the crystal in my cabinet.

At 8 p.m. I invoked, as usual, the C.A. in his mirror, and the action lasted till a few minutes to ten, when the C.A. left.

10 p.m.—Immediately Emma took up Mr Dresser's crystal, she observed: 'It is still clouded. The book is there open, and the man's face and shoulders. He has held his hand up, and the book has opened just in the same place. It looks very richly illuminated in gold and colours; there is an arch at the top, and one angel is standing upon a crushed ball. Now there are clouds of different colours coming up under the other figure at the bottom—white, like smoke, then purple, blue, pink and golden coloured which covers all up to their wings.

'In the oval the reading is not in English or like letters; it is large enough to be read. Two or three of the letters look like ducks with their heads under water.' Emma then copied the contents of the oval, and when finished she said: 'Now there's a little slip of paper come underneath the title page with these words on (9438 p.):

CHALDEE
MAGI
SACRI

Now the man is looking at you;' and I asked, 'Are these words a translation of the contents of the oval,' and he nodded his head. The figure then pointed to my papers upon the table, and I asked if I should make the title page of my 'Arcana Magica' similar, at which he again nodded. I then asked when he would appear again. He then pointed to the clock on the mantelpiece and turned his finger round a number of times. I asked him if he meant this day week. He nodded and departed.
10.20 p.m.

⊙ die 4th Jan., 1857
1 p.m.

Emma and I were conversing without meaning to invoke, when E. proposed inspecting the Dresser crystal, and upon taking it up, it immediately clouded without invoking, and she said:

'Now the book's coming—it comes in very slowly, from the

right to the left. Now it has opened one fly leaf and then the title. The colour of the paper is like your old MSS—the drawings are very beautiful. The light which comes from the top makes the figure on the left (of the title) all of a golden light. The other figure is altogether darker.'

I then requested that the characters on the title page might be deciphered, when she remarked:

'Now the leaf is turning over—the title is blank. At the back there is a formal pattern for the border of the next leaf, and reading in the middle. Those letters are all beautifully done in colours, but no gold. Thus, in amber, green and red (in capital):

SPIRITS

OF THE

SUN, MOON, AND STARS:

THEIR

TALISMANS

AND

POWERS.

———

TECIMO

———

Now that leaf has turned over on this side. There's the radiant spirit standing full face in a circle. The bottom of the circle hides the lower part of the figure, and underneath the circle is an oval. Now there's a round ball under the oval, divided into four parts; now there is a rod on one side, and three bright lines of colour—purple, green, and yellow—and on the small oval are the same characters as in the oval of the title. On the other side there is nothing but reading, and the same border as round the title.'

As the book in the crystal was only about two inches long, the reading was necessarily too small to peruse, and I took my oval mirror out of the cabinet, and requested (Unian) to transfer the vision from the crystal into the mirror, that the Seer might read it, for, although extremely distinct and beautifully executed, it was too small to read. The vision, however, did not pass into the mirror, and upon handing Emma a magnifying glass it enlarged the characters but rendered them less distinct. There appeared about two dozen lines upon the page.

I then requested the Spirit of the Crystal either to transfer the vision or send in the words one by one, and Emma remarked: 'There is an attempt at something like reading coming under the book in very straggling letters.

9440.—'The book would be shown plainly in an unconsecrated mirror or crystal.'

I asked, 'Shall it be a plain glass or silvered mirror?'

9442.—'Tuesday. Like that, but unconsecrated.'

'I am engaged on Tuesdays. Cannot it be on some other day?'

9443.—'Wednesday, Thursday, Friday, Saturday, Sunday—Noon.'

'Then we will inspect on Sunday at noon.'

Now it is gone, and the book is gone.

1.45 p.m.

Having duly prepared a mirror, on the following Sunday, Emma inspected the mirror.

⊙ die Jan. 11, 1857

UNCONSECRATED MIRROR.

1.45 p.m.

The Seeress immediately said: 'Here's the man come who had the book. He has on a brown stuff dress, close round the waist, straight black hair, black eyes, very thin, sallow complexion, his head shaved on the top. He has something like a hood hanging down the back of his dress.'

'May I ask your name?'

9511.—'I have no name now.'

'What was your name when on earth?'

9512.—'D.P.'

'Have you anything to communicate to us before you furnish us with the MS?'

9513.—'Yes. I made the book you have seen when I was alive. I was a Spaniard by birth, and was received early into the Catholic Church. I took the vows, and was a priest. I became acquainted with many secrets, and read many of the old Spanish manuscripts of the antient magicians. Such a study was prohibited, but not less desired by me. I had much time and little to occupy it, and I was devoted with my whole heart and soul to seeking into hidden things. At last my greatest wishes were fulfilled, and I saw beings disembodied.

'I was uneducated in the ways of the world, but brought up to be conversant with horrors. I was hardened by sights of penance and sufferings, and I was constantly employed in hypocrisy and deceit—my calling obliged me to be so. I saw and conversed with spirits to whom these things were hateful. By them I was persuaded, and I believe helped, to flee from the Brotherhood that would have persecuted me to death.

'I continued my communion with these spirits. I knew not, except from what they told me, their nature or office. I called them only with intense desire, and they left me when they pleased. I knew of no exorcism—those that I believed to be good then I know now to be different. I went away from the Convent and left the country with my book but half completed, and that I treasured more than my life, and, my spirit companions still attending me, I travelled to Rome. I was introduced by them into the society of the Rosicrucians, some of whom I cannot believe even now were human. If they were they had attained powers that man ought not to possess, for they did things that, callous as I was, and so well acquainted with sights earthly and ghostly, made me tremble with fear, and to believe that they had the working of the universe. At that place my book was completed. I sought the same powers that they possess. I learned nearly every form that they went through, every ceremony that was used at their meetings.

'I returned, I knew not why—impelled perhaps by spirits, careless of my temporal safety—to the town that I had fled from. It was at the time of the Inquisition. With my magic secrets and my talismans of powers, some harmless and others involving destruction, I performed many marvels before persons, who gave me up to its *"Justice."*

'I should have been more careful, for I might have saved myself even then, but I relied on the aid that had been given to me before. I did wonders that could not be reconciled with the action of nature. It was evident to all that I did them by the aid of spirits, but I did not know any more than they the nature or the quality of those who helped me.

'I was tried for being possessed by the Devil, and for practising black magic. I attempted to deny it, and I solemnly swear that I did not on that ocasion, when I knew the sentence would be death, use one word that I knew to be untrue. I would not compromise my dignity sufficiently to evade them or their questions, and when I denied their accusations it was with a sincere conviction of their falsehood. Every spirit that I had seen was of a pleasing form. I believed that the Enemy of Man was otherwise. The communication that I had with them tended to make me better than I should have been, or rather than I was, without their agency being sought. The knowledge they gave me, though startling and wonderful, was I believed innocent, for they in their charms and talismans did not mention him by any of the names known to me in all my reading of black magic. I had never used a "sacrifice", and on my conscience I could affirm that I had never used it for the purpose of injury to any living creature. I had never done with it one particle of the injury which they did with it every hour in their dungeons.'

Expecting I should be shortly disturbed, I requested the monk to appear at another time to continue his narration, when he replied:

'I will be as concise as possible. I have not much to say. I was tried and condemned to death by judges hearing only one side, but before death was allowed me the greatest blessing they could give—I was cruelly tortured—for they had a desire to possess the secrets for which I was punished, and out of the poor wretches they tortured they obtained secrets for which they might as justly been punished themselves. I had many such companions in the prison, and not until twenty-three days after the sentence did the end come that I had looked forward to and longed for with such agonised delight.

'I had been told that there was an after life, and realized it sufficiently peaceful, if not happy, as to make me bear with apparent composure the inflictions of my enemies. Up to this time I managed to keep my book undiscovered. I had sewn it in the mattress I had lain upon the first night, and that only after my imprisonment. With my teeth I had unripped, and with a nail found in the wall, I put the thread in again and made it appear the same as before, and when this mattress was taken away from me I may safely say that it caused me more pain, more uneasiness and anxiety than their inflictions or my doom—I was so fearful they should have the power I was so soon to lose.

'I was to be burned, and the night before it was customary to allow the prisoners the indulgence of a bed and a meal. Imagine my joy at that hour when my mattress was brought back. I picked out my book and concealed it in my dress until the last moment came, and then, with despairing energy, when that was no longer of avail, I clasped it in my hands and determined that it should be burned with me. I thought not so much of myself as of that, and I went to the stake as firm perhaps as the frailty of the flesh would allow a mortal to do. Many of us were burned, and to this circumstance or to those again interposing who were not of earth, I must owe the preservation of my book from the sight up to this time of the officials around me. It was not until a moment or two before my execution that they attempted to grasp it. The chains that they had put on my hands I had bound round my book, and I held it as tight as the will of a man nerved by death can, and I hurried quickly into the very flames to get it out of their reach. I succeeded, and I saw it in flames when only the soles of my feet were scorched. As the flames went on consuming me my senses left, delirium came on and I believed that I raved. My passing from life into immortality—from time into eternity—was certainly a fearful one. When my spirit was released and I was again whole as I am now—when I started into being, the same as life, yet how changed—I found my book with me and myself surrounded by those who had so often been my companions on earth.'

Just as I was about to be interrupted, the monk said:

'I will continue it with your permission when you have more time.'

2 p.m.—Action ended and the monk left.

⊙ die 18 Jan., 1857

2.15 p.m.

UNCONSECRATED MIRROR

Called the monk, and the Seeress instantly remarked, 'He is here as before.'

'I was burnt in 1693, in the summer, and I have not now progressed beyond the state I then found myself in. I had mistaken the appearance of the spirits that came to me upon earth. I had given myself up to their guidance without inquiring to what order they belonged, and I found when it was too late that I had been encouraging and communing with the planetary spirits, and not with those who can direct and counsel to their home. I believed from the information I received from those that visited me that the planets were the abode of men after death, that they formed the different degrees and modes of happiness, that some were evil and some good, and that the greatest felicity was enjoyed by those who were allowed to enter the sun. They never said one word to me of the spheres. I did not know that there was a short and direct mode by which I could obtain truth and profit by it everlastingly. I know now that I had the power of exorcising and dispelling them if they were not what they represented themselves to be, the only spirits of the universe.

'I know now that I might have enquired of them, and that they would have been bound to answer me rightly, but while receiving them and trusting implicitly to them I lost sight of the Being that could alone rule them and of the name by which, were they falsehood itself in their nature, they would be defeated and subdued. This was caused through my connexion with the

Catholic religion. I no more believed the doctrines I professed, the sanctity of vows that I took, than I did in my competency to give absolution for money or my efficiency in obtaining the intercession of saints that I ridiculed.

'I was soon after death aware of my sin, and with a consciousness of all my offences, with a knowledge of the right and a desire to obtain it, and through it peace and rest. I have remained as I died, and I am told that it is to the mercy of the Providence that I blasphemed upon earth I owe even this my present position, sorrowful and earth-bound as it is—they tell me that my sufferings on earth and my death by the hands of another prevented me from living a sufficient time to be repentant, even if I had been convinced of my errors—that such a conviction might have come before my natural life had closed, when the giver of it alone thought fit, and therefore the punishment that I might have expected with justice had I died a natural death was transmitted to those who caused my death; that they, when they deprived me of life, took upon themselves the whole burthen of my spirit and made me neutral, neither receiving increased happiness nor any punishment, save my own conscience, and as I sinned through error in my intercourse with spirits, I am not punished for that, because I believed them to be the highest. Those for whom I mistook them look upon me with pleasure and with pity, and they do all that is possible to keep me from falling a step lower. By their aid I shall be able to rise gradually to a better state of existence. But there is one thing that I want out of my possession, that I want to see back in reality upon earth before I can rest—the book that I have treasured at all times more than my life, and at the last, when I am well aware that my thoughts should have been directed to a far different subject, it was my only aim to take it with me, and if I could not do that to keep it from those who destroyed me.

'From that time to this I have incessantly wandered about trying to bring that book back into form before I lose sight of the earth. My only wish is to see it in material form as it was then, that the secrets that caused me such trouble to collect should not be lost when I was dead even to memory. I have tried to show it to men. So wild have been my endeavours that I have even presented it to them while asleep. They have dreamed of it, and I—oh, how hard have I tried to make it intelligible to them when waking has dispelled the illusion from their minds. I have sought other modes. I have tried to present it through writing mediums, but they have other spirits that, low as I am, I would not dare to mingle with or be near, for I shun their presence with as much abhorrence as I look with pleasure to the light which comes from those I trust may help me. They assure me that the more free I can keep my mind from the thoughts of earth, from the memory of the past, and turn them to things above me, I may hope for readier assistance.'

The monk here paused, and, mentioning to him some similar cases from Jung Stilling's Theory of Pneumatology, I earnestly exhorted him to pray for assistance and pardon. He replied:

'But I cannot pray sufficiently for Him to do so. More, I must show with my whole being that I am changed in turning my thoughts from earth to heaven. I must ask with humility by my actions as well as by my voice for His grace.'

I explained that although my time was fully occupied, yet, having received my G.S.'s permission, I would receive his book as often as possible, and, placing the title my seeress had copied, I asked if he could see it, and if the charcters were correct.

'The figures are the same; the spiritual characters are the same.

'It is the talisman of the sun, as I thought when I made it the highest that might be made. It is a key to the language of all spirits and their talismans that dwell there.

'That is, there is only one class of spirits, although numerous individuals. Each has a power peculiarly his own, which is felt or influences the material world. This power is obtained and kept up by a talisman, which each possesses separate and distinct from the other, and made up of different characters. These characters make a language that consists, I may say of 24 letters of the different modes of expression. These letters are joined and shortened—in the separate talismans it is so—there are conjunctions of characters that look to the uninitiated of quite a different description from the —— language of their originals. The one form which all their expressions are taken is the Talisman of the Sun, the one great talisman that belongs to their abode; their language you will see in my book.'

'I have long been desirous of penetrating the mysteries of the —— order of R.C. Will you give me the formula, or does your book contain it?'

'It does.'

'As I have now one hour to spare, shall we commence with a page of Chapter — of your MS?'

'I have not got it with me.'

'If I devote next Friday evening to it will you bring the book with you?'

'Yes, I will.'

'May I ask your age when you thus suffered under the tender mercies of the Holy Apostolic Inquisition?'

'Forty-three. The many years that I have passed since have made me no older. I would that the horrid religion that I professed, and which destroyed, was swept away from the earth, that its priesthood were extinguished, and the poor deluded wretches they drag after them in their misery were made partakers of the mercy of Him they blasphemed.'

'Do you know anything in your present state of the famous writer upon occult philosophy, Henry Cornelius Agrippa, who died in —— and published this work (R. Russell's translation of the three books, quarto 16.)?'

'He is not in my state—he has gone on far above me. He was a Christian and a student, that was all—I a believer and follower.'

'Do you suppose that he did not practise magic as well as study it?'

'He inquired into it before he could give that work (pointing to the book then on the table). He had a strong tendency to spiritualism, and used available means to elucidate apparent mysteries, but he always undertook the search with a deep reverence and a firm reliance on the Almighty, and a determination to let nothing that passed between him and spirits, be what they might, interpose between his own being and his Maker, and never to do aught at their instigation other than his own heart and conscience told him to be consistent with the laws of his Maker manifesting themselves in his being.'

'Did you ever know in the spirit world Joseph Balsamo, commonly called Count Cagliostro, who, like yourself died, under the pious and tender care of the Holy Inquisition in the Castle of St Angelo, at Rome, in 1793, just a century after your death?'

'I know he did. He was in my state—indeed, worse than mine, more degraded than I am, for he had made sacrifices to his gods, and yet he's gone on before me, I saw him leave this place and go on before me whilst I remain. I have seen murderers leave it.'

'I have often conversed with Cagliostro in my mirrors. Although a spirit, he held materialistic views. His appearances at first were very painful, but he has progressed onwards to happiness, and I hope it will be the same with you ere long; but you must pray for mercy.'

'I may be forgiven by mercy, if not by justice.'

'Did you ever know Guiseppe Francisco Borri, the Milanese,

the author of "La chiavo del Cabinetto"?'

'Yes, I knew him in my life.'

'I always understood that Romish priests who underwent the purifying by fire were first strangled at the stake?'

'There were some instances of it, but it was not a rule. It is left to the option of the supreme judge the mode of execution. If he had a purpose to effect he might do so, but not from mercy, for that was never a part of his nature. But whenever the torture of "the nails" was inflicted it was perfect evidence that the extreme would be gone into, and, instead of the fire being kindled after I was bound, it was made first, and I was then put in, and if necessary, an iron framework would have been thrown over me.'

'Surely the men who could inflict with fiendish pleasure such torments upon their fellow-creatures, however erring, cannot now be at rest?'

'No; I tell you the sins of their victims are visited on their own heads, and they are expiating their own offences and their victims' in the worst of all states that can befall spirits—in burning themselves in the fires that they have kindled for their victims.'

'Then there we will leave them.'

The Monk continued:

'Besides other means of torture, they drove splinters of iron, like fine nails, into the fleshy parts of the soles of my feet, a dozen in each at first, and then removed everything from my dungeon that I could either sit or lie upon. Standing or walking was insupportable. My hands were bound. On the damp floor, moist and slimy with vermin, in perfect darkness, except when the light came that was to bring me to punishment, and only dragged into full light to answer the repeated questions of the Ruler, and then dazzled and blinded with light, and voices, and curses, and the agony of walking, I was turned back into the dungeon for three-and-twenty days. But it is enough; you would be revolted at the horrors in detail.'

'Yours was indeed a shocking end. But let me ask if I, by again bringing into the material world your manuscript, and leaving it behind me when I die, may I not thereby lead some future possessor into evils which he might otherwise have escaped?'

'If a right use were made of it the work would only tend to enlighten and instruct.'

'When I complete your manuscript I shall put this narrative at the commencement as well as an introductory warning against its abuse.'

'It is not for the making of that book I am punished, but for the reliance I placed upon the spirits there treated of, and far more for the sins of my profession. They constitute my guilt.'

'Do you know anything of this MS—"The Key of Rabbi Solomon on Magic Telesms"?'

'Will you place it closer. I do know the characters. They were copied originally from some of the Rosicrucian works. There's some private libraries and manuscripts in Rome now that are kept quite secret from strangers to the order, that are full of the most curious seals and descriptions of spirits and spirit-places in their own language. You will find in my book the means of reading these. Each planet had a separate one.

'I know nothing of the means of communication between spirits of a higher state, or whether their modes of expression are the same.'

'May I ask how you became aware of my seer's faculty of spirit seeing, and my practice of invoking them?'

Px. 9534, vol. xi.—'You have seen so many spirits that it is well known that you are able to communicate with them. Were you to throw it open to all who would come there would be many and of different grades avail themselves of it. I was not prevented from appearing, therefore I may say I was allowed to do so. Higher spirits would not deprive me of the chance of making myself happier when they knew I had the desire to do so. They would not close every portal against me and make me an outcast from every one.'

'Then on Sunday evening I will await your appearance.' And my seer remarked, 'Now he has turned round and walked away.' 18th Jan., 1857—3.45 p.m.

iii
CORRESPONDENCE WITH ROBERT OWEN

[Robert Owen (1771–1858), the philanthropist and social reformer, became interested in Spiritualism late in life. As a result of published comments on the subject, he received a series of letters from Hockley which Owen published in his *The New Existence of Man Upon the Earth*. Appearing in seven parts between 1853 and 1855, the first five parts dealt with Owen's life and public speeches. Part VI had the subtitle 'with an Appendix containing a record of Spiritual communications' and includes Hockley's letters to Owen and a lengthy letter from Hockley to P. E. Bland and the members of the Harmonial Society of St Louis, Ohio. The letters say much about the Crowned Angel's, and Hockley's, religious views.]

Croydon
8 December 1853

SIR,

From the perusal of your *Quarterly Review* I have been induced to address you upon 'The Spiritual Communications' mentioned in that work,—a subject in which, for nearly thirty years, I have taken great interest, and I trust this will be deemed an apology for my presuming to offer any advice to one whose experience upon other subjects so far exceeds my own.

On a matter upon which so much has been written to so little purpose,—a subject so deeply interesting, yet so slightly understood,—it would be impossible adequately to remark in a letter; and I should not have thus trespassed upon your time and attention, but for the regard which even a stranger must feel for a gentleman whose endeavours to serve his fellow men have been so unceasing, and have extended over so long a period as your own.

Having for years past practised divining by the crystal, I have been led to make many inquiries as to the nature and quality of the spirits now so multitudinously entering into communication with mankind by means of writing and rapping mediums; and from the information thus obtained I am induced to believe that the far greater part of them, if not 'Evil', are at least illuding spirits, and not really the souls of those departed friends and others whom they assert themselves to be. Having through the kindness of a gentleman received an introduction to Mr S., I was much gratified by the *seance* with which I was favoured; and, my young seer proving a most excellent medium, I have since then had ample opportunity of satisfying *myself* upon the subject. Since reading the first communication in the *Rational Review* of your interviews with the Duke of Kent, Franklin, and others, I have been informed that you were misled as to their identity, and I beg to submit to your notice the following questions and the responses obtained by me in reference to your investigations.

On the 26th July, 1853, while in communication with the Crowned Angel, the spirit who the most frequently appears in the mirror, I said:—

1.—Robert Owen the philanthropist has writen to the Queen that he has been in communication with her deceased father the Duke of Kent, who states that he is in the 4th circle,—Is that so?

C. A.—It is——, the late——, whose spirit is now upon earth, which communicates with him.

2.—The spirit stated he was in the 4th circle and was very happy—Is that so?

C. A.—The —— who communicates with Robert Owen under the disguise of the Duke of Kent is an evil spirit, and still upon earth.

3.—I have not yet seen any of the communications, but Mr Owen states them to be very interesting, and of beneficial tendency. Will my writing to Robert Owen to test his spirit be of any service to him?

C. A.—In a very short time it will be of great use. At present it will not.

On November 1st, 1853, I said:—

1.—I perceive, by a late publication, that Robert Owen still believes it to be the spirit of the late Duke of Kent who raps to his questions.

C. A.—As Mr Owen has not much longer to live on this earth, it would be advisable that you write *soon*. It would be advisable for you to write to him as soon as possible after the 8th December.

2.—I will do so. Is there any information or advice upon the subject you would wish to favour me with?

C. A.—I will tell you before that time.

On November 29th, 1853.

1.—You were kind enough to say that, as I am to write to Robert Owen after the 8th December, you would tell me what to say. Is it convenient for you to do so now?

C. A.—I wish you to ask him if it would be agreeable to him to appoint an interview with you. You might tell him more than you would be able to do in writing.

2.—Can you furnish me with any proof I might give him that my writing to him is the result of spiritual advice.

C. A.—I cannot do that, because I cannot mix with evil spirits. Ask him to try exorcism on those spirits who state themselves to be the Duke of Kent and Benjamin Franklin. Tell him that you have written by my wish, and that his system of the Elevation of Society will never take place in England, but it will do so in America. Should he survive the 8th June next, he will live to see the time when America prospers under his social system of education.

The form of exorcism thus referred to is exceedingly simple. Upon preparing to enter into spiritual communication it is advisable to say, either aloud or mentally, but of course fervently, *three* times, this exorcism against evil spirits generally:—

'In the name of the Almighty God, in whom we live, and move, and have our being, I dismiss from this room all evil spirits that may be therein!'

And if any doubt arises whilst in communication with any spirit as to his identity,—use the following exorcism *three* times:—

'If thou, spirit, who art now in communication with us, art not really and truly the spirit of A. B., I dismiss thee hence, in the name of the Almighty God, in whom we live, and move, and have our being!'

Trusting most fervently that you may be spared to see the triumph of your long cherished hopes for the amelioration of society.

I beg to remain, Sir,
Your most obedient servant,

Robert Owen, Esq.   FRED. HOCKLEY

Croydon
18 January 1854

SIR,

I have now the pleasure of replying to your favour of the 11th December, and beg to refer you to my minutes for the cause of my not having answered it before.

Tuesday, 13th December, 1853.—In communication with the Crowned Angel through the mirror, I said:—

1.—I have written to Robert Owen; and he in return thanks me for the information; but he still expresses his firm belief that his spiritual communicants are the spirits of those deceased friends whom they represent themselves to be.

C. A.—I am gratified to know that you have done all you

possibly can to enlighten him. The issue, of course, is in the hands of God. By His grace I hope still to convince him of his error. I will know from his Guardian Spirit the best way of satisfying him.

2.—When will you give me any further information concerning him?

C. A.—Next Tuesday evening.

Tuesday, 27th December, 1853:

1.—Is it agreeable for you to give me the further information concerning Robert Owen, promised last Tuesday evening, if you have obtained it from his Guardian Spirit?

C. A.—I have obtained it. And as he wished to know the name of the spirit you communicate with,—give him mine. Perhaps by that means he will be able to find out that I am not one of the evil spirits he has been specially guarded against. His Guardian Spirit makes it known to me that it will not be advisable to write to him for a short time.

2.—I will write to him when you advise.

C. A.—In twenty days.

3.—May I ask the name of his Guardian Spirit?

C. A.—Solomia.

The responses thus obtained are given by the C. A. generally in a large mirror, eighteen inches by twelve; sometimes in a crystal. And although my seer is a rapping and a writing medium, I never use the first, and rarely the last. The process is so slow, and liable to interruption, and the spirits are so utterly beyond control, for even when we exorcise them we cannot tell whether they may or may not leave the room and return when it is over.

In the responses by the crystal, the answers continually come faster than I can write;—indeed I have had more than 1,200 words pass through the crystal consecutively, and often several hundreds, more rapidly than I could put them to paper;—an advantage, to me, incomparably superior to the slow and tedious process of rapping or writing, and infinitely less hurtful to the nervous system of the medium.

I have not yet seen your pamphlet, but will obtain it the first opportunity. In your *Rational Review* you do not mention your having in any way held conferences with the Atmospheric Spirits of living persons. These curious, and as yet little known existences, and the laws by which they are governed, have hitherto proved a stumbling block to Mesmerists in the revelations obtained through their Clairvoyants in the magnetic sleep.

'Every man,' says Swedenborg, (p. 203 of his life, by J. J. Garth Wilkinson,) 'has either a good or a bad spirit, who is constantly with him, but sometimes a little removed from him, and appears in the world of spirits; but of this the living man knows nothing—the spirit, however, knows everything. This familiar spirit has in the world of spirits the same figure, the same countenance, the same tone of voice, and wears also similar garments.'

Although in part, in my belief, Swedenborg is here, in error,—yet the existence of these Atmospheric Spirits of livng persons I have proved many, many times, and it is a spiritual manifestation of much interest.

I am, Sir,
Your obedient servant,
Robert Owen, Esq.   F.H.

Croydon,
29 May 1854

DEAR SIR,

Absence from town prevented my having the pleasure of waiting upon you at the date of your last letter, and I now beg to offer my best thanks for the portion of your life, just published, which you kindly enclosed with my MS.

The Appendix to the life is most interesting; and it is indeed an anomaly which I cannot yet fathom by the crystal,—That one man's unceasing efforts for so many years for the benefit of mankind should be so long, and apparently so hopelessly, retarded, by another man's insane ambition, plunging the civilized world into all the evils and horrors of a war and its consequence—retrogradation.

I took the opportunity of my return to call upon Mr S. for a tablet I had left with him, and was surprised to find that his medium's faculty had left her, though probably, under more judicious treatment, it may return.

May I be allowed to inquire if your researches by the rappists continue to develop themselves to your satisfaction, and to repeat that I shall be most happy to obtain responses by the crystal to any questions you may favour me with as a test of their relative value.

I have received from the spirit of my mirror a lengthened explanation of the Occult Law by which these visions are governed; but, as might be expected, the difficulty of conveying to corporeal ideas and beings living in time and space, any just conception of spiritual essences which do not seem to be under either of those conditions, has left me still much to seek. The response, which contains about 4,000 words, is, however, exceedingly curious, and I shall be at any time happy to show it to you.

I am, dear Sir,
Yours faithfully,

Robert Owen, Esq.   F. H.

Croydon,
9 June 1854

DEAR SIR,

I have the pleasure of sending you the responses obtained in reference to your conclusions. The answers are unusually short, owing, I conceive, to my having a friend with me, who, although a believer, has but rarely attended our sittings. I am to receive a further communication, which, when obtained, I will forward to you.

As the conclusions you have arrived at are utterly opposed to my own, and also to the whole tenor of the responses obtained by me from the C. A., I did not offer any remark; as I wished the answers to be as far as possible unbiassed.

I shall indeed feel great pleasure in sending you the first opportunity the explanation received of these occult laws. But from the difficulty experienced by spirits in conveying to our corporal senses and ideas, living as we do in time and space, the laws which govern the spirit world, I have much yet to enquire for.

Should you have any further queries, I shall always have great pleasure in obtaining replies.—And, trusting you may soon recover from your cold, and may live to see your ardent endeavours for the benefit of your fellow men in some measure realised,

I remain, Dear Sir,
Yours very faithfully,

Robert Owen, Esq.   F. H.

Tuesday, June 6th, 1854.
Responses obtained by the Crystal.

1.—Mr Robert Owen wishes to receive replies to the following questions. Is he right in coming to the following conclusions?

'1.—That nothing can never produce something.'

C. A.—He is right. All things are predestined, and one arises from another.

'2.—That therefore something has eternally existed.'

C. A.—It had. This world was created from a mass, without shape and without form.

'3.—That that something is the Elements of the Universe.'

C. A.—It was earth and air,—nothing more. I mean that the world was created out of something, and that that something was earth and air.

'4.—That these elements possess inherent unchangeable qualities.'

C. A.—He is right.

'5.—That some notion of the Almighty Power of these combined elements may be conjectured from observing the extent of motion, life, and instinct or mind, in one of the minute beings seen through a glass of great magnifying power in a drop of water.'

C. A.—He is right in that conclusion, but not in using the word *mind*.

'6.—That the aggregate of these elements constitute the supreme mind, or the God-head.'

C. A.—They do not.

'7.—That these elements,—their inherent unchangeable qualities,—and their aggregate power, or supreme mind,— co-exist externally.'

C. A.—They do not.

'8.—That, as nothing could have existed before them, they are the great first cause of all things; and that, as nothing can exist after them, they are first and last and everything.'

C. A.—They were first; but after the end of the world they will not exist; they are not necessary to a heavenly existence.

'9.—That these elements of the universe,—their inherent qualities,—and their aggregate power or supreme mind,—form the trinity—that which nations call Nature, the Laws of Nature, and God.'

C. A.—Although without them nature could not exist, they do not form part of it. They are not the laws of nature, neither are they God.

'10.—That they are three in one, and one in three,—separate, yet indivisible; for they eternally co-exist.'

C. A.—They are not united, and they have a separate existence.

'11.—That the inherent qualities of these elements are the laws of nature.'

C. A.—Although they are the most powerful of all things when used by God, they are not the laws of nature.

'12.—That the elements of the universe are matter and spirit; matter when condensed to human appreciation by our senses; and spirit when too refined or etherialized to be perceived by men except when mesmerised or out of the normal state.'

C. A.—The spirit of man can appreciate them more fully when separated from the body.

'13.—That God and nature are Omniscient and Omnipresent.'

C. A.—It is wrong for him to so closely connect nature with God. Although nature is His work, and He is the Supreme Ruler, He views it in the same way that an artisan would view a piece of elaborate machinery that he had made, and which would act under one principle until he chose that it should be stopped.

'14.—Omnipotent,—except that he cannot change the laws of nature, which would be to change his own qualities which are unchangeable.'

C. A.—As nature and God are quite separate, so He can change it without changing himself. They only exist in unity because it is His will and the most beautiful of all things.

'15.—Will Mr Owen succeed in convincing the world of the truth and superiority of the new system for governing and directing mankind, by the aid of the panorama now painting in Oxford?'

C. A.—It will be of benefit to his cause, but he will not be able to owe his success entirely to that. I think that at present there is nothing I wish to tell Mr Owen. You can send him the answer to his last letter; and in your next I will send some instructions. I have a reason for not sending them at present.

Croydon
24 June 1854

Dear Sir,

I herewith send you that portion of the responses obtained by me from the C. A. which has relation to yourself, and I will forward the promised 'instructions' as soon as possible after receiving them; but should you in the meantime have any further questions to propose, I shall be most happy to receive them.

Trusting this fine warm weather has removed your indisposition.

I am, dear sir,

Yours most truly,

Robert Owen, Esq.   F. H.

Tuesday, 13th June, 1854.

F. H. to the spirit in the mirror.

1.—Mr Owen has written me a letter returning his thanks to you for your kindly answering his queries. He also writes—'I have sent a memorial to the Lords of the Treasury to ask for a commission to investigate my views and practical recommendations:—perhaps to-morrow the C. A. will have the kindness to say if it will have any success or influence with them.'

C. A.—What day do you want to return an answer to his letter?

2.—Not until I receive your expressed wish.

C. A.—Do you want to answer it before next Tuesday?

3.—Not if it will be more convenient for you then to favour me with your views.

C. A.—I will give you the answer next Tuesday. But if you wish to write to him before, I will appear one evening for that purpose.

4.—I will wait your pleasure.

Tuesday, 20th June, 1854.

1.—Is it convenient for you to give me the promised information to send to Mr Owen?

C. A. He will not succeed in it.

2.—Have you any information or advice you wish me to convey to him?

C. A.—Does he intend visiting you?

3.—Mr Owen is aware that I should be very happy to see him here, but from his great age I fear it might be irksome to him to come so far; but I hope soon to have the pleasure of seeing him in London.

C. A.—You will not visit him before the 5th of July. Before that time I shall have some instructions to give you concerning him.

4.—May I ask if the spirits who rap and by the alphabet announce themselves as the deceased friends or relatives of the querents, are really so, seeing that they give names often unthought of by the querents, and state circumstances in some instances long forgotten, and even unknown.

C. A.—In most cases they are wandering or 'undeveloped' spirits; but in some cases they are really the spirits of the parties whose names they take; but then they are never happy, and are always evil. No good spirits—either angels, planetary spirits, or other—ever rapped for the gratification of mortals. They have rapped or made other noises to indicate the death of certain persons, or to announce events; but then it was unexpectedly and unknown to those who heard them.

Croydon
24 September 1854

MY DEAR SIR,

You will, I am afraid, think me a very dilatory correspondent,—but the limited hours I have to spare will I hope plead my excuse. I have now the pleasure of sending herewith the responses of the C. A. to the first six of your questions; and you will perceive that your views being so directly opposed to the C. A.'s, the C. A. could not give further answers to questions stated by him to be based on error. I therefore submit it for your judgment.

I also enclose the two parts of the '*Sacred Circle*,' for which I am much obliged to you; and also return you the pamphlet called the '*Harmonial Philosophy*.' And you will perceive in my minutes, which I have also sent herewith, that I selected from that pamphlet the 'Seven Theorems of Popular Christianity,' and the 'Seven Theorems on Spiritual Philosophy,' and submitted them to the C. A. And the responses thereto obtained will, I feel sure, be read by you with great interest.

I must premise that my seer had no possible idea of what I was going to ask until the Theorems were proposed; and the answers came so much faster than I could write, that I find a word or two in my rough copy which I cannot decipher. The responses are very interesting, and will serve, with replies to some other published Theorems, as a basis for future inquiry.

I have requested Mr John Chapman's assistant to obtain two copies of the pamphlet for me, if he can; but should I not be fortunate enough to get them,—shall I be taking too great a liberty in begging the present copy from you when you friends have perused it.

I was favoured last Tuesday with the company of your friend whom I had the pleasure of meeting at Sevenoaks on my visit to you, and I look forward for next Tuesday week for another pleasant meeting, as you will perceive by my book of minutes.

You will also therein observe, (*which from page 94 are all new to you*), that the C. A.'s views are not only orthodox, but perfectly consistent with all the answers he has hitherto favoured me with; and I should indeed be deeply gratified if they induced you to reinvestigate that all-important subject,—the truths of Christianity and its consequent scheme of redemption; and to that end I intend asking the C. A. if he can favour me with some questions to be proposed by you to the spirit rappers; as I cannot think that spirits, however powerful for evil, can be allowed to lead an earnest searcher after truth into irremmediable error.

I was also favoured on the 21st with a letter from ——, who informs me that upon his return from Germany in about a month's time he will visit Croydon, and will show me a Psycograph which it is said will return answers to inquiries. If this is possible I think you would find one a most interesting companion.

I have sent my book of minutes, and shall be much obliged by your returning it to me as soon as possible, to prevent my copy getting in arrear; and I will forward the earlier volumes as promised, and the Shekinah.

Trusting this will find you in good health,

I am, dear Sir,

Yours very sincerely,

Robert Owen, Esq.   F. H.

P.S.—Since writing the above, upon re-perusing your queries, I find Nos. 15 to 24 are such as I can ask without reference to your opposing views, and I will therefore ask them on Tuesday.

Tuesday, 12th September, 1854. The C. A. Mirror.
Invoked the C. A.
'He is here as usual.'

1.—Mr Robert Owen particularly requested that I would return you his best thanks, not only for the answers you were pleased to give to his propositions, but for the kind sympathy expressed in your former responses relative to him; and although he differs, with deference, from many of your views, he entertains for them the highest respect, and has written to me a letter containing twenty-four theorems or propositions, to which he solicits your kind and full response.

Proposition 1.—'That the universe is an eternal existence, consisting of space and all within it.'

C. A.—It is not eternal. 'Heaven and earth shall pass away, but my words shall not pass away, saith the Lord.' In the words of the most High we have the distinct assurance that the universe is at his will but a void.

Proposition 2.—'That space is illimitable.'

Proposition 3.—'That it is filled with the element or elements which are the materials or material of which all separate existences are formed.'

C. A.—In that he is wrong. Because in space there is no material for any thing. Space is the room in which —— material may be ——. Space has no limits; because the whole of creation,—every thing created, known and unknown,—there is room for them all.

Proposition 4.—'That this element or these elements contain inherent unchangeable qualities.'

C. A.—I cannot understand what he considers the nature of that element can be, which fills all space, and from which are created all things.

Proposition 5.—'That the element or elements filling the universe, with their inherent unchangeable qualities, are eternal, and constitute "Deity," or the "All in All" of the universe.'

C. A.—He does not recognise the Almighty as a distinct and separate power from nature. In that, of course, he is wrong. I cannot help remarking that he is too elaborate in his opinions. Strong opinions more simply expressed, would be better understood.

Proposition 6.—'That the eternal element or elements filling the universe is what men mean by nature; and the eternal unchanging qualities of the element or elements, what they mean by God.'

C. A.—Before I can distinguish the truth from the error of his arguments, I must better understand his way of expressing them. You must tell him, in the first place, that he makes the first false step when he recognizes nature and nature's God as the same power.

That they are entirely distinct:—

That *He* created the universe and the elements:—and

That He rules them.

2.—Accept my thanks. I will write to him as you direct. Mr Owen is a man who, as you once before kindly expressed it, has done so much through a lengthened life for the benefit of his fellow-men, without the hope of reward either here or hereafter, that he is pre-eminently entitled to the services of any one who may, by the blessing of God, be the means of placing him in the path of truth: and the more so as he possesses the great moral courage to boldly avow his belief, however opposed it may be to his own or his friends' previous opinions.

C. A.—That man has acted from his childhood from an inherent sense of right. No matter what it was, if he believed that he was right, he would publicly avow it.

That sense of right and truth has done a great, very great, good for his fellow men, by itself; but how much greater good would that do when guided by a religious sense of right;—when he can do those things under the blessing of God, how much happier would be his feelings, when he felt that he was chosen for a great work, and that it was the intention of the Almighty to give his reward accordingly.

I wish you to write to Mr Owen, to give him my answer to all those questions, express my hope that his opinions on that subject will be changed, and after that my pleasure in answering any questions that he may lay before me, as also in a communion through this mirror with himself.

Croydon
Monday Morning, 2 October 1854

My Dear Sir,

Having unexpectedly been engaged on business in the country, I have not been to town for some time,—but have no doubt the book has arrived safe. I have received your note, and am exceedingly pleased to find we may probably have the pleasure of seeing you with your friend to-morrow, though unfortunately it is Croydon Fair, and if you intend sleeping in Croydon, it would, I think, be best to defer your visit until the next or some other Tuesday. I only mention this for your guidance, as I am loath to postpone the pleasure of seeing you here.

I am, dear Sir, in haste,
Yours most truly,

Robert Owen, Esq.   F. H.

Croydon
13 October 1854

My Dear Sir,

I herewith enclose for your perusal the three first volumes of my experiments in this curious branch of Occult Philosophy. They will, however, I fear, be of little comparative interest to you, as it was not until the C. A. became my Guardian Spirit that I could bring my experiments to anything like satisfactory conclusions.

You will observe that I have had in this instance entirely to develop the faculty of crystal seeing in my young seer, who being at the commencement only just turned thirteen, and the inquiry strange to herself and her friends, I had to be very cautious not to alarm her fears or her friends' prejudices, and as at first evil spirits kept continually entering our crystal, their ugly faces and forms would have been a source of alarm to many other young persons. Fortunately on spiritual matters my young seer is not the least nervous, and I have now—thanks to the C. A.—but little to fear on that head.

In my haste to get my MS books copied complete, I have omitted in these volumes a great many notes which would tend to elucidate the visions, but which I hope to supply at an early opportunity.

I have also the great pleasure of sending your queries and the answers received when you were with us at Croydon; and at the end you will perceive a curious response as to the testing of rapping spirits, for which I was not at all prepared. Hoping to have the pleasure of hearing from you shortly,

I am, dear Sir,
Yours faithfully,

Robert Owen, Esq.   F. H.

Tuesday, 3rd October, 1854. 7-15 p.m. The C. A. Mirror. Invoked the C. A.

'The C. A. is here as usual.'

1.—I am favoured this evening by the company of Mr Owen and a friend of his who is a disbeliever in the objective nature of these communications. Mr Owen requests me to thank you for your kind responses to his former questions, and requests the favour of your answering the following queries.

C. A.—I will answer them, and I thank him for coming.

Mr Owen's questions:—

No. 1.—In reply to the question so often asked—'What is truth?' is it correct to reply that—'Truth is always consistent with itself, and in accordance with all known facts, and with all facts which may become known?'

C. A.—It is. But there are great truths that will still remain unknown to man.

2.—Is not belief involuntary? And is not every human being compelled to believe according to the strongest convictions made on the mind?

C. A.—Yes. When a person is convinced of a thing he can no longer disbelieve it.

3.—Are not love and hate involuntary feelings?—Are not human beings compelled to love that which is made to be very pleasant to their feelings, and to hate that which is made to be very distasteful to their feelings?

C. A.—No; it is not. Love arises from things which appear perfect. Hatred from deformities.

Question by Mr Owen's friend.—Are not love and hatred involuntary?

C. A.—No; they are caused by circumstances and actions.

4.—Can there be merit or demerit rationally attributed to individuals for their conscientious convictions? or for their loving or hating persons or things?

C. A.—A person should not dwell upon or nourish hatred for any worldly things. For their convictions they cannot be answerable.

5.—Cannot any child be easily trained to believe any religion or any absurdity which its teachers may say is Divine truth and must never be doubted without risk of eternal torments?

C. A.—He cannot. Because as he mingles with the world he must become convinced of other doctrines. And besides this, there is an inherent quality in man's nature, which teaches him by his reason to disbelieve in things monstrous and absurd.

Questions by Mr Owen's friend.—If that be so, how is it that so many persons retain even to the end of their lives the monstrous beliefs impressed upon them in their childhood, and even at a more advanced age believe in winking and bleeding pictures and crucifixes, in the legends of saints, &c., &c.?

C. A.—They believe in miracles, and that belief is not monstrous or absurd.

6.—Cannot any infant be trained to love goodness, wisdom, and union with his fellows over the world, and to have pure charity and sincere love for every one of them?

C. A.—It is not in man's nature to do this. Good training may make him better than his fellows; but no sort of government or education can make him perfect, as he must be if loving-kindness and mercy were thoroughly practised by him.

7.—Cannot every one be trained, educated, and have his or her character so formed from birth, that they shall have the greatest pleasure through life in actively contributing to the happiness of their fellow-men and of God's creation, to the utmost of their power?

C. A.—Yes; that may be their great object through life.

8.—Cannot new and universal conditions be now devised and

executed, to compel every child from birth, that shall be born and shall remain within those conditions, to become good, wise, united to his fellows, and happy through life?

C. A.—It could be done in a great measure; but there would be great difficulty in keeping all to that system of education.

9.—Is not the time arrived, in the due order of God's creative process, to introduce these conditions with this practice over the earth?

C. A.—It would be well now to begin any system of education that might tend to enlighten man, and make his after life wiser, happier, and better. The time has arrived; and I trust in God no opportunity will be lost.

10.—Is not the true and natural mode of forming the human character from birth, by sensible signs, or by seeing the things to be taught, and by familiar conversation between the instructor and instructed?

C. A.—I should recommend that while the character of a child is being formed, it should be secluded with other children, and with but few other persons, and those persons agreeing in their religion and their views of all material subjects. That his mind should not be overcharged, but gently and pleasantly instilled with things that it could understand according to its age. That that training should continue until the child's mind is so far matured as to distinguish alone the good from the bad in nature. Then he can be sent forth into the world, thoroughly knowing that he has a view of his own on all important subjects. Then, if by argument or intercourse with different people he becomes convinced, and believes in things different from those he was educated to believe, that conviction and belief is the right one.

11.—Is there any obstacle so formidable against the progress of mankind in wisdom, goodness, unity, and happiness, as the existing superstitions over the earth, called religion?

C. A.—Without religion, no education could make a man wise and good; because he could not have even a true knowledge of nature unless he believed in Nature's God. I cannot call any religion a superstition; as every sect of religion has true religion and sincere Christians.

Question by Mr H.—Does your last remark apply to those good men, whether Mussulmen, Hindoos, Bramins, or Buddists, who, convinced of the truth of their respective creeds, live piously and are of good moral character?

C. A.—Those men I call Christians; because, through the

death of Christ, they will be saved everlastingly.

12.—Does not true and undefiled religion consist in a neverceasing desire and action to promote the happiness of man and of all created life, to the extent of the knowledge and power given to the individual by the creator?

C. A.—That is a part of true religion; but not the vital part.

Question by Mr Owen.—May I ask what is the vital part?

C. A.—A belief in the almighty powers of God, and in the death of His Son.

Question by Mr Owen's friend.—Are the powers of God unlimited?

C. A.—He is Almighty.

13.—Does not the happiness of man and of all created life depend upon the goodness, wisdom, and power of God?

C. A.—'And mercy of God.'

Question by Mr Owen's friend.—What is the criterion by which good and evil may be known?

No reply.

Second question by the same.—Is not good, that which is conducive to happiness?

C. A.—It may be so distinguished; but the greatest goodness and the worst evil do not consist in that.

Question by Mr H.—In what do they consist?

No reply.

The question repeated by Mr H.

C. A.—The greatest good consists in saving, by the direction of God's word, and under the blessings of a special Providence, the souls of your fellow-men, as well as your own. The greatest evil in blaspheming the Holy Ghost, and willingly and knowingly directing others to misery and torture.

Mr H. then said:—If Mr Owen takes hold of my seer's hand, will it be agreeable to you to favour him with such information or advice as you may deem fitting?

C. A.—Since I told you I had something to say personally to Mr Owen, he has become enlightened on those points which I wished to explain. Any question on those points he may wish to ask, I will answer; but I look on Mr Owen as one greater than many of his fellow mortals;—as one destined by Almighty God to achieve a great end. I look upon him as a sincere Christian, although not a believer in the Cross. He will meet his reward.

Question by Mr Owen, put by Mr H.—The doctrine of rewards and punishments, Mr Owen says, is entirely opposed to his views. Man being in all things entirely the creature of God, cannot be entitled to reward for his good acts, nor to punishment for those which are evil.

C. A.—But if he believes in a life hereafter, he must hope for happiness, and having that would be a reward for his goodness here while on earth.

Mr Owen (to the C. A.)—I am very much indebted and obliged for the full manner in which you have replied to my questions; and I will well consider your replies, and will apply to you again for further information on these or on other points.

Croydon
29 October 1854

MY DEAR SIR,

Your favour of the 25th is to hand. I beg you will keep the MSS as long as you may require them. I am not likely to want them for some time, and am much gratified to find they interest you. As I mentioned in my last, the responses did not become of much import until the fourth and fifth volumes, which I am now transcribing, though they show the gradual development of my seer's powers. You will also perceive in the first volume a short vision we had relative to Sir John Franklin and his crew. At that time, unfortunately, my seer had not the faculty of discerning the replies,—the visions then appearing in my small crystal, which is only about one and a-half inches long, and an inch thick.

I shall be much obliged by receiving parts 4 and 5 of the '*New Existence.*' The C. A. has already expressed his consent and wish that the responses given by him might be printed; and, on the 10th October inst., I requested the C. A. to favour me with the means of testing, either by questions or otherwise, whether the spirits who rap to you and others are good or evil,—that if evil, they might be prevented from leading those persons astray who are actuated solely by a desire to attain truth. I received the following reply:—

C. A. 'The ways of the evil spirits are so numerous, and their powers so great, that no means can be formed of stopping them by tests or questions. If one place is shut, they find another opened, perhaps larger and more convenient.

'You as a man can do more under my guidance than I can spiritually.

'Will you write a work to the society, denouncing their spirits as evil . . . Give the passages from your minutes, and quote the answers you have received in support of the doctrine of truth.

However short it may be, let it be earnest, straightforward, and something that will compel them to answer.

'Select anything that I have given you, and use it in the way that you think best. When they have once been roused to attention, I will deal with them.

'Do so; and, guided by truth, reason, justice, and mercy, on a Christian errand, you cannot do wrong. And remember that the intentions, as well as the actions, are indeliably written in the book of life. If the purpose should fail, the intention remains unsullied.'

The society here alluded to by the C. A. is 'The Association of the Friends of Progress at Cincinnatti, Ohio,' who are the authors of the pamphlet you kindly favoured me with. I have therefore drafted out a letter which I intend to address to them on the subject, and which, when complete, I will do myself the pleasure of sending for your perusal.

If either of your mediums are seers, I shall be most happy to lend you my large crystal, which —— did me the honour to present me with, and also to obtain the promise of your Guardian Spirit to appear therein, and to respond to your questions, should your medium possess the requisite faculty; at the same time furnishing you with the necessary instructions for its use.

With my and my young friend's best regards,
        I am, Dear Sir,
                Yours faithfully,
Robert Owen, Esq.   F. H.

[Croydon]
13 November 1854

MY DEAR SIR,

I duly received your esteemed present of the fourth and fifth parts of the '*New Existence*,' by which I am much obliged; and I should have acknowledged their receipt more promptly, but I wished first to obtain the C. A.'s opinion upon them. And I also was in hopes of sending for your perusal a letter which I purpose sending to the Harmonial Society of Cincinnati, Ohio; but my time is so limited that I shall be obliged to defer that pleasure until I see you in town.

If I understand your letter right, I am much gratified to find your communicating spirits are now of a superior order to the rappers, and I much wish to learn the particulars.

The three volumes of MSS are safe to hand; but I am sorry to say my fourth and fifth volumes are as yet only partly fair copied; but so soon as I have one finished, it shall be at your service.

On Tuesday the 7th inst., I asked the C. A. if the fourth and fifth parts of the *'New Existence,'* which I had that morning received, but had not read, would have a beneficial tendency. The reply was:—

C. A.—'I am of opinion that they are of great service to his cause. I regard Mr Owen very highly; and his works are equal to himself; but in some things he is wrong. Could he but believe in the redemption of Christ, and look for salvation through his atonement, and believe that nature owes its existence to God, and that He is the Supreme Ruler of all things, I should firmly believe him to be a man with few equals upon earth.'

I shall be engaged as usual on Tuesday the 21st inst., but I purpose, if agreeable, calling upon you on Wednesday the 22nd, and I can then arrange which evening will suit you for me to bring my young friend with me to London.

Trusting you are in good health,

I am, Dear Sir,
Yours faithfully,

Robert Owen, Esq.   F. H.

Communication to P. E. Bland, Esq., and the Members of the Harmonial Society of St Louis,—Ohio. By F. Hockley.

[Croydon]
16 November 1854

GENTLEMEN,

Mr Robert Owen, the philanthropist, having favoured me with a copy of your pamphlet, entitled 'Correspondence between the believers in the Harmonial Philosophy in St Louis, and the Rev. N. C. Rice, D.D.'—I am induced, from the great interest now taken in Spiritual Philosophy, to offer some remarks, obtained by Spiritual Communication, upon the Theorems contained in your two papers, marked A. and B.,—in the hope that yourself and friends, 'being actuated, so far as you can discover your own minds, by a desire for truth,' may be led seriously and carefully to sift the pure Christian precepts of the New Testament, and its substantial principle of the atonement through Jesus Christ, from the dogmas and practices of its professed disciples, and more especially its mammon-loving priests, and may thereby be enabled to guard yourselves from the irremediable evils into which you may otherwise be led by a blind reliance upon an invisible infallibility.

This precaution I believe to be the more needful, as I have not observed in any work which I have yet read upon American Spirit Manifestations, that any exorcism or other test is used to prove whether the spiritual presence be good or evil. But, on the contrary, there appears a strange disregard of the formulas for testing spirits so copiously given and urgently insisted upon in all ancient MSS upon Magic Science,—a precaution which, when invoking spirits, by the crystal or mirror, is found to be continually and peremptorily necessary, to prevent those wandering spirits who are ever ready to appear therein from replying to the questions proposed, and leading the enquirers into hopeless error. And although I may appear to be reasoning in a circle by referring you to John, ch. 4, v. 1, 2, 3, 6, as an example for your guidance, yet the precept there given merits the most serious attention from all who in these latter days seek to enter into communion with the spirit world.

As a perfect stranger to you, I can only offer the following upon the good faith of one who now for thirty years has been a searcher in spiritual diviniation, and during that time has seen its believers increase a thousand fold.

The extraordinary impulse lately given to spiritual intercourse, renders it the more urgently necessary that its practisers should, if possible, be placed at their very outset in the path of truth.—And although I hope I may ever be one of the last to form an overweening assumption in favour of the spiritual responses received by myself, yet I feel that it becomes a duty which every one owes to his fellow-men, to avow unreservedly that which he deems to be the truth. I address you the more confidently and earnestly as the authors of the above pamphlet, thus given by you to the world; because its effects,whether for good or evil, now being utterly beyond your control, you have voluntarily taken upon yourselves a most serious responsibility,—remembering, as we must do, 'That whatsoever a man soweth, the same shall he reap.'

It would be out of place to endeavour in the compass of a letter to elucidate the strange coincidence of doctrines derived immediately from the indwellers of the Spirit World, with those of the modern German rationalists, who, denying spiritual intelligence altogether, profess to ultra-Christianise Christianity by leaving out Christ. Equally impotent would it be on my part to attempt to discuss the truths of the theorems contained in paper A. of your pamphlet, when the piety and learning of the Christian world has been engaged thereon for so many centuries.

The purport of my present letter is deferentially yet earnestly to suggest that yourself and friends, before placing implicit faith in the revelations received by you, should first thoroughly satisfy your selves that your spiritual communicants are good and truthful.

Convinced as I am that *all* responses given by good spirits, whatever may be their relative development or attainments in spiritual knowledge, tend to the one only to-be-coveted point,—that of truth, I would advise all parties, upon commencing a circle for rapping or writing manifestations, having first resolved not to enter knowingly into communication with evil spirits, earnestly and mentally to offer up a prayer that they may be preserved from the presence or contact of any evil, wandering, or undeveloped spirits, and that, immediately upon any manifestation taking place, and the name of the communicant being made known,—they should exorcise it with a strong and fervent will, *three* times, in the words of this ancient though simple formula:—

'If thou, spirit, who now rappest, or movest the arm, &c., of A. B., art evil, *I dismiss thee, in the name of the Almighty God, in whom we live, and move, and have our being.*'

Or,

'If thou, who now rappest, &c., art any other than the spirit of C. D., now deceased, *I dismiss thee, &c.*'

Or,

'If thou, spirit who now rappest, art evil, or other than what thou declarest thyself to be, *I dismiss, &c.*'

If the communicating spirit remains, let the members of the circle propose your 5th theorem A., and again exorcise it thus:—

'I conjure you, spirit C. D., *in the name of the Almighty God, in whom we live, and move, and have our being,* truly, explicitly, and without equivocation, to state if that doctrine is correct or otherwise.'

I may appear to attach an undue importance to a formula of exorcism so simple in itself as the above, but I could not find words sufficient to express my own conviction of the great benefit resulting from its practice in all cases of spiritual intercourse, when used with a strong and fervent will, and with an earnest reliance upon the preserving power of the Almighty. It is moreover urgently insisted upon by all the old MS authors upon magic, with whose works, judging from what has appeared in print, the American spirit circles seem so remarkably unacquainted.

The most singular feature to me of these recent spiritual manifestations is, that the communicants have almost invariably announced themselves as being the spirits of deceased mortals only, and not as being spiritual inteligences who never had been embodied on earth, whilst the existence of co-existing atmospheric spirits of living mortals has never been alluded to as such, although, I perceive, they have in numerous instances developed themselves in the spirit circles.

'Every man,' says Swedenborg, (see page 203 of his life by Garth Wilkinson, 8vo. London 18—,) 'has either his good or bad spirit, who is constantly with him, but sometimes a little removed from him, and appears in the world of spirits; but of this the living man knows nothing—*the spirit, however, knows everything.* This familiar spirit has in the world of spirits the same figure, the same countenance, the same tone of voice, and wears also similar garments.' Although in some points Swedenborg is, I believe, in error, yet these co-existing doubles of the human race, who perform over again in the spirit-world our actions in this, however minute, exert, a very important part in the phenomena of mesmeric clairvoyance, self-somnambulism, the revelations of Cahagnet's extatics, and particularly in visions by crystal, mirrors, ink, water, &c.—phenomena the Occult Laws of which are at present so inscrutable to materialists.

My opinion of the quality of the spirits who have now so numerously entered into immediate communication with mankind, is the same as is given in the response—'Evil, Wandering, or Atmospheric;'—and,—convinced as I have for many years been, that human ideas and actions, once formed, become existing entities, capable of being reproduced, not only to the individual mind that gave them birth, but to the mind, and by the crystal to the vision, of others,—I can easily imagine that those wandering spirits,

—who are ever surounding us, and eagerly seeking to enter into rapport with man, especially those whose will is directed towards them, (by circling,) and whose spiritual peculiarity or faculty as mediums enable them more readily to do so,—are, by some as yet unknown law, enabled to discern these co-existing ideas, and thus become possessed of the knowledge of certain facts and matters appertaining to the members of the circle invoking.

The worldly knowledge thus obtained by evil spirits,—being communicated to the members of a circle by invisible intelligences, of whose entities, though unseen, they have thoroughly convinced themselves, clothed in language generally high-flown and often eloquent,—acts all the more strongly upon those members who were previously the most sceptical, and causes them, by the reaction consequent thereon, to be the more easily seduced into the grievous error of receiving whatever communication they may thus obtain from the world of spirits with implicit faith in its truthfulness, and to reject with contempt the prophecy now nearly 2,000 years old:—'For there shall arise false Christs, and false Prophets, and shall show great signs and wonders; insomuch that, if *it were* possible, they shall deceive the very elect.' *Matthew, ch. 24, v. 24.*

Actuated by an earnest desire that those who seek the truth for its own sake, and not for gain, might, so far as my belief extends, be guarded against error, I beg to send you the following result of my inquiries relative to the Theorems contained in the pamphlet published by yourselves.

Tuesday, 12th September, 1854.
Invoked the Crowned Angel.
The Crystal veiled, and the Crowned Angel appeared.
I said:—I have just perused an American work, published by a society of believers in spirit manifestations at St Louis, Ohio, containing a statement of their having challenged the Rev. N. C. Rice, D.D., to publicly discuss two sets of propositions,—the first containing the doctrines as generally accepted by Protestant and other dissenting Christians, the second embodying the views and Theorems laid down by the members of the society in their endeavour to establish an 'Harmonial Philosophy':—Unfortunately, Dr Rice, instead of openly and candidly declining the

challenge, as he had a perfect right to do, if so minded, attempted to shuffle out of the debate by unworthy and untruthful logical and metaphysical quibbles:—The correspondence now thus published contains the following propositions, which being of great interest, I shall be much gratified by receiving your views thereon. May I now ask them seriatim?

C. A.—'Yes.'

PROPOSITIONS A.
Denied by the Harmonial Society, and to be supported by
Dr Rice:

Proposition 1.—'The Bible is the word of God, being a full revelation from Him to man, in itself complete, and never to be either enlarged or diminished.'

C. A.—It is the word of God, because it was written by His will, and the New Testament by His inspiration; but it is not all correct. The original manuscript was in some places wrong, and that is much altered now. The material points were quite right, and now remain so.

Proposition 2.—'A being exists, the antagonist of God, and all righteousness, called the "Devil," "Satan," "Beelzebub," &c.'

C A.—A body of evil does exist in direct opposition to God, and that evil is the enemy of mankind.

Proposition 3.—'Man was, at, and sometime after his creation, perfect in his intellectual, moral, and physical nature.'

C.A.—He was perfect in his physical nature, but his mind was undeveloped, even as a child's; he was to attain knowledge by intercourse with his Creator and the rest of creation.

Proposition 4.—'Man being thus perfect, he yielded to the counsels and the persuasions of the Devil, and violated a divine command, and in consequence fell down from his high estate, cursed of God with total depravity and eternal death.'

C. A.—It was in his imperfection that he sinned; and they are wrong to suppose that one act committed by the first man should so entirely change his situation.

Proposition 5.—'That God so loved man in his present fallen condition, that He sent His only son to die upon the Cross, and thereby redeem man from the effect of the curse. This son was Jesus Christ,—very God and very man,—and He, together with God the Father, and God the Holy Ghost, constitute the Holy Trinity—the Everlasting God.'

C. A.—That is right. By His redemption the three are united, and the salvation of man is complete.

For the redemption, salvation, and happiness of the very worst of all, the Saviour died upon the Cross.

He was the Essence of the Father,—the Spirit of the Father,—one with himself,—sent by Him on earth amongst men in their own form, to enlighten them according to His word. The body was sacrificed for their sins, and the spirit again returned to be one as before.

Proposition 6.—'Men are saved by the favour of God, through faith in Jesus Christ; and those dying out of his favour and faith are heirs of eternal death by inheritance from the original progenitors of the race, and remain to all eternity in the torments of hell.'

C. A.—As all men are born sinful, it is by the mercy of God that they are saved.

He showeth that mercy to those that seek it. But through the intercession of His son he also showeth His loving kindness to those who sin more; and although they cannot be saved, as those who are righteous, by their own merits, they are not consigned to everlasting punishment. They are punished for a length of time that seems to them, while in that state, a punishment eternal; but it comes to an end.

Proposition 7.—'After death, and at some remote day in the future,—the day of General Judgement,—the souls of men will be arraigned, tried, and a decree rendered in each case, by virtue of which the faithful pass into Heaven, becoming angels of light and transcendent bliss, on the one hand, and the unfaithful, on the other, are cast into Hell.'

C. A.—That is wrong. Because they believe that all spirits pass the time between death and judgment in a state of unconsciousness. But it is not so. A man does not enter the presence of his Maker ★ ★ ★ ★ as they leave the earth. They are there to receive judgment; but they have all been progressing towards good since their death. By that time a great part of the punishments awarded to the wicked are over;—most of them, indeed, are entirely happy. Then the gates of paradise are unfolded, and they are eternally and supremely blest. Even the best who die, do not have the most perfect bliss until that day. Although they cannot imagine a state happier than their own, they look forward to it with great pleasure.

There are no torments that are everlasting. Can any Christians imagine that God,—and, when I say that, I mean the Highest of all Angels, the Disposer of beings, and the Author of all blessings and goodness,—could consign those creatures that He made with His own hands and moulded after His own fashion—that He could let them taste the blessings of life, and allow them to commit crimes in that life, and then consign them to the most frightful tortures for ever without end?—that no space of time, known to God, Angels, or Man, should in the least relieve them from their frightful torments?

You know, from my former answers, that eternal damnation does not exist. There is very terrible punishment,—more terrible than a human being can conceive; but it is not everlasting. But fire and brimstone are not part of that punishment. Fire is not a spiritual body, and brimstone is very earthy:—then how can that exist where things are purely spiritual? (This referred to my having previously asked some questions relative to the Rev. Mr Godfrey's absurdities, in his book on spirit rapping.)

PROPOSITIONS B.
Affirmed by the Harmonial Society, and to be disproved by Dr Rice.

Proposition 1.—'That Nature is God's revelation, and her laws the only infallible standard of truth.'

C. A.—They are entirely wrong in that supposition. Nature entirely obeys the laws of God; and so far it is truth. But Nature of itself is powerless without God. It ceases to exist,—it is nothing.

Proposition 2.—'That man is a progressive being,—becoming, by a law of his nature, better, nobler, and more God-like, and will in time as a race become pure and righteous.'

C. A.—Man's moral and intellectual faculties are becoming more and more developed through every generation,—but they are not getting more God-like.

Man in his outward and physical form is not so perfect as when first created. He is weaker,—not even capable of sustaining life for a lengthened period, which he then did. But that in some measure can be attributed to the development of his intellectual faculties.

The race of man will never become perfect. For while man is flesh, there is iniquity.

Good training may make him better than his fellow-men; but no sort of government or education can make him perfect, as he must be if loving kindness and mercy were thoroughly practised by him. Without religion, no education could make a man wise and good; because he could not have a true knowledge of nature unless he believed in Nature's God.

Proposition 3.—'That "Evil" is a relative term, and originates in the misuse of things, principles, and faculties, in their use good; which misuse is occasioned by ignorance or misdirection.'

C. A.—Evil is a separate power in opposition to God. It is that in itself which misdirects man, and leads him to the abuse of those things which were intended for his good. Of himself, although he never would be good, it is not in his nature to be entirely evil.

Proposition 4.—'That death is the process of transition from the earthly to the spiritual life. That by this process the man is separated from the body for ever, and in his spiritual form commences his new life, possessing precisely the same mental and moral attributes which he possessed before.'

C. A.—Death is the transition from the corporeal to the spiritual state. But in passing from life into death, man only loses his flesh. The mind, faculties, and desires, are exactly the same as those with which he quitted the earth. As he loses those faculties, so he loses the perception of the things he left; and when he has entirely lost sight of them, he then begins his progress.

The corporeal body ceases to exist, and they rise spiritually; but the spiritual body is in the form of the corporeal body, as that of angels might be in the shape of a man; still purer, but preserving the shape and form.

Proposition 5.—'That the spirit entering the spirit world is drawn by spiritual attraction to such society as corresponds to his or her mental and moral condition — *similes similibus* — and the enjoyment of all is in just proportion to their moral and intellectual elevation.'

C. A.—When they have lost all that feeling which binds them to earth and to those that were there known to them, they can appreciate all that is within their knowledge; but still there are sympathies existing between them when in the lower spheres.

Proposition 6.—'That all, even the lowest, entering the spirit world, may progress for ever, rising higher in the scale of being, and becoming purer, and lovelier, and grander.'

C. A.—They depend upon others for many things. They progress with them; they show each other kindness;—they have their differences of opinion concerning things known to them; but when they rise, they are a perfect being in themselves. They are at peace with all; because there is no difference of opinion.

They all recognise the same law; and they all are governed by the same desires.

Proposition 7.—'That men, women, and children, from the spirit world, may, and do communicate with those on earth, and that such communication is full of good to the race.'

C. A.—Spirits, both good and evil, but more especially the latter, can communicate with man, before their gradual rise towards happiness. After that, they lose all knowledge of men, and therefore have no will or desire to communicate with them. But when a manifestation is desired by good though undeveloped spirits towards man, they choose an appearance to the party themselves, and to them alone. By rappings or other noises they are never heard.

Evil spirits, and evil spirits alone, feel themselves justified in giving man the opportunity for deception and imposture, that will make them in the end gain the wealth of a world, and lose their own soul.

In most cases they are wandering spirits. But in some cases they are really the spirits of the parties whose name they take. But then they are never happy, and are always evil. No good spirits,—either angels, planetary spirits, or others,—ever rapped for the gratification of mortal.

No person ever yet left the earth in so pure a state that he could leave without one thought or regret the things that he left behind. It is impossible that they could do so. The less regret they have at leaving it, and the less their thoughts are fixed on worldly things, the more rapidly they lose consciousness of it in the atmosphere and Hades, but none (of those who attain Hades) through that are doomed to any punishment, further than their own thoughts.

The soul, for the first time after being disembodied on earth, will take a material shape. It will have the appearance of the human body, with all grossness, all deformity removed. It will be spiritual,—angelical,—light, even as air,—swift as thought,—transparent,—and yet have a human form,—the form of its Creator, and nothing can be more lovely than that. Angels know that to be perfection; and man has always the blessing of this.

A spirit, even in his first stage, is so different from mortal, that I cannot give any idea of his occupation.

He does all that he wishes; and he wishes to do nothing that he knows will not advance him towards a higher state. To him things are great pleasures which would be perfectly incomprehensible to man.

I next asked:—

1.—May not 1 Cor. ch. 14, v. 22—'Wherefore tongues are for a sign, not to them that believe, but to them that believe not; but prophecying serveth not for them that believe not, but for them which believe,'—apply also to spirit rapping, seeing that many have come thereby to a belief in the spirit world and a future state, who neither by argument nor scripture could have been convinced?

C. A.—Every evil as well as good comes under the direct knowledge of God. And He could not permit any evil to come, unless some good should come from it. The rappings, the movings, the appearance on earth of deceased persons, and the gift of tongues, are sent for no actual divine purpose, but to convince the outward and bodily sense.

The finer, higher, and more secret communications of spirits with man, are utterly destroyed by disbelief and ridicule.

2.—In Acts ch. 23, v. 8 and 9, it is written—'For the Sadducees say that there is no resurrection,—neither angel nor spirit.'—And again—'But if an angel or spirit hath spoken to him, let us not fight against God.' May I ask what is the distinction between spirits and angels here made?

C. A.—There are many kinds of spirits. Angels are spirits; but every spirit is not an angel. There are Planetary Spirits,— Atmospheric Spirits—Wandering Spirits,—and Spirits that animate the body. The Heavenly Host are a band of Spirits; but they are also Ministering Angels. There are many evil spirits in the atmosphere and upon the earth; but they cannot take the form of an angel of light. The man who has the power of second sight, has also the power of discerning betwixt good and evil spirits.

If knowingly he seeks the evil spirits instead of the good, he deserves the errors they may lead him into.

3.—In Matthew, ch. 15, v. 18, and ch. 22, v. 37, and in many other places in the Old and New Testaments, the heart of man is spoken of as the seat of the soul—the *brain*, as such, being never referred to. May I ask where in man is the seat of the soul?

C. A.—It pervades the whole being. It is contained in the body, and has no separate existence while life lasts. The spirit is the life which animates the body. The soul is the reason and the feelings. The life is in the blood; it is something besides the spirit. The soul is distinct from the body. The spirit animates the body; but when the body dies, the spirit does not cease to exist.

The spirit that animates the earthly body, and the atmospheric spirit, make the form of the spiritual being joined; and the soul is the life and existence of that spiritual being. The spirit and the soul, as belonging to the body, are distinct. They are like thought, confined to the body, and known only to it; having no visible appearance while life lasts. The soul really is a spark, as it were, of the Almighty's own being, given to man, that he may, with the knowledge that that soul will have life hereafter, govern his actions by reason, so that life hereafter may be full of bliss.

When the soul is disembodied, it has instinct instead of reason. It does not therefore think of one thing at a time. It acts upon all that it has the intention of doing.

The soul is the reason,—the knowledge,—the intellect,—the will,—and every invisible faculty that is possessed by man. While confined in the body it has no painful longing, any more than any Christian would possess, of being in a better state. It is happy in the body, because he has no knowledge of another state. It is guided by belief.

19.—In John, ch. 3, v. 3, Jesus said to Nicodemus—'Except a man be born again, he cannot see the kingdom of God.' Will you favour me with your view of that passage?

C. A.—It means that a person after death must pass through a state, and emerge from it in entire ignorance of every thing connected with the world, the flesh, and the life.

That may be said to be created again. It is then communicated to them, (good persons, I mean,) the way to make themselves acceptable to the Saviour. And they then progress onwards. But they will not enter the presence and dwell with God, until the world is at an end and all are judged.

They do not immediately after death face their maker; but they enjoy a spiritual existence, according to their deserts. When they have passed so much time as is required to pass from one sphere to another, and have left behind them seven, they lose all recollection of the other spheres, and they are in the Divine presence.

20.—Is it sinful to use 'the gift of discerning spirits,' (Cor. 12, v. 10,) as practised in cabalism and crystal working?

C. A.—It is wrong to use means for developing any mysterious powers that are forbidden by the laws of God; but there are means of foretelling things and knowing things belonging to other worlds consistent with the Holy Bible.

There is no evil in developing these to the extent of all power on earth.

When a person has that gift, and tries to develop it for good purposes, there is not much danger of his going astray. It is attractive; but it is so peculiar that no very bad influence could work by it. That a person should guard against any evil attending that power of course is right; but it is not necessary for them to be always in a state of anxiety concerning it; for the being that gives that power, directs and controls the use of it.

When you have done as much as is in your power for preventing evil spirits from taking any hold upon you, you have done sufficient.

21.—Is it advisable that I should develop my faculty of being a writing medium?

C. A.—It would be prejudicial to you. In the first place you could not ascertain whether those spirits who guided your hand were really and truly what they profess themselves to be.

You might receive communications from them which would so prey upon your mind that it would incapacitate you from the every day duties of life. The statements they made would most probably, one half of them, be untrue, or much exaggerated. They would begin by giving what would appear to you or any other mortal, good and sound advice, given in high-flown and eloquent language. They would then work upon and get you to agree with them in their opinions, and so work upon your *in*credulity, that they would entirely get you in bondage, and lead you, as I fear in the case of A. B., into great error.

But at the same time I wish you to exercise that judgment which it has pleased the divine purpose to give you for investigating all matters, that you may be able at the end of a short time to see if your hand is guided by a spirit. It is most advisable that you should use the exorcism that you use in exorcising this mirror, every time you feel an inclination to take your pen.

The nature of evil spirits is deceit; and were they to say what they truly are, they would be for the time honest. Besides,—by declaring themselves as relatives and friends, they claim attention more readily than if they were to make themselves known by a strange name.

The knowledge of the evil spirits is almost boundless, so far as concerns mortals or spirits of low degree. If questions were proposed to those spirits such as this—'Are there a number of ministering angels who have never been embodied, constantly in the presence of God, His Son, and the Holy Ghost, interceding for man's eternal happiness and welfare?'—they would stoutly deny it.

The foregoing responses I give, word for word, as received by me. I have not knowingly altered a letter; and I must now conclude. I trust you will accept this in the good faith with which it is sent; and if it may be the means—D.V.—of inducing but one of your members to give the formula an earnest and sincere trial, I shall indeed feel myself more than a thousand times repaid.

I remain, Gentlemen,
Yours faithfully,
FRED. HOCKLEY

Croydon
5 December 1854

MY DEAR SIR,

I have the great pleasure of sending you the response obtained this evening from the C. A., who as usual enters earnestly into your views, and, as you will perceive, expresses a wish that you should have another communication with him personally before your intended meeting takes place. However much pleasure it will give me to see you here again, I am afraid travelling at this time of the year must prove irksome to you. But if you can name any Sunday it would be convenient for you to pass the day with us, I feel sure the C. A. would appear for the purpose of affording you his further opinion.

I have this evening been engaged with my friend, who is as incredulous about our spirit manifestations as your good friend ——. We had, however, an interesting evening, and if I shall on Thursday have finished my volume, I will send it at once to you for your perusal.—My seer, who is quite recovered, joins me in kind regards.

I am, dear Sir,
Yours faithfully,

Robert Owen, Esq.   F. H.

Tuesday, 5th December, 1854.

Addressing the C. A., I said:—Mr Robert Owen has written to me this letter, enclosing an advertisement of the meetings he intends calling for the purpose of propounding his plans for 'the permanent happy existence of the human race, or the commencement of the millennium in 1855.'—He requests your kind opinion of his views.

C. A.—He is truly a kind and good man, ever ready to sacrifice his own comfort and happiness for the welfare of others, and yet receiving more happiness from the knowledge that he has in his heart of doing good, than those who, high in the English State, pass it over with such lightness and contempt. Tell him it is my firm opinion, as well as earnest prayer, that that meeting will do great good to his cause. That as far as possible those advertisements should be circulated, and they cannot fail to bring together a large portion of thinking people, and amongst them there must be those that will act as well as think. He will, I have no doubt, before his arrangements are quite matured as to the proceeding which he intends to take place on that day, again have communion with me on the subject. I shall then be able to give him my more decided opinions as to what will be best.

Croydon
4 December 1854

My Dear Sir,

Your favour of the 1st is to hand. I will ask the C. A. for his opinion upon your advertisement, and forward it to you forthwith. I intend, (D.V.,) to be at the proposed meeting on the 1st of January, 1855, and I trust your philanthropic exertions will at length meet the much coveted *'reward'*—the happiness of *seeing* 'the permanent happy existence of the human race' actually commenced.

With reference to the Christian doctrine of the atonement, which you deem 'contrary to all your previously received ideas of the Almighty God of the Universe,'—I can only repeat the words of your friend William Allen, addressed by him to you in October, 1815;—'If a man will believe nothing which cannot be mathematically demonstrated to him,—nothing which is not beyond the reach of his limited capacities and powers,—he must remain in darkness so long as it is impossible for *finite* to comprehend *infinite*.'

I am still engaged upon the subject with the C. A., and through him receive that by faith, which reason could never give me. If the doctrine could be demonstrated by argument, Professor Newman's earnestly written works,—'*The Soul, its Sorrows and its Aspirations*,' and '*The Phases of Faith*,'—would not still remain unanswered; for I cannot receive the much lauded '*Eclipse of Faith*' as an answer;—indeed, I do not think an effectual antidote to his views can be given, except by him. That he will ultimately do so, I believe, from the response given to me by the C. A.:—

'Five years ago there was no probability of Mr Owen's believing in a life hereafter. As long a time will make the same difference to Mr Newman.'

I shall be much pleased to receive any further information as to the manifestation at Brighton which you mentioned to me the other evening. If it is corroborated, we must send —— down as 'Our own Correspondent,' that he may become converted.

With best wishes,
I remain,
Dear Sir,
Yours faithfully,

Robert Owen Esq.   F. H.

Croydon
23 January 1855

MY DEAR SIR,

I am favoured with the proofs of the Appendices A. and B. of your forthcoming Part 6. Were I to presume to criticise either the questions or the answers contained in Appendix A., simply because they are opposed to the views stated in Appendix B., it would on my part be an unwarrantable impertinence; still I cannot but think it is to be regretted that the name of Jesus Christ should be thus inserted without any comment or qualification upon the simple announcement of an invisible-spirit rapper, inasmuch as it is a needless and profitless shock to the feelings and opinions of your Christian readers and well-wishers. Upon receipt of your letter of the 16th November last, I stated to the C. A.—

1.—Mr Owen informs me by letter that at a recent *seance* the presence of Jesus Christ was announced. Now although we are told by Jesus himself, (Matt. 18 v. 20,) 'Where two or three are gathered together *in my name*, there am I in the midst of them'—yet the present statement being repugnant to my feelings and belief,—may I ask if it is possible that any spirit can assume his name and appearance?

C. A.—A vision of him appeared to Swedenborg,—and Mr Owen is as great as he.

2.—When you say a vision of Jesus appeared to Swedenborg, and to Mr Owen,—do you mean that he appeared personally.

C. A.—No I do not. The vision of the spirit appeared—the likeness of the spirit of the Son of God.

3.—If the likeness of the spirit of the son of God so appeared to Robert Owen,—would it not, or the spirits attending it, have enlightened him upon the subject of the atonement and redemption of mankind through Jesus Christ?

C. A.—His belief is so much nearer to the right path, than it was at first, that I firmly believe the time will come when he will be thoroughly convinced of all the true doctrines of Christianity.

4.—The answer you have given me as to this spiritual vision is so surprising, that I beg you will give me some further explanation or reason for its appearance.

C. A.—Great purposes are used to meet great ends. If two founders of great and distinct sects of religionists needed assurance of things which they may doubt, nothing would be too great that conduces to that end. Under these circumstances, or for any worthy cause, the Son of God would condescend to allow the light of his spirit to illuminate the way of truth.

He who when upon earth went about doing good for the sake of good, and going amongst every disease that he might heal for the sake of his fellow-men, when he was as pure in spirit as he is now, would assuredly guide right at last the man who in so many instances had followed in his path.

On Tuesday the [   ] inst., I read the question and answer, page 8, Appendix A., and requested the C. A.'s view of it.

C. A.—I wish it had not been written; but as it is done, I do not wish it to be altered. I am not sure that communication was received rightly.

Jesus Christ is the Messiah, or rather will be at the second coming. He *is* the regenerator of mankind, because through him all have life everlasting.

His influence was there; his knowledge and part of his spirit was there; together they formed a spiritual body representing him. All persons who believe in the divinity of Christ, believe that he is an all-pervading influence, and that his spirit enters into the heart of those who follow his guidance and do what they believe their duty.

They all believe that he is there to do good, to enlighten them, to purify their hearts, sanctify their actions, and lead them in salvation.

Then if they believe this, they can scarcely doubt that that same influence can take any form to do the same work for others which He is doing for them.

Why is it unreasonable to suppose that he should take the only means which a man will allow to be used in any way to convince him?

Mr Owen was more readily open to conviction this way, than

any other; and what the argument of man could not effect, a spirit would be able to do by aiming at the weakest part.

If Jesus Christ left the most perfect bliss, came upon earth full of sorrow, lived here for more than thirty years amongst the hardships and privations of life, and amongst the poorest of mankind—persecuted as no man has been since, and died an ignominious death, when he could have prevented it, solely for the love of man, do you not think he would use his influence,—small perhaps at first, but great if necessary,—for the enlightenment and true teaching of any of those mortals who were willing to believe?

No Christian can deny that he *can* do this; and if he will do this for those who have denied him, done wrong to their fellow-men, and yet died in his belief at last,—why should he not do it for a man who, through his long life, has had no aim but the good of mankind; who, as a man, has followed the example that Jesus Christ set—'Love one another'—'Love thy neighbours as thyself'—'Do unto others, even as you would they should do unto you?'

I returned thanks.

[I hasten to send the above. Any comments of mine would be superfluous; but I trust shortly to have the pleasure of showing you the whole of the C. A.'s remarks in relation thereto. Trusting you are in good health,

I am, dear Sir,
Yours faithfully,
F. H.]

Croydon
February 1855
My Dear Sir,

Enclosed I have the pleasure of forwarding you the responses given by the C. A. in relation to your introduction to Part 6, of which you sent me a proof, and also upon the MS portion of Part 6 enclosed in your letter of the 3rd inst.

I also send you the first question your friend —— has favoured me with, and the response given by the C. A. in answer thereto,—the first I hope of a long series. I have had some very curious communications lately, and so soon as I have written up my minutes, I will forward them for your perusal.

I am, Dear Sir,
Yours faithfully,

Robert Owen, Esq.   F. H.

Tuesday, 30th January, 1855.

1.—Addressing the C. A., I said:—Mr Robert Owen requests your view of this 'Introduction to the Second Edition of the report of his meeting in St Martin's Hall, on the 1st instant, containing his reasons for calling his meetings.'

C. A.—I know what it contains, and I believe it to be another step towards the success of his much desired plans.

2.—I then said:—As his scheme for the amelioration of society is not founded on a religious basis, do you think it will succeed?

C. A.—I do. And it is also much best that in this peculiar system which he has founded, and which, if carried out strictly, would 'sow the good seed' in the hearts of man, and which is intended to be universal education, no religion should be named. Were he to mention that, he must name one particular sect; and were that one sect mentioned, all others would be excluded. Where it is founded to teach piety and benevolence, it is unnecessary that any particular Doctrine should be argued upon. Children brought up under his method could not fail to have religious feelings.

3.—Mr Owen illustrated his axiom that 'man's character is formed *for* and not *by* him,' at his lecture on the 1st January, by observing that it was possible to take seven children of the same parentage, and to bring them up in different places, in different languages, nationalities, and creeds, and to make them most religiously hate each other; and that it was equally possible to take seven children of different parents and nationalities, and to bring them up in one language, one creed, and one brotherly love to each other.

C. A.—Man's character is formed for him in the first place, because, had he no education at all he would be little better than a savage. But if that education is performed rightly, it develops *his own will* and *his own character*.

4.—Mr Owen's friend —— has favoured me at my request with the first of a series of questions—which he places as curtly as possible, that it may not be 'a leading question.' It is:—'What is the human will?'

C. A.—The mind concentrated on one object. Thought, and the powers of the mind directed to obtain it. But I may here state to you, that the will of man can only exist in opposition. It is a dormant power of the mind, which only rises under restraint.

And that which is deemed impossible to be gained by any other agency of the soul, is obtained by the will.

Tuesday, 6th February, 1855.

Addressing the C. A., I said:—Mr Robert Owen has sent me the MS of Part 6, and requests your opinion thereon.

C. A.—Will you put them against the seal?—It is very well; but you know my opinion on the spirit manifestations. You can tell him that as his opinion remains unchanged on the spiritual manifestations, he is right to express them;—but, at the same time, I can assure him they are undoubtedly wrong.

iv

CONTRIBUTIONS TO *THE ZOIST*

[*The Zoist* was a periodical published in thirteen volumes between 1844 and 1856. It consisted principally of correspondence and book reviews mainly concerned with mesmerism, natural medicine, and, in later volumes, Spiritualism. Hockley stated that he had made four contributions but only the following three have been traced.]

On the Ancient Magic Crystal, and its Connexion with Mesmerism.
By Mr Hockley.

'My brethren, there are men who, whether designedly or not, are in league with the fallen spirits—*wizards* and *necromancers*, using *enchantment* and *divination*, and producing divers effects beyond the power of man—real and natural effects, by the *help of the devil*, upon both the minds and bodies of their fellow-creatures. I shall endeavour this evening, by God's help, to follow that branch of the subject, and to shew you what I conceive to be the connexion between the agency of those fallen spirits and the *lying wonders* performed in these later times, amongst which I have no hesitation in reckoning this *mesmerism*, which is now performing its real effects—real, supernatural, but *diabolical*.'— Rev. Hugh McNeil, Liverpool, April, 1842.

'Were we to believe nothing but what we could perfectly comprehend, not only our stock of knowledge in all the branches of learning would be shrunk up to nothing, but even the affairs of common life could not be carried on.'—Tucker.

TO THE EDITORS OF *THE ZOIST*

The surprising coincidence of the phenomena elicited by the ancient practice of invocation by the crystal with the later discoveries of animal magnetism has for some years attracted the attention of the curious, and I have long been desirous of seeing the subject investigated by some of your able contributors with the attention which it eminently deserves: and, although there may be cause to fear that those opponents of mesmerism who, like the Rev. Mr. McNeil, are already too prone to attribute to satanic agency every thing connected with animal magnetism which is beyond their limited comprehension might, by its apparent alliance to the art of divination by the crystal, find an additional reason for denouncing it; yet, considering that the very surprizing revelations made by clairvoyants under magnetic influence, whether attributable 'to the agency of spiritual beings' or to 'the divinity that stirs within us and points out an hereafter,' have opened a wide field of enquiry into some of the hitherto least understood arcana of psychology, and that many of your readers, whether rationalists or spiritualists, notwithstanding the rhapsodies of the above learned and reverend gentleman, may feel desirous of investigating those occult laws of nature which, in spite of the poet, yet 'lie hid in night,' I have been induced, upon a perusal of Gamma's article in the last number but one of *The Zoist*, to offer the following notes upon the subject, trusting they may prove the germ of a more full and able essay by one of your learned correspondents.

It would trespass too much upon your space to attempt to elucidate the origin and various modes of divination by the crystal, of the antiquity and wide-spread belief in which there exist innumerable testimonies, sacred and profane; from the divine responses by the Urim and Thummim, mentioned in the Old Testament,* to Josephus, who in his history declares it to be more than 200 years since the stones of the ephod had given an answer by their extraordinary lustre; and from Porphyry, Iamblichus, and Psellus, to the magicians of Cairo and the peepers and speculators in England at the present day. With respect to the 'superstitious rites, the long fastings, the mystical words, the concentric

---

*It would seem from the observations of Sir Gardner Wilkinson that this form of divination was employed by the Egyptians before the time of Moses. Not only the form, but the symbols, and even titles, connected with it, are all related to those of Egypt. The Urim and Thummim, connected with, if not part of the breast-plate of judgment of the High Priest (Exodus xxviii, 30), and interpreted as Light and Truth, or Revelation and Truth, correspond most remarkably with the figure of Re (the Sun) and Thmei (Truth) in the breast-plate of the Egyptian priest: and Ælian and Diodorus Sicidus are quoted as authorities for the custom of the Egyptian priest when acting as arch-judge, hanging around his neck a sapphire stone which was called Truth. (*Manners and Customs of the Ancient Egyptians*, ii., 22, v. 28.)

Good accounts of the Urim and Thummim, or rather of what is understood concerning them, may be found in Winer's *Biblisches Realverterbuch*. In the Rev. D. Kitto's *Cyclopædia of Biblical Literature*, are extracted the observations and wood-cuts of Sir Gardner Wilkinson, before whose researches ultra-theologians endeavoured to make the world believe that the immense and ancient Egyptian nation had only copied the Jews, whose Urim and Thummim they had learnt after Solomon had married a daughter of Pharaoh! Dr Kitto, though we dare say quite orthodox, is not among these, but cheerfully admits the force of Sir G. Wilkinson's observations: just as other orthodox divines cheerfully allow us to admit the fact of the existence of the countless worlds for millions of years, and of the sun not going round the earth but the earth round the sun, and to agree with the Chevalier Bunsen and others that the current views of history derived from the Old Testament are untenable.— *Zoist*.

circles, the perfumes,'* which 'Γ' deems only worthy of the knaves who employed them, it is to be regretted that many mesmerists, who justly deprecate their favourite science being deemed a deception and its professors impostors, yet so readily bestow the same abusive epithets indiscriminately upon the advocates of any doctrine which may be opposed to their own preconceived opinions. It is to be remembered that divination by the crystal is, more than any other species of modern magic, derived immediately from the Jews—a people whose numerous ceremonials of the same kind were enjoined, we are taught to believe, by divine command; and their followers, the Cabalists, though not perhaps strictly speaking the utilitarians of their day, yet remembering 'how much better it is to get wisdom than gold, and understanding rather than fine silver,'† were diligent investigators of the occult properties of nature, and the efficacy of their 'concentric circles' we must leave undecided until it can be explained how an invisible line drawn across the path of a somnambulist instantaneously arrests his progress—a fact which, although of daily occurrence, as yet remains equally inexplicable. Of the use of strict previous fasting we have continued examples from Exodus xxxiv., 28, where Moses 'did neither eat bread nor drink water,' to Matthew iv., where Jesus 'led up of the spirit into the wilderness fasted forty days and forty nights.' Now as Jesus was 'harmless, undefiled, and separate from sinners,'—had no fleshly lust to mortify—no sluggishness of spirit to overcome, why then did he fast? Fasting was also enjoined to the candidates previously to their admission to the ancient mysteries; thus proving how old is the belief that the rude health, so needful for the laborious struggles of every-day life, is incompatible (as mesmerists also experience) with a high degree of spiritual perception and clairvoyance, but that by such fasting, prayer, and other purifications, it is possible to attain an insight into physical causes, which by constant contemplation becomes at length an intuitive perception. And passing over for the present the esoteric doctrine of the vestments and pentacles, it must be observed that the extraordinary, though little known and appreciated, properties of perfumes derived from the animal, vegetable, and mineral kingdoms, has long been known to students in the occult sciences,

---

*'Γ' is rather unfortunate in his 'most approved modern author.' Barrett was a mere book-maker, and his *Magus* (the original MS of which was for years in my possession) is a transcript from Agrippa and a MS of Rabbi Solomon, and the conjurations therein given were never intended for crystal work.

†Proverbs xvi., 16.

and amongst others the following remarkable relation is to be found in Eckhartshausen's *Key to Magic*, p. 57; Munich, 1791; and is thus related by Jung-Stilling in his admirable theory of Pneumatology.*

'Eckhartshausen became acquainted with a Scotsman, who, though he meddled not with the conjuration of spirits, and such like charlatanry, had learned however a remarkable piece of art from a Jew, which he communicated also to Eckhartshausen, and made the experiment with him, which is surprising and worthy of perusal. He that wishes to raise, and see any particular spirit, must prepare himself for it, for some days together, both spiritually and physically. There are also particular and remarkable requisites and relations necessary betwixt such a spirit and the person who wishes to see it; relations which cannot be otherwise explained than on the ground of the intervention of some secret influence from the invisible world. After all these preparations, a vapour is produced in a room, from certain materials, which Eckhartshausen with propriety does not divulge on account of the dangerous abuse which might be made of it, which visibly forms itself into a figure which bears a resemblance to that which the person wishes to see. In this there is no question of any magic-lantern or optical artifice, but the vapour really forms a human figure, similar to that which the individual desires to behold. I will now insert the conclusion of the story in Eckhartshausen's own words.

' "Some time after the departure of the Scotsman, I made the experiment for one of my friends. He saw as I did, and had the same sensations.

' "The observations that we made were these; as soon as the ingredients were thrown into the chafing dish, a whitish body forms itself, that seems to hover above the chafing dish as large as life.

' "It possesses the likeness of the person whom it is wished to see, only the visage is of an ashy paleness.

' "On approaching the figure, one is conscious of a resistance similar to what is felt when going against a strong wind, which drives one back.

' "If one speaks with it one remembers no more distinctly what is spoken; and when the appearance vanishes, one feels as if awaking from a dream; the head is stupified, and a contraction is felt in the abdomen. It is also very singular that the same

*Longman, 12mo., p. 200; 1834.

appearance presents itself when one is in the dark, or when looking upon dark objects.

'"The unpleasantness of this sensation was the reason why I was unwilling to repeat the experiment, although often urged to do so by many persons.

'"A young gentleman once came to me, and would *par force* see this phenomenon. As he was a person of tender nerves and lively imagination, I was the more reluctant to comply with his request, and asked the advice of a very experienced physician, to whom I revealed the whole mystery. He maintained that the narcotic ingredients, which formed the figure, must of necessity violently affect the imagination, and might be very injurious according to circumstances; he also believed that the preparation which was prescribed contributed much to excite the imagination, and told me to make the trial for myself with a very small quantity and without any preparation whatever. I did so one day after dinner,* when the physician had been dining with me; but scarcely had I cast the quantum of ingredients into the chafing dish, when a figure presented itself. I was however seized with such a horror, that I was obliged to leave the room. I was very ill during three hours, and thought I saw the figure always before me. Towards evening, after inhaling the fumes of vinegar, and drinking it with water, I was better again, but for three weeks after I felt a debility; and the strangest part of the matter is, that when I remember the circumstance, and look for some time upon any dark object, this ashy pale figure presents itself very vividly to my sight. After this I no longer dared to make any experiments with it."'†

And in support of this singular development of the hidden properties of nature, the following curious receipt, '*How to make a Ghost*,' is extracted from the *Monthly Magazine* for June, 1848:—'If chloride of barium is put upon a plate in a dark cellar, and the hand placed beneath it, so soon as the warmth of the hand has penetrated the plate, the form of the hand is delineated in phosphoric delineations on the upper surface of the plate.' Thus the heat communicated by the hand to the chloride of barium gives rise to certain luminous emanations,

---

*It is surprising that Eckhartshausen should have thus violated the rules expressly laid down for his guidance, and then complain of the unpleasant sensations he experienced.

†See also a very singular narrative by John Howlson, Esq., of the East India Company's Service, in his *Foreign Scenes and Travelling Reminiscences*, London, 1825.

which have the extraordinary property of seizing at the same time the form of that which gave them birth, and proves that the minutest atom of creation possesses elementary powers which it would be far wiser to attempt to explain than to deny.*

In this mode of divination, crystal has not solely been used; its scarcity and the difficulty of cutting having caused it, from the earliest ages, to be superseded by olive-oil, black liquids, glass, and particularly by bottles and basins of water. Porphyry, under the heads of Hydro- and Lecano-mancy, says that demons were compelled by invocatory songs to enter a vessel filled with water, and give answers to the questions propounded, or represent therein the issue of any required event. Psellus also states that the Assyrians were much addicted to prophesying in a basin of water. And Dr Kerner relates† that the Seeress of Prevorst appeared to him to have had her inner or spiritual eye excited by soap-bubbles, glass mirrors, &c. Dr K. relates that, 'a child happening to blow soap-bubbles, she exclaimed, "Ah, my God! I behold in the bubbles every thing I think of, although it be distant, not in little, but as large as life; but it frightens me." I then made a soap-bubble, and bade her look for her child that was far away. She said she saw him in bed, and it gave her much pleasure. At another time she saw my wife, who was in another house, and described precisely the situation she was in at the moment—a point I took care immediately to ascertain. She was

---

*Of the desirableness of investigating the physiological influence of perfumes, gases, and exhalations, there can be no doubt: and, in the history of witchcraft and of ancient divination, we find these influences so closely connected with quasi-mesmeric phenomena, that the recent discoveries of anæsthetic agents—'weak masters though they be,'—that took so many by surprise, only came as instalments of the expectations and partial fulfilment of the predictions of observers of mesmeric nature and students of its antiquities. At the same time, there is nothing in the anecdote of Eckhartshausen as related with its unspecified drugs and uncertified results, that enables us to say that it is more than a case of intoxication by narcotics. It is very unsafe to say positively what influences and incidents will not produce the mesmeric states: but caution is always required in judging of matters so liable to mistake; above all, we have a right to demand the best evidence in the best form so far as obtainable.

If the illustration said to be gained from the experiment with the plate of *barium* goes for anything, it goes to prove that the image in the vapour was that of the experimenter himself: and 'ashy paleness' and 'stupified head,' not to say alarm, may account for the non-recognition of it. If the warmth of the hand gave rise to emanations, these must, we suppose, take place at the portions warmed by the hand, and therefore represent its figure.—*Zoist.*

†*Seeress of Prevorst,* p. 74. London, 1845.

however with difficulty induced to look into these soap-bubbles. She seemed to shudder, and she was afraid that she might see something that would alarm her. In one of these she once saw a small coffin standing before a neighbouring house. At that time there was no child sick; but shortly after the lady who lived there was confined; the child lived but a few months, and Mrs K. saw it carried from the house in a coffin. If we wished her to recall dreams which she had forgotten, it was only necessary to make her look at a soap-bubble, and her memory of them immediately returned. She often saw persons that were about to arrive at the house, in a glass of water; but when she was invited to this sort of divination, and did it unwillingly, *she was sometimes* mistaken.'

Aubrey, in his Miscellanies,* gives the form of the crystals as commonly used in his time. Dr Dee used several stones, one of which is now in Case No. 20, of the Mineral Room, at the British Museum; it belonged, with his MSS, to the collection of Sir R. Cotton; another, composed apparently of a flat circular and highly-polished piece of Cannel coal, about six inches in diameter, came to the hands of Lord Peterborough, and from thence passed into the possession of Horace Walpole, and was sold at the Strawberry-hill Sale, in 1842, and most probably was the one alluded to by Butler.†

Upon referring to that very remarkable and scarce work, entitled 'A true and faithful Relation of what passed between Dr John Dee and some Spirits,'‡ edited by the learned Dr Meric Casaubon, which although a goodly folio of 500 pages, formed but a small portion of Dr Dee's Experiments, or as he termed them, 'Actions;' yet sufficiently attest that both Dee and Kelly (his seer) were *firm believers* in the truth of their researches; and the very singular coincidences arising from a perusal of this work with the revelations made to Dr Kerner by the Seeress of Prevorst, and by the somnambulist described in Dr Henry Werner's work, entitled, 'Guardian Spirits; or, Remarkable Cases of Vision by two Seeresses into the Spiritual World,'§ will well repay an attentive perusal, although, unfortunately, it would

---

Miscellanies by J. Aubrey, Esq., 8vo., 1696, p. 128.
†*Hudibras*, Canto III., line 631.

> 'Kelly did all his feats upon
> The devil's looking-glass a stone,
> Where, playing with him at bo-peep,
> He solved all questions ne'er so deep.'

‡London. Folio: 1659.
§Stuttgart, 1839. New York, 1847. Translated by A. E. Ford.

occupy too much of your valuable space to allow of parallel passages from such voluminous works.*

Dr Collyer, the able lecturer on mesmerism, appears to see the subject only in a rationalist point of view, and in support of his theory, gives, in his Psychography, or the embodiment of thought, the following account of a modern magical experiment performed at the instance of Lord Prudhoe and Major Felix, a British officer, when travelling in Egypt, who were among the first persons who astonished the European world with their report of the magic mirror experiment; being men of high character and sense, their statement created a considerable sensation, (although a matter of almost daily occurrence in many parts of England, especially in Lancashire), and was first reported by the interlocutors in the Noctes Ambrosianæ of *Blackwood's Magazine*, for August, 1831.†

'Lord Prudhoe and Major Felix, being at Cairo last autumn, on their return from Abyssinia, where they picked up much of that information which has been worked up so well by Captain Bond Head, in his life of Bruce, found the town in a state of extraordinary excitement, in consequence of the recent arrival in those parts of a celebrated magician, from the centre of Africa, somewhere in the neighbourhood of the mountains of the moon. It was universally said, and generally believed, that this character possessed and exercised the power of shewing to any visitor who chose to comply with his terms, any person, dead or living, whom the same visitor pleased to name. The English travellers, after abundant enquiries and some scruples, repaired to his residence, paid their fees, and were admitted to his *sanctum*. They found themselves in the presence of a very handsome young Moor, with a very long black beard, a crimson caftan, a snow-white turban, blue trousers, and yellow slippers, sitting cross-legged on a Turkey carpet three feet square, with a cherry stalk in his mouth, a cup of coffee at his left elbow, a diamond-hafted dagger in his girdle, and in his right hand a large volume clasped with brazen clasps. On hearing their

*Dr Dee relates in his Diary, published by the Camden Society in 1842: '16th March, 1575. Her Majestie (Elizabeth) willed me to fetch my glass so famous, and to show unto her some of the properties of it, which I did; her Majestie, being taken down from her horse by the Earle of Leicester, did see some of the properties of that glass, to her Majestie's great contentment and delight.'

†See also an article in No. 356 of *Chamber's Edinburgh Journal*, which contains an account of some of the Egyptian magicians' failures.

errand, he arose and kindled some spices on a sort of small altar in the midle of the room; he then walked round the altar for half an hour or so, muttering words, to them unintelligible; and having at length drawn three lines of chalk about the altar, and placed himself upright beside the flame, desired them to seek a *seer*, and he was ready to gratify them in all their desires. There were in the olden days whole schools of magicians here in Europe, who could do nothing in this line without the intervention of a *pure seer*, to wit, a *maiden's eye*. This African belongs to the same fraternity. He made them understand that nothing could be done until a virgin's eye was placed at his disposal; he bade them go out in the streets of Cairo, and fetch any child they fancied under ten years of ago. They did so; and after walking about for half an hour, selected an Arab boy, not apparently above eight, whom they found playing at marbles; they bribed him with a few halfpence, and took him with them to the studio of the African Roger Bacon; the child was much frightened at the smoke, and the smell, and the chatter, but by and by he sucked his sugar candy, and recovered his tranquillity; and the magician made him seat himself under a window, *the only one that had not been darkened*, and poured out a table-spoonful of *some black liquid into the boy's right hand*, and bade him hold the hand steady, and keep his eye fixed upon the surface of the liquid; ("here," the doctor says, as with the magic mirrors of old, "is the medium used to embody the idea, which has been conveyed by the operator to persons in correspondence; the angle of direction from the boy's mind, must be in accordance with the angle from the person in correspondence;") and then resuming his old station by the brazier, sung out for several minutes on end, "What do you see? Allah Bismillah—what do you see?" All the while the smoke curled up faster and faster; presently the lad said, "Bismillah, I see a horse—a horseman—I see two horsemen—I see three—I see four—five—six—I see seven horsemen, and the seventh is a sultan!" "Has he a flag?" cried the magician. "He has three," answered the boy. "'Tis well," says the other; "now halt." And with that he laid the stick right across the fire, and standing up, addressed the travellers in these words: "Name your name; be it of those that are upon the earth, or of those that are beneath it; be it Frank, Moor, Turk, or Indian, prince or beggar, living and breathing, or solved into the dust of Adam, three thousand years ago; speak, and this boy shall behold and describe."

'The first name was *William Shakespear*. The magician made

three reverences towards the window, waved his wand nine times, sang out something beyond their interpretation, and at length called out, "Boy, what do you behold?" "The sultan alone remains," said the child; "and beside him I see a pale-faced Frank—but not dressed like these Franks—*with large eyes*, a pointed beard, a tall hat, roses on his shoes, and a short mantle!" The other asked for *Francis Arouet de Voltaire*, and the boy immediately described a lean, old, yellow-faced Frank, with a huge brown wig, a nutmeg-grater profile, spindle shanks, buckled shoes, and a gold snuff box. Lord Prudhoe now named *Archdeacon Wrangham*, and the Arab boy made answer and said, "I perceive a tall grey-haired Frank, with a black-silk petticoat, walking in a garden with a book in his hand,—he is reading in the book; his eyes are bright and gleaming, his teeth are white; he is the happiest looking Frank I ever beheld!" Major Felix now named a brother of his, who is in the cavalry of the East India Company, in the presidency of Madras; the magician signed, and the boy again answered, "I see a red-haired Frank, with a short red jacket and white trousers; he is standing by the sea-shore, and behind him there is a black man in a turban holding a beautiful horse richly caparisoned!" "God in heaven!" cried Major Felix. "Nay," the boy resumed, "this is an old Frank; he has turned round while you are speaking, and by Allah he has but one arm!" Major Felix's brother lost his arm in the campaign of Ava.'

'It is here evident,' says Dr Collyer, 'that he did not see any real spirit or apparition, but merely the *embodied idea* of the travellers, who depicted in their minds the image of Shakespear as he is *generally* represented,' &c., &c.

Dr Collyer then proceeds to state that he has proved the 'possibility of mental transfer' beyond the remotest chance of doubt: he relates several experiments in which the recipients exactly described what the spectators wished them to perceive, it being necessary that the latter should form clear and vivid images, in their own minds, of what was to be seen by the patients. One of these experiments is described as follows:—

'New York, Feb. 1841.

Magnetized Miss——; found her condition one of the most exalted. At the request of her father, who is one of the most eminent artists in the country, I brought before her *spiritual* vision the shade of Napoleon, whom she recognized at once, then Byron and Alexander the Great; the experiment was

performed with much care, so that she could not have previously
known our intention. I repeated the experiment on a series of
persons with a like success. I was obliged to embody the image
of those personages in my own mind, before they could be
recognized by the recipients; whose brain during the congestive
state was so sentient, that the impression was conveyed to the
mind, similar to the photographic process of Daguerre.'

In the *Albany Argus,* Dr Collyer says, 'I have always advocated
the philosophy, that the nervous fluid was governed by the same
code of laws which governed heat, light, &c., as radiation and
reflection actually made a lady perform the same class of
phenomena which is the wonder of travellers in the East. She
was desired to look into a cup of molasses (any other dark liquid
will answer the same purpose) and when the angle of incidence
from my brain was equal to the angle of reflection from her
brain, she distinctly saw the image of my thoughts at the point of
coincidence, and gave minute descriptions of many persons
whom she could have no idea of; she saw the persons and things
in the fluid, only when the angles of thought converged.'

With due deference to Dr Collyer, is it not most probable that
these ladies were influenced by the well known mental control
which magnetizers possess over their patients, and which has
been aptly termed 'suggestive dreaming'? Upon considering the
relations just made it cannot for a moment be supposed that
Lord Prudhoe and Major Felix could have heard the persons
and costumes thus described, in the same sequence in which
they were formed in their own minds, without remarking the
coincidence; still less could Major Felix have felt such
astonishment at the description of his brother, with the
accessories of the red-haired Frank, &c., when, according to Dr
Collyer's theory, it was merely the reflex of his own imagination.

Mr Salt, the late British Consul, a gentleman intimately
acquainted with the language, people, and country, and less
liable to be deceived than a passing traveller, found himself
completely puzzled on many occasions by the results of the
magic mirror experiment. Having once, for example, private
reasons for believing that some one of his servants had stolen
various articles of property; Mr Salt sent for a celebrated
Mugh'-reb'-ee magician, with the view of intimidating the
suspected person, and causing him voluntarily to confess if he
were really guilty: the magician came, and at once declared that
he would cause the exact image of the guilty person to appear to

any boy not above the age of puberty. A boy was taken incidentally from a band of several of them at work in Mr Salt's garden, the forms were gone through and the magic mirror properly formed; after seeing various images, the boy finally described from the mirror the guilty person, stature, dress, and countenance; said that he knew him, and ran down into the garden, where he apprehended one of the labourers, who, when brought before his master, immediately confessed that he was the thief.

Mr Lane, the eminent Orientalist, who lived for several years in Egypt, and witnessed personally the operations of the Egyptian magicians, of which he has published many curious relations: states, that on one occasion the magicians' performances were ridiculed by an Englishman present, who said that nothing would satisfy him but a correct description of his own father, of whom he was sure no one of the company had any knowledge. The sceptic was a little staggered when the boy described the man in a frank dress, with his hand placed to his head, wearing spectacles, and with one foot on the ground, and the other raised behind him, as if he were stepping down from a seat.

The description was exactly true in every respect, the peculiar position of the hand was caused by an almost continual head-ache, and that of the foot by a stiff knee caused by a fall from a horse in hunting.

I am assured, continues Mr Lane, that on this occasion, the boy described accurately each person and thing that was called for, and I might add several other cases in which the same magician has excited astonishment in the sober minds of Englishmen of my acquaintance. Mr Lane candidly confesses that there is a mystery in the matter to which he cannot discover any clue. How then are such phenomena, so perfectly coincident with the higher order of mesmeric clairvoyance as developed by Alexis Didier, and by Mr Hands's patient, as recorded in No. XXV. of *The Zoist?* Dr Collyer would certainly confess that it is utterly improbable, that these gentlemen should have been in that peculiar position in respect to the boy-seer, that the angle of incidence in all these cases equalled the angle of reflexion, and a very slight perusal of Dr Dee's work, will convince the reader, that Dr Dee could not have been so besotted during more than twenty years experiments (with different seers) not to have discovered that the visions and *responses* given by the crystal were but the embodiment of his own thoughts.

That the phenomena thus elicited has a closer connexion with the spiritual world than the rationalists of the present day are disposed to allow: the following extracts are given from that remarkable piece of autobiography, *William Lilly's History of his Life and Times, from the year 1602 to 1681.*

'All the ancient astrologers of England were much startled and confounded at my manner of writing, especially old Mr Wm. Hodges, who lived near Wolverhampton, he swore I did more by astrology than he could do by the crystal and use thereof, which indeed he understood as well as any one in England. His angels were Raphael, Gabriel, and Uriel. John Scott, my partner, having occasions into Staffordshire, addressed himself for a month or six weeks to Hodges, assisted him to dress his patients, let blood, &c., being to return to London, he desired Hodges to shew him the person and features of the woman he should marry. Hodges carries him into a field not far from his house, pulls out his crystal, bids Scott set his foot to his, and after a while wishes him to inspect the crystal, and observe what he saw there. "I see," said Scott, "a ruddy complexioned wench in a red waist-coat, drawing a can of beer." "She must be your wife," said Hodges. "You are mistaken, Sir," said Scott, "I am, so soon as I come to London, to marry a tall gentlewoman in the Old Bailey." "You must marry the red-waistcoat," said Hodges. Scott leaves the country, comes up to London, finds his gentlewoman married. Two years after, going unto Dover, on his return, he refreshed himself at an inn in Canterbury; as he came into the hall or first room thereof, he mistook the room, and went into the buttery, where he espied a maid, described by Hodges as aforesaid, drawing a can of beer, &c. He then more narrowly viewed her person and habit, found her in all parts to be the same as Hodges had described; after which he became a suitor unto her, and was married unto her, which woman I have often seen; this Scott related unto me several times, being a very honest person, and made great conscience of what he spoke. Another story of Hodges is as followeth, which I had related from a person who well knew the truth of it.

'A neighbour gentleman of Hodges lost his horse; who having Hodges' advice for recovering of him, did again obtain him. Some years after, in a frolic, he thought to abuse him; acquainting a neighbour therewith, viz., that he had formerly lost a horse, went to Hodges, recovered him again, but saith it was by chance, "I might have had him without going unto him. I will leave some boy or other at the town's-end with my horse, and then go to Hodges' and enquire for him." He did so, gave his horse to a youth, with orders to walk him till he returned; away he goes with his friend, salutes Hodges, thanks him for his former courtesy, and now desires the like, having lost a horse lately. Hodges, after some time passing, said, "Sir, your horse is lost, and never to be recovered." "I thought what skill you had," replies the gallant, "my horse is in a lane at the town's-end." With that Hodges swore, (as he was too much given into that vice,) "Your horse is gone, and you will never have him again." The gentleman departed in great derision of Hodges, and went where he left his horse; when he came there he found the boy fast asleep upon the ground, the boy's arm in the bridle. He returns again to Hodges, desiring his aid, being sorry for his former abuse. Old Will swore, "Begone, begone, go look for your horse." This business ended not so, for the malicious man brought Hodges into the Star Chamber for sorcery, bound him over to the assizes, put Hodges to great expence; but by means of the Lord Dudley, if I remember aright, or some other person thereabouts, he overcame the gentleman and was acquitted.'

And again Lilly says, 'I was very familiar with one Sarah Skelhorne, who had been speculatrix unto one Arthur Gauntlett, about Gray's Inn, a very lewd fellow, professing physick; this Sarah had a perfect sight, *and indeed the best eyes for that purpose I ever yet did see.* This Sarah lived for a long time, even until her death, with one Mrs Stockman, in the Isle of Purbeck, and died about sixteen years since. Her mistress one time being desirous to accompany her mother, the Lady Beaconsfield, unto London, who lived twelve miles from her habitation, caused Sarah to inspect her crystal, to see if she, viz., her mother was gone, yea or not; the angels appeared and shewed her mother opening a trunk and taking out a red waistcoat, whereby she perceived she was not gone. Next day she went to her mother's and there, as she entered the chamber, she was opening a trunk, and had a red waistcoat in her hand.'

Lilly wrote the account of his life to and by the request of Elias Ashmole, (the founder of the Ashmolean Museum, Oxford,) and in reference to these and similar relations, says, 'I may seem to some to write *incredibilia*, be it so, but knowing unto whom, and for whose only sake I do write them, I am much comforted therewith, well knowing you are the most knowing man in these curiosities of any man now living in England.'

So far as my own experience extends, I feel convinced that nothing approaching a transmission of thought takes place between the caller and the seer, in fact, the vision in the glass is often quite unconnected with what is passing in the minds of either. In this country the seer generally inspects the crystal for himself, and the object he perceives is known only to himself, and concerns alone his own private affairs. Upon referring to a diary I formerly kept, I find the following entry.*

' ♃ *die*, Oct. 9, 1834. This evening I charged my crystal (a glass sphere), and J—— N—— inspected it, she wished to see her mother who lived at Worcester. Upon commencing the call a second time, she perceived a straight streak of light, which appeared to open like a pair of compasses, and she then saw the head, and gradually the whole person of her mother, shoulders, waist, &c., but she could not see any feet. She described her mother as dressed in a green gown with yellow spots, and a purple silk handkerchief with blue spots over her shoulders, her dark hair parted over her forehead. She said her mother appeared to be well.

'M. inspected the crystal, but had no vision.'

This J. N. was a young woman, about twenty years of age, and although I knew the purpose for which she inspected, yet having no knowledge of the absent party, it certainly could not be a transmission of my thought. But, says the rationalist, it was the embodiment of her own. Granted—still the following experiment will shew even that might not have been the case.

'☉ *die*, Nov. 9, 1834. I charged the crystal for E. T. She wished to see a gentleman of her acquaintance (but a perfect stranger to myself), and who then resided a short distance from London. Upon my first charging the glass, she perceived only an eye looking at her; but upon repeating the charge, the whole face and body to the waist formed gradually. So distinctly did the vision appear, that she perceived even a scar he had on his right cheek, he was dressed in black, with *white* neckerchief and *white* shirt studs.

'I afterwards charged for another person, but they had no vision.'

*Nothing is more likely than that John Lilly may have encountered and even have produced many genuine phenomena of the class now known as clairvoyance: but he is a confirmed charlatan, in whose hands truth itself,—to parody Burke,—loses half its goodness in losing all its purity. His autobiography is, nevertheless, capital; it reads like a foretaste of Defoe, and, as it is difficult to think that Defoe, as he wrote fiction, did not sometimes come to believe that what he related was fact, so Lilly, it is not at all impossible, was once or twice so far carried away by fervour and habit of invention as to feel as if he was telling the truth.—*Zoist.*

In this case the speculatrix had never seen the party in question in any other than a black silk neckerchief and jet studs, but it afterwards appeared that the gentleman, being then in mourning for his deceased wife, he on Sundays wore a white neckcloth and diamond studs, a circumstance she was at the time perfectly unconscious of, and consequently the vision could not be the embodiment of her own thoughts. I will just add one more relation to prove the fallacy of Dr C.'s opinion.

In 1842, an old and worthy friend, of whose strict veracity I have no possible reason to doubt, came from Burnham with a relative to transact some business in London, and during the time of my absence from home with his relation, he took up from sheer curiosity a small oval mounted crystal, which I had been using (without effect) shortly before, and then stood upon the table; and after examining it and trying to guess its use, he observed it to become clouded, this at first he attributed to his breath, but upon further observing it, the cloud, as he expressed it, appeared to open like a pair of ostrich's legs, which gradually resolved itself into the form of a skeleton. He has since told me that at the same time he felt so great an oppression of giddiness and alarm, that he immediately replaced the crystal, and was a considerable time before he could throw off the unpleasant sensations it had produced. It was not until nearly two years after this that he ventured to tell me the circumstance; but I could never by any means induce him to inspect it again. It is remarkable that a few months after this happened his relative, with whom I was absent, *died.*

In this case there was no embodiment of thought, no angle of incidence equalling the angle of reflexion, and it would be difficult to persuade my friend, a hale and hearty farmer of fifty, that at noon-day he was dreaming.

'Γ,' in p. 69 of *The Zoist,* considers this mode of divination as precisely analogous to one of Mr Braid's methods of inducing sleep; but in that he is most certainly in error; there is not the slightest analogy between Mr Braid's process of producing sleep by fatiguing the rectus and levator muscle of the eye, and the method of inspecting the crystal. Mr Braid's method is to fix a small but conspicuous object above the level of the eye, (the stopper of a bottle was the first object he employed,) and then desiring his subjects to fix their gaze steadfastly upon its outer extremity, their eyelids generally closed in sleep in a few minutes, often a few seconds, thus causing congestion by a rapid exhaustion of the natural sensibility of the retina and motive nerves of the eye and eyelids; or, in Mr Braid's own words, 'My phenomena, I consider, arise entirely from the patient keeping his eyes fixed in one position, *and the greater the strain* on them the better, and the mind rivetted to one idea.'

On the contrary, when inspecting the crystal, it is held in the party's hand, in the position most easy to himself, and he retains the full possession of his faculties and conversational powers. But if '*Γ*' is still wedded to his hypnotic theory, perhaps he will try a few experiments by squinting, say at a decanter stopper, and then favour us in the next *Zoist* with his revelations. As for the visions in the crystal being as '*Γ*' supposes, the result of merely 'the earnest gaze and concentration of the mind to one idea;' as well might he assert that Sir John Herschell, Adams, or Gasparis, when scrutinizing every point of the starry heavens with telescopic eye, were self-hypnotized, and their resplendent discoveries, which have placed them foremost in the ranks of science, were but the revelations of a neuro-hypnotic trance.

For myself I am content to believe that the faith of our forefathers were not such 'wretched superstitious absurdities;' and that 'there are really things in nature of which our modern philosophy does not permit us to dream.'

London   FRED. HOCKLEY.

[Printed in *The Zoist*, No. XXVII (October 1849).]

Remarks upon the Rev. George Sandby's Review of M. Alphonse Cahagnet's *Arcanes de la Vie Future Dévoilés, &c.* By MR. HOCKLEY.

'Many rich mysteries are lockt up in the nature of angels, which, by degrees, will break out.'—Rev. R. Dingley's *Deputation of Angels.* London, 1654.

In common, I doubt not, with all the readers of *The Zoist*, I with great pleasure perused the valuable review of M. Cahagnet's Arcanes in the last number of *The Zoist*: and, as any article from the pen of the learned author of *Mesmerism and its Opponents* well merits the earnest consideration of the magnetic world, both from the very liberal and truth-seeking spirit of his writings and his position as a clergyman of the church of England, I have, with great diffidence, ventured to differ from that gentleman on the subject of his review; but, emboldened by his admission that, although 'many would probably dissent from his views, still some portion of truth might be elicited from the enquiry,' I have, after a careful perusal of M. Cahagnet's work, come to the conclusion that Mr Sandby has not placed before his readers a correct analysis of his author, inasmuch as that gentleman's objections rest more upon M. Cahagnet's logic than his facts; and the two examples selected are of little value while others are omitted which seem perfectly to establish his book as 'a step farther towards the unknown.'

The *Celestial Telegraph* appears to me to prove more forcibly than any other work on animal magnetism, with the exception of I. Hernrich Jung's (called Stilling) *Theory of Pneumatology*, the existence of guardian angels, of Hades, and the materiality of the human soul, but to be as far removed from Swedenborgianism (by which term I mean a belief in the *doctrines* and doxology of the New Jerusalem Church, and particularly articles xxi., xxii., and xxiii.,*) as from Behemenism, Mahometanism, Buddhism, or Polytheism, all, there is little doubt, equally indebted to the hitherto occult but ever existent law of nature which we now term animal magnetism. Mr Sandby has sufficiently shewn there 'is no reason to question either the good faith of M. Cahagnet or the credibility of his witnesses,' and 'that the work is written in an earnest and truth-loving spirit.' This opinion I readily adopt, as, after a careful reading, I do not perceive in the work or correspondence anything *new*. 'There is no new thing under the sun;' and scarcely a statement but to which a parallel can be readily produced.

In any treatise upon ghosts, the oft-repeated, but much to be esteemed, advice of Mrs Glass, as to cooking a hare, occurs on the very threshold as a startling difficulty; for in these dark ages a (not *the*) sensible majority of the public require, upon this subject, confirmation a vast deal stronger than Holy Writ. Fortunately, the ensuing pages are addressed solely to *the* sensible readers of *The Zoist*—the readers who have arrived at

---

*'Art. XXI.—That unless a new church be established by the Lord, no one can be saved; and that this is meant by these words, "Unless those days should be shortened, there should no flesh be saved." Mat. xxiv., 22.

'XXII.—That the opening and rejection of the tenets of the faith of the present church, and the revelation and reception of the tenets of the faith of the new church is meant by these words in the Apocalypse, "He that sat upon the throne said, Behold, I make all things new; and he said unto me, Write, for these words are true and faithful." Chap. xxi., 5.

'XXIII.—That the new church about to be established by the Lord is the New Jerusalem, treated of in the Apocalypse, chap. xxi. and xxii., which is there called the Bride and the Wife of the Lamb.'

the conviction that there are, midst nature's laws, operations whose method of working, though beyond our finite comprehension, are still full of sublime truths—readers who believe that the phenomena of clairvoyance, soul travelling, transference of thought, taste, and feeling, 'are established truths, and who differ only as to the questions of degree.'

Mr Sandby, in placing before his readers a proof that M. Cahagnet's revelations are the result of transference of thought and not a connexion with the spiritual world, has selected two cases of clairvoyant communication with persons actually declared by the somnambulist to be *living*; and although, in stating them, that gentleman has given us the truth (of which there could be no possible doubt), still, if he had not most ingeniously disjointed it, I think very few of his readers would have coincided with him in opinion; and as the case appears to me a very strong proof of soul travelling, and remarkably corroborative of the very singular statement given by Mr Hazard in No. XXVI. of *The Zoist*, I must crave room for the sitting in detail.

In the ninety-eighth sitting, M. Lucas, desirous of learning the fate of his brother-in-law, who had left France twelve years before, in consequence of an altercation with his father, applied to M. Cahagnet for a sitting.

Scarcely was Adèle asleep, than she asked for this man by his name, as she usually does for deceased persons. She then said to us, 'I see him: he is not dead; he is on the earth, and not in the spiritual world.' She then gave so exact a description of him to M. Lucas, that the latter declared even the very gestures true to life. A few days later, M. Lucas and the mother of the man had a second sitting. Adèle once asleep, said, 'I see him.' Where do you see him? 'Here present.' Give us, once more, a description of him, as also of the place where he is. 'He is a fair man, browned by the heat of the sun; very corpulent, features pretty regular, hazel eyes, mouth large; air sombre and meditative. He is in the garb of a working man—a sort of small blouse. He is at work, gathering seeds like peppercorns, but I don't think they are, as they seem bigger. This seed is found in small shrubs about three feet high. I see a negro near him, who is doing the same thing.' Try and obtain an answer to-day: let him tell you the name of the country where you see him. 'He won't answer me.' Tell him that it is his good mother, whom he was so fond of, who bids you enquire after him. 'Oh!' at the name of his mother he turned round and said to me, 'My mother! I shall not die before seeing her again: comfort her, and tell her that I am always thinking of her, that I am not dead.' Why does he not write to her? 'He has written to her, but he presumes the vessel was wrecked, as he received no answer. He tells me he is at Mexico. He followed the emperor Don Pedro; was five years a prisoner, suffered much, and will make every effort to return to France: they will see him again.' Can he name the place he lives in? 'No, it is far up in the country: such places have no names.' Is he with a European? 'No, with a man of colour.' Why does he not write to his mother? 'Because, where he is, no vessels come; he knows not to whom to apply: then, again, he scarcely ever knew how to write, and now less than ever. No one near him can render him that service: no one speaks his language. He has much difficulty in making himself understood: withal he never was of a communicative dispositon; he has a somewhat unsociable look. It is a hard matter to get a word out of him; one would think he was dumb' (In short, how are we to manage to write to him or hear from him?) 'He can't tell: all he can say is, "I am in Mexico: I am not dead: they will see me again."'

The mother melted into tears as she recognized the truthfulness of each detail given her by Adèle. She had not a word to retrench from this description; the character, the instruction, and the departure of her son, were precisely such as described by Adèle: but what gives an air of greater probability to the clairvoyant's recital as to the country he lives in is, that some of his relatives entertained the idea that he had enlisted into Don Pedro's army, and took steps, at the time, to acquire a certainty of it. M. Lucas furnished me with this particular some time after, when on a visit to Paris. No information, however, could be obtained in this respect. But what astonished all present at this sitting was to see Adèle, who, to screen herself from the burning rays of the sun of these countries, put her hand up to the left side of her face, as if suffocating with heat. But the most marvellous part of the scene was, *that she received a violent coup-de-soleil that rendered all this side of her face, from the forehead to the shoulder, of a reddish blue*, whilst the other side remained perfectly white; and full twenty-four hours elapsed before this deep colour commenced disappearing: *the heat was so violent there for a moment, that it was impossible to keep one's hand on it.*

Mr. Haranzer Pirot, formerly a magnetizer, and honourably known for more than thirty years in the magnetic world, was present at this sitting, and declared he had never seen the like. The good woman took her leave quite consoled, unable to account to herself how her son who was in Mexico could be between her and Adèle, and how the latter could have received a *coup-de-soleil* when nobody felt the heat, the weather that day being very gloomy.

Now were we to suppose it possible that any sane persons could sit and listen to their own thoughts thus revived before them without recognition, still the *coup-de-soleil* could not be the result of mental transfer, nor could the circumstance thus minutely particularized be mistaken. It is either true, or the whole work is indeed a scandalous fabrication. Fortunately, in p. 179, Vol. VII. of *The Zoist*, we have a case in point, thus related by Mr W. Hazard, of Ann Bateman, who, sitting in a mesmeric state, at Bristol, thus described the condition of a vessel, then (as afterwards proved by the captain) to the westward of Madeira.

'Ah, there's the ship; but oh! how dark. How she tumbles. *I shall be sick.*' At the same time she was in that kind of unsteady motion so usual to persons unaccustomed to the sea. 'How the wind roars, and the sea so high and black: it's dreadful!' Do you see Captain C.? 'Yes, there he is on a high deck, calling to the men; now there's an Irishwoman at the cabin door asking for medicine; others saying they would all be drowned: now there's Capt. C. leaning over a rail, saying, "Go down, my good women, there's no danger."' Now she said, 'There's such a noise down stairs: there's a man,—he looks like a parson or a quaker—with a great flat hat on, talking to the people; now he has put a large tin horn to his ear, and is lifting up his hand.'

Now these,—may I say facts?— are thus to be accounted for, according to Mr Sandby's hypothesis. The trees, the seed-gathering, and the negro, 'love of the marvellous;' the correct description and part of the answers, 'thought reading;' a part of the description and a portion of the answers, 'suggestive dreaming;' the *coup-de-soleil* of twenty-four hours' duration, 'a remarkable instance of the power of the imagination over the body;' and the perception of the circumstances taking place in the vessel and afterwards proved to be minutely correct, 'old mesmeric principles of thought reading and clairvoyance.' 'What's in a name?'

But similar objections had been made to M. Cahagnet personally, and he has given a host of sittings—many of them at the instance of experienced magnetists—to prove their utter fallacy; and in support of M. Cahagnet's views, and to shew how far relations of events, which have taken place nearly a century apart, confirm each other, I subjoin the following anecdote as related by Jung.

A respectable man in Stockholm bought an estate of another, paid for it, and received an acknowledgment. The purchaser died soon after, and a long time had not elapsed before the seller demanded payment of the widow for the estate, threatening her that he would otherwise take possession of it again. The widow was terrified: she knew that her husband had paid for the estate, and made search for the receipt, which, however, she was unable to find anywhere. This greatly increased her fright; and as her deceased husband had been on friendly terms with the Russian ambassador, she had recourse to him.

The ambassador knew from experience what assistance Swedenborg had occasionally afforded in such cases; and as the widow was not known to him, the ambassador undertook the matter. He spoke, therefore, with Swedenborg; and recommended the cause of the widow to him. Some days after, Swedenborg came to the ambassador, and requested him to tell the widow, that on such a night *her husband would appear to her and tell her where the receipt lay.* However terrible this might appear to the widow, yet she was obliged to consent to it, because the paying for the estate a second time would have rendered her poor, or even been impracticable to her. She therefore resigned herself to her fate, sat up on the night appointed, and retained a maid with her, who, however, soon began to fall asleep, and could by no means be kept awake. At 12 o'clock the deceased appeared. He looked grave, and as though displeased, and then pointed out to the widow the place where the receipt lay, namely, in a certain room, in a little desk attached to the wall; on which he disappeared. The widow went the next morning to the place he had indicated and found the receipt.

Mr Sandby observes that the tendency of this work, as well as those of Davis, Kerner, &c., is to support the *doctrines* of Emanuel Swedenborg. But to this also I must, with due deference, object: in the first place, it is plain that M. Cahagnet and Davis are neither of them believers in Swedenborgian*ism* or any other *ism* but pure Theism, although their revelations strongly confirm a multitude of *statements* made by the Swede. That Swedenborg sincerely believed in his own being a special and divine commission, it would be a libel upon humanity to deny; that he was, though ignorant of it himself, a natural somnambulist, I think no one, conversant with animal magnetism, can reasonably doubt, and it has been held by many magnetizers, whose opinions well deserve attention, that in this magnetic state he became possessed of the faculty of clairvoyance, fell into a connexion with the world of spirits, and also possessed the power (so rare in mesmerised persons) of evolving the ideas thus raised, and embodying his visions, in his normal state; endued, also, with a prodigious amount of varied knowledge, which he brought, by his peculiar idiosyncracy, to bear in support of dogmas founded on the doctrine of Hades, the possibility of a communion with the souls of the departed and the spirit world, particularly the ministry of guardian angels—doctrines which appeared novel to the great body of the Protestant faith, though strictly scriptural and strenuously asserted by the ancient fathers and numerous modern authorities of the Church of England.

The claims of Mahomet, Jacob Behmen, or Swedenborg, to a divine mission arose from their cases being isolated, though exceedingly elevated, instances of spontaneous somnambulism; but surely the demonstration of the existence of animal magnetism by Mesmer, the discovery of clairvoyance by De Puysegur, and the phenomena since elicited by an almost countless number of somnambulists, tending incontestibly to prove that the Great Disposer of all things has thus placed the same powers in the hands of every man, irrespectively of his creed or station, ought to be deemed sufficient to strip from their revelations every particle of a belief in their being the result of a *special interposition* of the divine will, but leave their statements as to the spirit world to be attested or refuted by subsequent investigations.

In M. Cahagnet's theorem 'that the soul is an intelligent being or fluid, independent in that (the magnetic) state of the material body, and able to see, hear, feel, and converse with another being at a distance,' Mr Sandby demurs to the logical accuracy of the term *independent*. To msyelf it appears only to mean that when the body is in a magnetic, cataleptic state, the soul is loosened, untrammelled, and no longer biased or controlled by the material body. That it is not entirely unconnected with the body is shewn by M. Cahagnet in his fifty-third experiment, when, wishing to test whether (as asserted by the somnambules) there were any real dangers in leaving the soul of the somnambulist to its own guidance, he states that, relying on Bruno,—

> I had paid little attention to Adèle, whose body, in the mean time, had grown icy cold: there was no longer any pulse or respiration; her face was of a sallow green, her lips blue; her heart gave no sign of life. I placed before her lips a mirror, and it remained untarnished. I magnetized her powerfully in order to bring back her soul into her body, but for five minutes my labour was vain. I thought for a moment that the work was consummated, and that

the soul *had departed from her body.* Falling on my knees, I asked back of God, in my prayer, the soul that I had in my doubts suffered to depart. I seemed, by an effect of intuition, to know that my prayer was heard: after a moment's farther anguish I obtained these words, 'Why have you called me back.' I paid but little attention to her complaints; I was only too happy to hear her speak.

In truth, the majority of the magnetic world will care little about M. Cahagnet's theory, or whether his logic is of the school or not, any more than for the theories which almost every new aspirant for mesmeric fame seems impressed with the necessity of expounding, and which generally turn out as valueless as the 'wonderful' experiments of Dr Scoresby,* who gravely places before his readers, as startling discoveries† of his own, a number of experiments, common as household words, abounding in mesmeric works almost to nausea, and which, after all, only prove that the eccentric author has, indeed, caught something 'vastly like a whale.'

As Mr Sandby, at p. 428, rather summarily disposes of all those 'who may still have a leaning towards these developments of spiritualism,' he will, perhaps, in proof of his assertion that 'in revelations to be credited, there should be a complete harmony between the different parts,' oblige us by pointing out an example; for, judging from the discord, to use the mildest term, between the members of the Christian world, we might be afraid of seeking it even in the *Bible.* To myself, 'the manifest discrepancies' in the works of H. Werner, Hauffe, Davis, and Cahagnet, are the greatest proofs that they are written with a

---

*That any tyro in the sciences should jot down the (to him) surprizing phenomena elicited would be most commendable; but that a learned D.D., an F.R.S., and a member of the Institutes of Paris and Philadelphia, should *publish* such crudities, with the modest avowal (p. 53) that of a science which during 80 years had successively engaged the attention of such men as La Fayette, d'Espremenil, De Puysegur, Deslon, Gmelin, Eschenmeyer, Oken, Deleuze, and Elliotson, he, to a considerable extent, had *refrained from reading,* may well cause us, like his philosophic friend, Mr S. (p. 19.), to 'throw up *our* hands, exclaiming, Astonishing! Wonderful!'

†Amongst other 'discoveries,' permit me to say that the very curious analogy of thought-reading to the daguerreotype did not originate with your corerspondent, W. F. G. of Clifton, but belongs to Dr Collyer of Philadelphia, and forms the chief feature in his *Psychography or Embodyment of Thought,* and also in his lectures, which he delivered at Bristol and most other large towns in England.

truth seeking spirit, and even those discrepancies may be referred to our own limited information. To any one possessed only of the knowledge of the *attraction* of iron by the magnet, the fact of the opposite pole *repelling* it would be 'a discrepancy equally at variance with his common sense and reason.' Mr Sandby also objects that departed souls, on their arrival in the other world, retain their antecedent habits and opinions; in other words, 'a Jew seems to remain a Jew, a Catholic a Catholic, and a miser as fond of his gold as before.' Exactly so; and what idea more rational than the soul, which I presume Mr S. allows to be the reasoning faculty when on earth, retaining its erratic dogmas for a short period (for what is 1000 years or so to eternity?), and when it becomes illumined by the divine mind, and capable of solving *our* doubts, being placed beyond the reach of mortals however magnetic. Had these clairvoyants affirmed that the souls of the defunct became immediate converts to Romanism or even orthodox Church of England, I should have become a rationalist at once. Notwithstanding Jung, whose *Theory of Pneumatology** I conceive to be the best in our language, has the following for the 35th and 37th theorems of his *Brief Summary*.

35. The souls of all such as have only led a decent civil life, and who, though not vicious, are still no true Christians, must undergo a long purification in the waste and desert Hades, by enduring the deprivation of all that is dear to them, and of every enjoyment, whilst longing most painfully after that earthly life which has for ever fled, and thus be gradually prepared for the *lowest* degree of bliss.

37. The souls of true Christians, that have trodden the path of sanctification, and who expired in the exercise of true faith in Jesus Christ, in the grace of his atonement, and in complete renunciation of everything earthly, are received immediately on awaking from the sleep of death, by angels without delay, conducted upwards to the pure regions of light, where they enjoy the fulness of bliss.

Doctrines such as these may have been a pleasant contemplation for a steadfast Lutheran, as Jung undoubtedly was, but would afford cold comfort to the myriads of devout Jews, or pious Mussulmans, and truly worthy men of all denominations.

I have long been of the opinion that the soul is the luminous *material* atmosphere which surrounds the body, described by

*London. 12mo. Longman and Co, 1834. Translated by Samuel Jackson.

many somnambules as appearing like a lambent flame. *The outer and not the inner man*, and, so far from not being in connection with the spirit world, is, in fact, never out of it; and, as the opposite pole of a magnet repels the needle which the other attracts, so does the body, when in its normal state, by overpowering by its will the soul, repel all other soul atmospheres: but in the magnetic state, the body being rendered inert, the soul is left free to exert itself, and in that state exists, irrespective of time or space, and endued with the power of attenuating or expanding itself to whatever point it desires to be in, with 'QUASI-electro-telegraphic-wire-like speed,' and of acting on other human soul atmospheres, thus becoming cognizant of the past transactions of others like Heinrich Zschokke—the Swiss historian—of the present, how far soever distant, like the American *solitaire** and Mr Hazard's patient; and, in like manner, becoming possessed by an intuitive perception of the floating ideas of other coexistent souls, thus accounting for the phenomenon of Jacob Behmen—a rude, unlettered shoemaker—who, falling, like his predecessor—Mahomet, and his successor—Swedenborg, into a 'quasi-mesmeric state,' produced those admirable and voluminous works, the *Teutonic Philosophy*, which thus engendered were merely the reflex of the Christianity of his time mixed up with the then all-engrossing theories of the triune, body, soul, and spirit—the sulphur, salt, and mercury of the magi-alchemical philosophers, and *expressed* in their peculiar language and phraseology. Thus Swedenborg anticipated, in his revelations,

---

*Zschokke in his *Selbstschau* states: 'It has happened to me occasionally, at the first meeting with a total stranger, when I have been listening in silence to his conversation, that his past life, up to the present moment, with many minute circumstances belonging to one or other scene in it, has come across me like a dream, but distinctly, involuntarily and unsought. Instead of recording many instances I will give one. On a fair day at Waldshut we went into an inn called the Vine; we took our supper with a numerous company at the public table: when it happened that they made themselves merry over the peculiarities of the Swiss, in connexion with the belief in mesmerism and the like. One of my companions begged me to make some reply, particularly in answer to a young man of superior appearance, who sat opposite, and had indulged in unrestrained ridicule. It happened that the events of this very person's life had just previously passed before my mind. I turned to him with the question, whether he would reply to me with truth and candour if I narrated to him the most secret passages of his history? he being as little known to me as I to him. He promised if I told the truth to admit it openly. Then I narrated the events with which my dream-vision had furnished me, and the table learnt the history of the young tradesman's life,—of his school years, his

Much science of the nineteenth century; anticipated in astronomy, the discovery of the seventh planet, but unhappily not also the eighth; anticipated the views of modern astronomy in regard to the generation of earths by the sun; in magnetism, some important experiments and conclusions of later students; in chemistry, the atomic theory; in anatomy, the discoveries of

peccadilloes, and finally of a little act of roguery committed by him on the strong box of his employer. I described the uninhabited room with its white walls, where to the right of the brown door there had stood upon the table the small black money chest, &c. A dead silence reigned during this recital, interrupted only when I occasionally asked if I had spoke the truth. The man, much struck, admitted the correctness of each circumstance, even, which I could not expect, of the last. Touched with his frankness, I reached my hand to him across the table, and closed the narrative. He asked my name, which I gave him. He may be alive yet.'

This extraordinary power Zschokke afterwards found also possessed by a *beggar man*.

The anecdote of the Solitaire is thus related by Jung, *Theory of Pneumatology*, p. 74:—

'In the neighbourhood of Philadelphia there dwelt a solitary man in a lonely house. He was very benevolent, but extremely retired and reserved; and strange things were related of him, amongst which were his being able to tell a person things that were unknown to every one else. Now it happened that a captain of a vessel belonging to Philadelphia was about to sail to Africa and Europe. He promised his wife that he would return again in a certain time, and also that he would write to her frequently; she waited long, but no letters arrived: the time appointed passed over, but her beloved husband did not return. She was now deeply distressed, and knew not where to look either for counsel or consolation; at length a friend advised her to go to the pious solitary, and tell him her griefs: the woman followed his advice, and went to him. After she had told him all her troubles, he desired her to wait awhile there until he returned and brought her an answer. She sat down to wait, and the man opening a door, went into his closet. But the woman thinking he stayed a long time, rose up, went to the window in the door, lifted up the little curtain, and looking in, saw him lying on a couch like a corpse; she then immediately went back to her place. At length he came and told her that her husband was in London, in a coffee-house which he named, and that he would return very soon: he then told her also the reason why he had been unable to write. The woman went home pretty much at ease.

'What the solitary told her was minutely fulfilled; her husband returned, and the reason of his delay and his not writing were just the same as the solitary had stated. The woman was now curious to know what would be the result if she visited the friendly solitary in company with her husband. The visit was arranged, but when the captain saw the man he was struck with amazement. He afterwards told his wife that he had seen this very man, on such a day (it was the very day that the woman had been with him), in a coffee-house in London, and that he had told him that his wife was much distressed about him; that he had then stated his reason why his return was delayed and of his not writing, and that he would shortly come back; on which he lost sight of the man among the company.

Schlichting, Monro, and Wilson; and first demonstrated the office of the lungs.*

Thus also enabling Andrew Jackson Davis, whose education, like Behmen's, 'scarcely amounted to reading, writing, and the elements of arithmetic,' in his magnetic sleep, mesmerically induced to pour forth a mass of recondite matter (filling 800 closely printed octavo pages), explaining the laws of nature and giving us the minutiæ of her operations in myriads of by-gone ages, revelling in the deepest profundities of geologic speculations and central-sun systems in the technical phraseology of the day, but stopping short precisely where his revelations would be most useful and most convincing—the limits of our present knowledge and ideas,†—detailing to a nicety the vegetation of the planet Saturn, the complexions of the inhabitants of Jupiter, and the very forms of the cerebrum and cerebellum of the inhabitants of Mars, but unable to give us the diameter of the sun to within 114,000 miles—'its diameter has not been as yet correctly determined;' becoming dogmatical upon the *origin* of the asteroids, but stating 'Their rotations have been scarcely decided upon, their revolutions have been *nearly* correctly calculated.' But the (to me) most convincing proof that our soul atmosphere has the faculty of receiving, when in a mesmeric induced sleep, the influx of all the floating, though unpublished, ideas of the time is Professor Bush's note, at p. 227.

> What is here said of the dia-magnetic principle was entirely new to me at the time, having never heard of the term. On subsequently asking the speaker (Davis) for a more particular explanation, he replied, in substance, that an imponderable element had recently been discovered, the motion of which intersected the current producing the direction of the magnetic needle. On my enquiring the name of the discoverer, the clairvoyant passed off (*i.e.*, spiritually, the body assuming the inclined position, as is explained on p. 38), and on returning, he remarked, 'It *sounds* like—he is known as Professor Faraday.'

*Emerson's *Representative Men*, p. 51. Bohn.
†'The statement here, concerning the revolution of the sun as a planet around a centre in the depths of immensity, is verified by the recent discoveries of Maedler, a Russian astronomer; of which discoveries the clairvoyant, in his normal state, had no knowledge, neither had either of his associates until many months after this was delivered.' p. 160.
'Numerous witnesses can testify that what is said about an eighth and ninth planet was in manuscript months before Le Verrier's calculations and conclusions had been announced in this country. Ib. 161

In conclusion, it must still depend on our individual idiosyncracy, whether we believe the revelations of the spiritual world thus obtained are parallel truths or mere repetitions; but M. Cahagnet has promised us a tangible proof in a volume of alchemical revelations, and we must forewarn him that in these sceptical days we shall expect from him, with such a goodly host of defunct Adepti, 'real sons of the fire'—from Synesius to Philalethes—for interlocutors, who, if judged from their voluminous writings, must doubtless prove most loquacious fellows, and who, having indulged when on this dull earth so copiously in dark and mystical enigmas, will now throw an unerring light upon the first matter, will truly give us an open entrance to the shut palace of the king, a lucid explanation of the Tabula Smaragdina of Hermes, the sophic fire of Pontanus, the doves of Diana, the fountain of Count Turisan, and the green lion, and all other monsters of Paracelsus, Ripley, Flamel, and Co.,—not omitting the assistance to be derived from those thrice learned ladies, Miriam the prophetess, Perrenelle, and Quercitan's daughter. Let them do this, M. Alphonse Cahagnet, and your revived art of projection will make more converts to animal magnetism than Anthony Mesmer and the whole of his disciples.

I remain, Sir,
Your obedient servant,
Fred. Hockley.

London.

*** Not wishing to continue a controversy in another number, we showed Mr Hockley's manuscript to Mr Sandby and to a philosophical layman; and the following are their remarks.— *Zoist.*

I. Mr Sandby begs to thank the editor of *The Zoist* for the perusal of Mr Hockley's manuscript, and at the same time he thanks Mr Hockley for his friendly observations; and in reply he can assure him, that he has a pleasure in meeting so well informed a writer, though it is his misfortune still to dissent from his conclusions.

There are many questions alluded to in the above 'Remarks,' on which Mr S. would be glad to comment; but he will confine himself to one point, where his argument seems misunderstood, or rather is altogether overlooked by Mr Hockley, and it is the argument by which the fallaciousness of M. Cahagnet's *facts* is attempted to be proved.

This argument has respect to the *conversation* maintained

between Adèle, the clairvoyante, and the mother of M. Lucas, an alleged resident in Mexico. Here Mr Hockley says, that 'Mr S., in placing before his readers a proof that M. Cahagnet's revelations are not a connection with the spiritual world, has selected two cases of clairvoyant communications with persons actually declared by the somnambulist to be *living*, and, although in stating them that gentleman has given us the truth, still if he had not most ingeniously disjointed it, I think very few of his readers would have coincided with him in opinion,' &c., &c.

Now the reason why facts, which are in themselves curious, were thus 'ingeniously disjointed,' and the whole story not given, was partly the desire of brevity, but mainly the fact of their not bearing upon the actual argument, which argument related solely to the *conversation* held between two persons some hundred miles asunder.

The case is this. Adèle, in addition to her power of calling up and conversing with the souls of the departed, travels in spirit to Mexico, and professes to hold a dialogue with a gentleman dwelling in that country. Now that gentleman was either dead, or he was living. If he were dead, there is an end of the matter, and the illusive character of the vision is at once demonstrated. But if he were living (as Adèle's power of clairvoyance would lead us to assume), then it is contended that that gentleman's spirit or 'reasoning faculty' must have been conscious at the time of so strange a transaction as this interesting conference, and could, if he had been questioned, have given much the same version of the interview as that communicated by Madame Adèle; for, in addition, it must be remembered that he was not asleep mesmerically or otherwise, but engaged at work with a negro in gathering seeds like peppercorns.

Now, according to Cahagnet, Adèle's power of conversing with the stranger in Mexico was as easily brought into action, as her power of conversing with the soul of Swedenborg or of Louis XVI. The fact then is readily tested. Let Cahagnet, or any lady or gentleman in London, who has the same faculty of raising the dead by the aid of a spiritualized clairvoyant, hold a conversation after the same fashion with some third party resident in some accessible locality, who shall be quite unprepared for the conference; and if that third party shall subsequently confirm the *procés verbal* of the dialogue, and admit that his 'reasoning faculty' did really feel conscious of the same spiritual conversation; and if this fact be well established by repeated trials, then Mr Sandby will admit that a *prima facie* case is made out in favour of M. Cahagnet's statements, and he will be prepared to reconsider the secrets of the 'celestial telegraph.'

But if the communication cannot be obtained at home or at Paris, and the distance of Mexico is required to 'lend enchantment to the *interview*;' then it is contended that this spiritual intercourse with the brother of M. Lucas was simply a spectral illusion by the aid of clairvoyance, and the dialogue but 'a coinage of the brain;' and then it follows next that the faculty, which at one moment could thus depicture a living man, could with equal facility raise up the ideal figures of a whole host of departed beings, and hold imaginary colloquies with them; and thus it follows next that the large army of Cahagnet's ghosts *may* be little else than airy nothings, or that—

> 'Bodiless creation ecstacy
> Is very cunning in.'

The cerebral power of *seeing ghosts at will* is the great point established and explained by this Mexican dialogue: and though there may be several other facts in M. Cahagnet's volumes which a *most imperfect acquaintance with the extensibility of clairvoyance* renders at present difficult of solution, still this is the great physiological feature in the subject, while all the other perplexing points are of inferior moment.

Flixton Vicarage.

II. If we apprehend Mr Hockley rightly, his purpose in giving this extended extract is to support the deduction drawn from it as from others by M. Cahagnet, and which is combated by Mr Sandby in his more brief citation. The facts, cleared of inferences, are admitted or assumed by the several parties to the discussion, but the deduction from them 'that spirits can and do make their appearance to an ecstatic sleep-walker, and can hold conversations with him,' Mr Sandby demurs to, while Mr Hockley, we presume, supports. The text, however, furnishes us with no assistance in the work of connecting the premises and the conclusion, and we can find none for ourselves in the full report of the sitting, least of all in the *italicized* passages. Surely the anecdote of the *coup-de-soleil*, however interesting in itself, in no way elucidates the theory of conversing apparitions.

At the same time we are bound to say that Mr Sandby appears to narrow his own ground too strictly. At page 421, *Zoist* XXVIII, he well states, that when the transference of thought is once established as a truth, the other points,—can a brain which is not in *apparent rapport* with the sleeper, (a brain which is at a distance, or which in years long past had been in sympathetic intercourse with some person that is present), can this brain conduct its impressions to the brain of the ecstatic,—are only *questions of degree*; additional experience, it is added, tends to extend our notion of the capabilities of the human brain in these respects. Now why should we deny to the cases of M. Cahagnet the character of evidence on the question of degree? and if they are attested, authenticated, admitted, what other course remains for us? The step in degree may be so vast—from transference of thought at the interval of an hour and a street, to an interval of a hemisphere and half a century—that we may withhold assent, waiting an example more completely exempt from all chances of mistake, misapprehension, and misreport; but a question of degree it still remains, and we must not allow the enormity of the application to frighten us out of recognition of the principle. What view then may we form, consistently with the principle, of the conversation reported between Adèle in France and the stranger in Mexico? If, as we have seen, it be an admitted possibility that the brain of a person at a distance, at Mexico, may conduct its impressions to the brain of a person, in this case a brother, which in years long past had been in sympathetic intercourse with it, another link in the mysterious chain conducts those impressions to the brain of the somnambule; and it is quite within the range of experience in these matters that the more sensitive organism should alone have distinct perception of the impressions conveyed to it through an unconscious recipient. The particular forms in which the impressions are enunciated by the somnambule, as a conversation, a vision, &c., are known to be matters of casual association and habit and predisposition, and the liabilities of mixed failures and success are also notorious.

There seems then no impossibility, according to the conditions of the argument, in a positive communication of thought taking place between a brain in Mexico and a brain in France; nay, if we suppose the brain in Mexico as sensitive and clairvoyant as the French one, the transference of thought may be mutual, and there may be consciousness of the communication on either side. But in the absence of such coincident sensitiveness there seems no reason, under the assumptions, for requiring that the absent person should become 'conscious of the communication, and agree in the accuracy of the conversations ascribed to them,' and to which they did in fact furnish their part, and in default of this for concluding that the 'unreality of the supposed perception is at once obvious, and we have incontestable proof that the whole is a mental delusion.'—*Zoist*, p. 426.

But furthermore, if any one chooses to claim the manifestation thus hypothetically admitted,—the perception in a room at Paris of the personal condition and present thoughts of a person in Mexico,—as virtually an apparition, as something much more to the purpose of a profitable apparition than is often to be had in the market, we know not what objection can be made on the part of those who have brought the question to this point. The sound of a voice is as much an apparition as a face and form seen, and what are externals of any kind to actual communication of mental impressions?

The differences, however, must not be lost sight of between assenting to such matters as theoretically possible and actually facts; between instances again that are authenticated and those that are not; and in authenticated instances, between the criticised residuum of philosophical truth and the accretions of error and false inferences at every step, from the somnambulist in chief to the last avoucher. It must be said that facts of this class recommend themselves too often to those who are so fortunate as to encounter the best specimens, not by their proper and essential value and significance, but by their supposed bearing in illustration and furtherance of a pre-adopted theory, not to say superstition; and painful it is to the student who would fain be the minister and interpreter of nature, to see her choicest productions mangled and bleeding, and smoking as sacrifices on the altars of every idol of den and tribe that physiology and philosophy have reason to abhor.

For the rest, after the exposition by Mr Sandby of the 'contradictions' and 'poverty of ideas' exhibited in these developments of spiritualism, we fancy it is needless to enter farther into their claims as transcendental and authoritative revelations and 'unveilments of the secrets of future existence.'"

London   W. W. LLOYD.

[Printed in *The Zoist*, No. XXIX (April 1850).]

Cure by Mesmerism, without medicine, of a condemned Diseased Knee.
Communicated by Mr Hockley

'The incredulity of the learned is hardly less hurtful to truth than the credulity of the vulgar. When a discovery like animal magnetism is announced, in the disbelief of which he has been trained from his youth, the learned sceptic dogmatically declares it impossible, and contradicted by the established laws of nature;—forgetting that these laws are merely certain modes of acting which we have discovered nature to follow. Such an objection, in fact, assumes that we have a complete knowledge of physical science; whereas, the philosopher most deeply versed in it will be the first to confess, like Newton, that he is but a boy gathering pebbles on the seashore, and knowing almost nothing of the vast ocean of truth that rolls at his feet.'—*Editor of the Dublin University Magazine*, vol. xxxviii., p. 384.

TO THE EDITOR OF THE ZOIST

Sir,—I beg to submit to your notice a mesmeric cure, effected without medicine, of a 'declared hopeless case,' through the untiring zeal and attention of Mr Laurence Moreton, of Burnham, Bucks, an amateur mesmerist; and as the case shews the inestimable blessings which may be conferred upon suffering humanity, even by the most unpractised hand when under medical supervision, however slight. I must observe that the mesmeriser was absolutely ignorant of mesmerism and its manipulations until almost immediately before the commencement of the present case.

Having the pleasure to be an old friend of Mr Moreton's father, and my advocacy of mesmerism being known, I was requested one day to shew the members of his family the process by putting, in a few minutes, one of his sons into the mesmeric sleep, producing rigidity, &c., at will. This induced Mr L. Moreton to turn his attention to the subject, and procuring a Deleuze, and Mr Barth's excellent manual for a guide, he made his first essay upon a young woman, aged 20, who had long suffered from repeated attacks of severe head-ache, which he immediately relieved to her great comfort and his own surprise, producing sleep in about a quarter of an hour, and by two further mesmerisings she has been permanently relieved.

His next essay was upon John Holden, a labouring man, aged 60, during an attack of gout, to which he had been continually subject during many years. The first mesmerising produced great relief, and mesmerising him each evening for a week effected a cure; for, although about six months afterwards he had another attack, it yielded to a couple of manipulations, and he has been perfectly free ever since, now two years.

My young friend now had confidence in himself, and doing as all good mesmerists should do—subscribe to *The Zoist*, he determined not to hide his portion of light under a bushel, and, as erring man is ever 'infringing organic laws,' he speedily found *a case*—one which many older mesmerists, myself included, would have shaken their heads at, and then 'passed over on the other side.'

Not so with Mr Laurence Moreton: with the ardour of youth, and a determination to prove to the parish wiseacres that mesmerism is a great truth, its advocacy having with him produced its usual fruits—sneers and ridicule from its opponents instead of argument, be on the 31 August, 1853, commenced operations upon the subject of this paper.

George East, a last-maker, aged 33, a much more powerful and older man than his benevolent mesmeriser, suffering from a diseased knee, the effects of a fall when about eight years old and a subsequent injury, had previously placed himself under the advice of Dr Robarts, of Burnham, for a lengthened period, but without success, and amputation was advised. He then went to Guy's Hospital, and was advised by Mr Cock and other gentlemen at that institution to rest the leg and make a stiff knee of it, for which purpose a gutta percha bandage in a warm state was applied. But this caused such severe pain that at the end of three or four days it was removed.

He then placed himself under Dr Boddy of Windsor, who tried the homoeopathic system upon him without any benefit. He then exhausted all the medical science within his reach, in addition to the equally efficacious remedies of all the old women in the parish, &c. After several months' rest his leg became daily more painful, when in August, 1853, Mr Laurence Moreton, seeing him at the door supported by crutches, unable to put his foot to the ground, and, as he expressed himself, 'in despair of ever walking again,' advised mesmerism and offered his services gratuitously.

On the 31st August, 1853, Mr L. Moreton commenced mesmerising his patient by long passes without contact from head to foot for half an hour, and then local passes were continued every evening for about a month; the long passes were then discontinued, the patient shewing no tendency to sleep. Little benefit was experienced until the end of the second month, when the pain was much relieved. About the end of the fourth month, during the process of mesmerising, several violent pains, *'like shocks of electricity,' passed through the knee, returning at intervals during the night, and were reproduced upon mesmerising the following evening.** A small red spot was then observed below the knee, which gradually became larger and very painful, and about the middle of January ulcerated, discharging very freely. Mr Moreton was here assisted by the kind advice of a medical friend, who advised the continuance of mesmerism. In about three months the ulcer closed; it reopened shortly afterwards, and the case having progressed thus far, and the good result though existent not very apparent, he on the 31st May, 1854, took his patient to the Mesmeric Infirmary, and had the good fortune of bringing him under the notice of Dr Elliotson and Dr Symes. Those gentlemen pronounced it a favourable case, enjoined the continuance of mesmerism, and deemed a cure might be expected in about *two years*.

Now it must be allowed that a two years' case would prove a damper to most mesmerists, but as my young friend wrote me word, 'Dr Elliotson, the apostle of mesmerism, had pronounced a cure possible, and he was determined to achieve it,' and D.V. he has done so.

At the end of June the ulcer discharged very copiously and then healed up, but was followed by two others about an inch higher up, which, by his medical adviser's direction, was poulticed, and mesmerised water was given, for which the patient had considerable relish. Mr Moreton also constructed a tube, by which he could breathe strongly upon the affected part. His patient's leg now began to improve in shape and strength fast, and by the middle of January, 1855, was so much restored that mesmerism was only applied every other evening for half an hour, and in July the patient could walk with ease aided by a walking stick.

*The occurrence of pain from successful mesmerism has been often noticed.

In No. XXXIII., p. 45, is the cure of ulcers in the leg with varicose veins, by a lady, the sister of a recently deceased distinguished Cabinet Minister. The passes caused sharp, and at length intolerable, pain, even if a piece of paper intervened. Even if the ointment was mesmerised it produced pain, but otherwise not: and the comparative trials were made without her knowledge.

In No. XXV., the Rev. Mr Sandby relates a cure by himself of intense tooth-ache; and states that, after mesmerising the patient, an athletic man, for ten minutes, and making him drowsy, 'suddenly a shock or sensation passed over the top of his head, and he roused up in a most vigilant and active state.'

In the splendid cure of ovarian dropsy related in the last report of the Mesmeric Infirmary, the pains were extreme which the passes produced in the abdomen. See No. L., p. 182; or the Report, p. 16.—*Zoist.*

I was in Burnham in August last, and met the patient walking in the town, walking with that very leg which *ought* to have been amputated; and he with great glee told me that in the previous week he had passed a day at Slough with his friends, walking there and back—a distance of eight miles; eight miles which, according to orthodox rules, he ought to have stumped on a wooden pin. But let me add, to the honour of a profession which numbers in its ranks so many generous men—a profession preëminent for the sacrifice of time and talents and services to the poor and needy, that Mr Moreton was aided and encouraged during his long and tedious case by the kind advice of — Barrett, Esq., Surgeon, of East Farnham.

Mr East is now able to stand all day at his work without fatigue, and I have this day received from him—three months after mesmerism had been discontinued—the following letter which I enclose:—

'Burnham, Nov. 12, 1855.

'Sir,—A great many years ago I had the misfortune to hurt my knee. In November, 1852, I was obliged to give up my work, and go to Dr Roberts, but he could do me no good; he said I must have the leg taken off, or I should shortly lose my life; but I felt anxious for further advice. Then I went to Guy's Hospital, and there I saw Dr (Mr) Cock, and his advice was the same as Dr Roberts's. Then I came home, and tried all the remedies that could be thought of: but nothing did me any good, when Mr Moreton offered to mesmerise me, and in two months I found great benefit, and he continued for two years.

'Before Mr Moreton mesmerised me I could not put my foot to the ground, now I can stand all day at my work, or walk seven or eight miles, without feeling tired. I am sure I am very thankful to Mr Moreton for what he has done for me, and I believe he has saved my leg.

'Sir, I feel it my duty to let the public know what benefit I have received from Mr Moreton's mesmerising, although I was much ridiculed at first; but, I thank God, Mr Moreton continued, and now the people can see that his labour was not in vain.

'Your humble servant,

'G. EAST.'

Mr Laurence Moreton has thus the happiness of seeing his gratuitous and untiring devotion to his patient during the long period of two years crowned with signal success—*not having, Mr East told me, missed one evening's manipulation for a year and a half*—and without any of the clap-trap marvels of mesmerism to excite him on, his patient having only once gone to sleep during the process. As he has sown, so may he reap.

I am, Sir, your obedient servant,

FRED. HOCKLEY.

Croydon, 12 November 1855.

[Printed in *The Zoist*, No. LII (January 1856).]

Also in this series:

THE ALCHEMIST OF THE GOLDEN DAWN: Letters of the Revd
   W. A. Ayton to F. L. Gardner and Others 1886–1905
Edited and Introduced by Ellic Howe

THE MAGICAL MASON: Forgotten Hermetic Writings of W. W.
   Westcott
Edited and Introduced by R. A. Gilbert

THE SORCERER AND HIS APPRENTICE: Hermetic Writings of
   S. L. MacGregor Mathers and J. W. Brodie-Innes
Edited and Introduced by R. A. Gilbert

Books of related interest:
THE MAGICIANS OF THE GOLDEN DAWN: A Documentary
   History of a Magical Order 1887–1923
Ellic Howe

THE GOLDEN DAWN: Twilight of the Magicians
R. A. Gilbert

MASONIC FACTS AND FICTIONS
Henry Sadler
Edited by John Hamill

EGYPTIAN MAGIC
Florence Farr
Introduced by Timothy d'Arch Smith

A. E. WAITE: A BIBLIOGRAPHY
R. A. Gilbert